RAND NATIONAL DEFENSE RESEARCH INSTITUTE

T0294885

Implications of Integrating Women into the Marine Corps Infantry

Agnes Gereben Schaefer, Jennie W. Wenger, Jennifer Kavanagh, Jonathan P. Wong, Gillian S. Oak, Thomas E. Trail, Todd Nichols

Prepared for the United States Marine Corps

For more information on this publication, visit www.rand.org/t/RR1103

Library of Congress Cataloging-in-Publication Data is available for this publication.
ISBN: 978-0-8330-9203-8

Published by the RAND Corporation, Santa Monica, Calif.
© Copyright 2015 RAND Corporation
RAND® is a registered trademark.

Support RAND
Make a tax-deductible charitable contribution at
www.rand.org/giving/contribute

www.rand.org

Preface

On January 24, 2013, the Secretary of Defense and Chairman of the Joint Chiefs of Staff announced the rescission of the 1994 Direct Ground Combat Definition and Assignment Rule (DGCDAR). The 1994 DGCDAR restricted assignments of women to occupational specialties or positions in or collocated with direct ground combat units below the brigade level, in long-range reconnaissance and special operations forces, and in positions involving physically demanding tasks. The effect of this rescission will be to open previously closed occupations—including the United States Marine Corps (USMC) infantry—to women who can meet occupation-specific, gender-neutral standards of performance. This decision to rescind the DGCDAR could open more than 230,000 positions in the U.S. armed forces to women. The services were required to report their implementation plans to the Department of Defense (DoD) by May 2013, and they have until January 2016 to seek exemptions if they want any positions to remain closed to women.

In response to this change in policy, the Marine Corps Combat Development Command asked RAND's National Defense Research Institute to assist in identifying the issues that may arise if women are integrated into the Marine Corps infantry, describe efforts that have been successful in addressing these issues in the past, and estimate the potential costs associated with integration. This research should be of interest to USMC and other DoD policymakers, as well as others interested in the potential implications of integrating women into the USMC infantry.

This research was sponsored by the United States Marine Corps and conducted within the Forces and Resources Policy Center of RAND's National Defense Research Institute, a federally funded research and development center sponsored by the Office of the Secretary of Defense, the Joint Staff, the Unified Combatant Commands, the Department of the Navy, the Marine Corps, the defense agencies, and the defense Intelligence Community. For more information on the RAND Forces and Resources Policy Center, see www.rand.org/nsrd/ndri/centers/frp or contact the director (contact information is provided on the web page).

Questions and comments regarding this research are welcome and should be directed to the leaders of the research team: Agnes Gereben Schaefer (Agnes_Schaefer@rand.org) or Jennie Wenger (Jennie_Wenger@rand.org).

Contents

Figures

Tables

Summary

In January 2013, the Secretary of Defense and Chairman of the Joint Chiefs of Staff announced the rescission of the 1994 Direct Ground Combat Definition and Assignment Rule (DGCDAR). The effect of this decision will be to open previously closed occupations—including those within the United States Marine Corps (USMC) infantry—to women who can meet those validated occupation-specific, gender-neutral standards of performance. In response to this change in policy, the Marine Corps Combat Development Command asked RAND's National Defense Research Institute to assist in identifying the issues that may arise if women are integrated into the Marine Corps infantry, describe efforts that have been successful in addressing these issues in the past, and estimate the potential costs associated with integration.

Study Approach

This study consisted of four tasks: (1) review the literature on the integration of women in ground combat and other physically demanding occupations, (2) conduct interviews with representatives of organizations that have integrated women into physically demanding occupations, (3) estimate the costs of potential initiatives to promote successful gender integration, (4) develop an approach for monitoring implementation of gender integration of the infantry.

In order to carry out task one and task two, our review of the literature examined

- the expansion of the role of women in the U.S. military
- the integration of other U.S. military services and other Military Occupational Specialties (MOSs)
- the current literature on cohesion
- the current literature on *critical mass* (the notion that minorities have different experiences as their numbers in a group increase)
- the integration experiences of foreign militaries
- the integration experiences of domestic civilian organizations.

Our findings in task one and task two informed our effort in task three to esti-mate the costs associated with integration. Lastly, our findings from all three of the previous tasks fed into our last task: the development of a gender integration monitor-ing framework. In this summary, we briefly discuss the main findings and implications from our study.

Research on Cohesion

In general, prior research demonstrates that more cohesive groups perform better than less cohesive groups. Importantly, there is evidence that the link between unit cohe-sion and performance is bidirectional. In fact, the evidence suggests that the effect of performance on cohesion is stronger than the effect of cohesion on performance. Research has also demonstrated that the impact of gender integration on the cohe-sion of traditionally male groups depends on the culture of the group—groups more hostile to women experience lower cohesion after gender integration than do groups less hostile toward women. Therefore, gender integration is more likely to have nega-tive consequences for unit cohesion when the social context of the unit creates a hostile work environment for women. Where the environment is not hostile toward women, integration is less likely to negatively affect cohesion.

Implications

Although the integration of women into male-dominated groups can potentially have detrimental effects on group cohesion, these effects can be mitigated through a variety of methods. Good leadership is key to increasing the acceptance of women. Leaders that treat both women and men fairly, provide support for women, and emphasize the good of the group create cohesive groups in which women are fully integrated into group life. In addition, women generally perform better in groups in which they are not the only woman in the group,[1] but the optimal proportion of women for group cohesion is not clear from the existing research. Finally, there are cohesion-building activities that the Marine Corps can put in place to build cohesion in gender-integrated groups, and it is important to understand that cohesion in integrated groups is likely to increase over time as groups work together and develop a sense of shared group identity.

---

[1]   Charles G. Lord and Delia S. Saenz, "Memory Deficits and Memory Surfeits: Differential Cognitive Con-sequences of Tokenism for Tokens and Observers," *Journal of Personality and Social Psychology,* Vol. 49, No. 4, October 1985, p. 918; Denise Sekaquaptewa and Mischa Thompson, "Solo Status, Stereotype Threat, and Perfor-mance Expectancies: Their Effects on Women's Performance," *Journal of Experimental Social Psychology,* Vol. 39, No. 1, 2003, pp. 68–74.

Insights on Critical Mass

The concept of *critical mass* focuses on the notion that the experiences of women in minority status in a group change as their numbers increase. As the Marine Corps analyzes how best to integrate women into infantry units, it may consider whether it should assign a minimum number of women to a given unit to achieve a particular critical mass threshold. Unfortunately, the findings from the literature on critical mass offer limited insights for the Marine Corps. Even among foreign militaries using the critical mass approach, there remains little consensus among them about what actually constitutes a *critical mass*.

Implications

The experiences of foreign militaries suggest that attention to critical mass and to the numbers of women assigned to integrated combat units is important. Assigning women in groups of a sufficient size does seem to increase their satisfaction and success—particularly in occupations that have small numbers of women. However, the experiences of foreign militaries do not recommend a precise threshold or standard for what constitutes a critical mass. Those experiences also suggest that setting a single, rigid standard or proportion may be difficult and counterproductive. Therefore, the Marine Corps should consider experimenting with various gender mixes for infantry units of varying sizes to determine whether there are optimal gender proportions in different-sized units. However, even if the Marine Corps determines a specific critical mass policy, there may be cases in which women in solo status cannot be avoided. In such cases, additional mentoring mechanisms should be put into place.

Lessons Learned from the Experiences of Foreign Militaries

Our analysis of the experiences of foreign militaries suggests a set of key insights and cross-cutting observations that span cases. These lessons fall into four primary categories: (1) the importance of leadership commitment and accountability, (2) issues related to implementation, (3) the need for resource management strategies, and (4) issues related to physical standards.

The Importance of Leadership Commitment and Accountability

The first set of lessons has to do with the importance of leadership commitment and accountability. According to senior leaders and key stakeholders in the integration process, without this commitment and without visible involvement by senior leaders, progress on integration is difficult or impossible to achieve. Integration needs to be supported by legal and policy changes, and senior leaders are uniquely positioned to implement and enforce these types of changes.

Issues Related to Implementation

The second set of lessons has to do with implementation. According to the opinions and observations of military leaders and researchers, phased integration (in which integration occurs within only a specific set of occupations or units at first before being gradually expanded to all units and occupations) often appears to support progress, as it allows integration to occur gradually alongside training. It also facilitates frequent status checks and course corrections as needed. A clear implementation plan is another key element of more-successful integration programs.

The Need for Human Resource Management Strategies

Our analysis also suggests the need for human resource management policies that support integration—specifically the need for targeted recruitment and retention policies that attract women into combat arms occupations and retain them there. Countries that have been relatively more effective at integrating women into combat arms occupations have employed these strategies. This might include flexible workplace policies and childcare resources, as well as procedures to ensure that women receive equal training and promotion opportunities. It might also include well-defined, updated, and clearly communicated sexual harassment policies.

Issues Related to Physical Standards

Finally, our analysis suggests a few lessons related to physical standards. First, the experiences of countries in our analysis suggest that gender-neutral standards should be frequently monitored and revised. Gender-neutral standards may actually reduce barriers to integration because they help to establish an equal foundation among all new recruits. Second, in several cases, countries have sped the integration process by providing additional training for female recruits, either before or after enlistment. This training has helped increase women's ability to complete basic training and, in some cases, meet physical standards for combat arms occupations by ensuring physical readiness. Along the same lines, integrated training also appears to improve cohesion and improve the physical readiness of women more than gender-specific training alone.

Lessons Learned from the Experiences of Domestic Police and Fire Departments

In order to extract applicable lessons from domestic nonmilitary organizations, we first identified gender-integrated civilian occupations that require physically demanding work. In order to compare these civilian occupations to the infantry occupation field, we next developed a rubric that summarizes the characteristics of the infantry occupational field.[2] We also created a scale to rate the comparability of a given organization to the infantry occupational field. Using this rubric, we found that, among the organizations we analyzed, fire departments are most similar to the Marine Corps infantry and have the greatest potential to provide insights to infantry gender integration. Police departments are also similar, but less so.

Four main findings came out of our analysis of the integration experiences of civilian organizations:

- Equipment and uniforms must meet the needs of women.
- Small-unit dynamics and discipline need to be closely monitored.
- Integration challenges change and mature over time.
- Being open to external perspectives can better facilitate the integration process.

Implications

While no civilian organization is directly comparable to the USMC, the long history of gender integration in some physically demanding civilian occupations, such as policing and firefighting, do offer some insights for the Marine Corps. The specifics of the integration process will be different for the Marine Corps, but the experiences of civilian organizations highlight that integration is a process in which issues arise in correspondence to the career progression of women in those occupations. Initially after integration, issues and challenges tend to focus on recruiting and hiring. As time progresses, integration challenges related to promotion and retention arise. These experiences of civilian organizations indicate that the Marine Corps should expect integration issues and challenges to change over time. By proactively monitoring the progression of these issues, the Marine Corps could potentially identify and address them quickly. Our analysis also highlights the importance of both internal and external oversight of the integration process.

Costs Associated with Integration

In our cost model, we focus on the largest MOS in the Marine Corps infantry, that of "Rifleman." However, many of our results generalize to the other MOSs in the infantry. As a first step to estimating the monetary costs associated with opening the Marine Corps infantry to women, we divided costs into two categories: (1) one-time costs and (2) recurring costs. We define *one-time costs* to include all costs that occur only in a single time period (generally in preparation for or during the initial period of integration). Examples of one-time costs include any costs for research and development, as

---

[2] See rubric in Appendix A.

well as costs associated with necessary changes to equipment or facilities. Costs of establishing gender training and communication plans, gender advisers, or other specific resources to assist women (such as hotlines) would also fall in this category.

We define *recurring costs* as those that occur repeatedly over multiple years as a result of opening the infantry to women. A main driver of recurring costs will be differences in attrition or retention rates. To the extent that women complete training at a lower rate, or spend fewer months on average in the infantry, substituting women for men will eventually result in fewer personnel serving in the infantry. Therefore, the Marine Corps will need to recruit or retain additional personnel to maintain the size of the infantry. Recurring costs could also include additional physical conditioning time as necessary, lost time necessary to recover from increased injury rates, as well as any other alterations to training or continued implementation of policy changes. Costs associated with maintaining gender training, gender advisers, or other specific resources also would fall in this category.

Our methodology for estimating costs rests on a detailed literature review and interviews with key personnel in organizations that have integrated women into physically demanding occupations; in the case of recurring costs, we also use a straightforward model based on personnel data to estimate the number of women in the infantry at each point in time over a 15-year framework. Because our estimates of recurring costs are based on personnel data, we are able to capture differences in attrition rates and overall length of service, but we are *not* able to capture or predict costs based on time lost due to differential injury rates.

Results: Basic Model

Figure S.1 provides an example of the outputs produced by our model. Figure S.1 demonstrates that the growth of female representation in the infantry is heavily dependent on the number of women who enlist with the intent to serve in the infantry, and that growth is likely to be fairly slow, taking at least seven to ten years to level off. For example, if 100 women enter the Marine Corps each year with the intention to serve in the infantry, our model predicts that women will eventually make up about 2 percent of the infantry. In contrast, to exceed 8-percent representation would require that about 400 women per year enter the Marine Corps with the intention to enter the infantry and about 300 per year actually enter the infantry after boot camp and training attrition, for most of the next 15 years. Moreover, these estimates are based on quite optimistic rates of training completion. Specifically, here we assume that 88 percent of women complete boot camp and that 85 percent of women who enter infantry training complete the training. In Chapter Seven, we demonstrate how the outcomes change when we alter the rate of training completion.

Figure S.1
Predicted Representation of Women Among USMC Infantry Enlisted Personnel Based on Initial Assumptions of Accession and Training Completion Rates

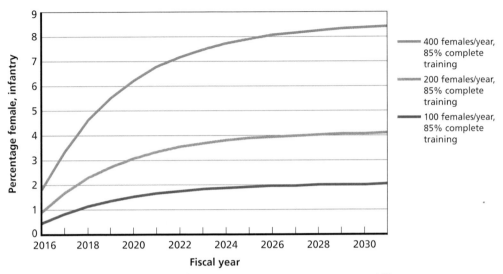

SOURCE: RAND analysis based on Defense Manpower Data Center personnel files.
RAND *RR1103-S.1*

Findings and Implications

Based on our exploration of costs and our model of recurring costs, there are a number of implications and takeaways that will be relevant as the Marine Corps considers opening the infantry to women. Here, we provide a brief list:

- Our estimates, as well as experiences when the Marine Corps opened previously closed occupations to women in the past and the experiences of foreign militaries, suggest that the number of women entering the infantry will be modest, and the increase in representation will be slow.
- Our model suggests that opening the infantry to women will have costs, because we expect women to have higher levels of attrition during training and fewer months of service in the infantry than men, but we expect the overall costs to be modest when compared to recruiting and retention budgets.
- The Marine Corps will be able to make up any shortfall in the infantry effectively through increased recruitment, increased retention, or both.
- Both the rate at which women successfully complete infantry training, and the retention of women who do not complete the training, will be linked to costs. Retaining women who do not successfully complete the training in other MOSs offers a mechanism for cost savings; retaining men who do not complete the training also has significant cost implications.

Developing a Monitoring Framework

We also developed a short- to medium-term monitoring framework to provide an example of common practices of other organizations that have implemented gender integration. This plan is broken into two phases: the Planning Phase (before the decision whether or not to integrate has been made) and Phase One (up to five years after integration). At the five-year point, we recommend that the USMC conduct a comprehensive evaluation of the integration process to reevaluate monitoring priorities. Regardless of the outcome of this evaluation, we also emphasize the need for long-term, sustained monitoring to identify potential problems quickly as they evolve over time.

Our monitoring framework is organized by levels (individual, unit, MOS, and institutional), categories, and subcategories. For the categories, we followed the Doctrine, Organization, Training, Materiel, Leadership and Education, Personnel, Facilities, Policy structure, with the addition of a category termed *Attitudinal*, which includes well being, welfare, morale, and misconduct. In this monitoring framework, we included issues ("what are you measuring?"), metrics ("how are you measuring progress, and what information do you need?"), and methods ("how are you collecting the information that you need to measure progress?"). The metrics are deliberately designed to track progress over time. See Appendix D for the complete spreadsheet of the monitoring framework and Appendix E for a summary of our approach to developing the monitoring framework.

Strategic Monitoring Considerations

In addition to our suggestions in the monitoring framework regarding specific issues to monitor over time, there are several broader strategic monitoring considerations that should also be taken into account. These include

- importance of internal and external oversight
- significance of gender advisers
- cultural change and understanding of gender issues
- importance of consistent monitoring.

Implications

As indicated by the experiences of foreign militaries and domestic civilian organizations, gender integration will not happen overnight; rather, it could be a long process that will not be without challenges and obstacles. Monitoring something as sensitive and important as gender integration in combat roles in the USMC requires constant vigilance from leadership and from the institution itself. A monitoring plan must consist of long-term and deliberate methods for measuring progress, including personnel policy and collection of data or statistics, and must include strategies to measure institutional and cultural change over time.

Cross-Cutting Implications and Recommendations for Implementation

As the Marine Corps moves closer to the January 2016 deadline, the findings in this report offer critical insights into the integration planning and implementation process. The planning phase presents the Marine Corps with a critical window of opportunity to develop integration strategies, plans, and policies, as well as to put the necessary data systems in place to monitor integration progress over time. When looking across all of our study findings, we identify the following areas as particularly relevant to informing the Marine Corps' implementation planning process: (1) leadership is key to integration success on many fronts, (2) development of a detailed implementation plan and assignment of accountability, (3) establishment of oversight mechanisms, (4) consideration of long-term career progression issues, (5) development of customized integration strategies through experimentation, (6) monitoring integration progress over time, and (7) management of expectations. We discuss each of these issues below.

Leadership Is Key to Integration Success on Many Fronts

Across the findings from our study, it is striking how much agreement there is on the importance of leadership during the integration process. Leadership (at all levels of the chain of command) is also key to setting the tone for the integration process and ensuring that cohesion is not negatively affected by integration. Our findings from the cohesion literature indicate that integration can rarely succeed without the support of leadership. Leaders can set the command climate and enforce good order and discipline to prevent issues of misconduct (e.g., sexual harassment) that can have negative impacts on cohesion. In addition to setting the tone for the integration process, leadership also plays a critical role in disseminating a consistent message about integration to both internal and external audiences. Our findings suggest that a clear communications strategy can help facilitate the integration process as a whole by clarifying integration goals.

Development of a Detailed Implementation Plan and Assignment of Accountability

Our analyses of the integration experiences of foreign militaries and of civilian organizations indicate that the development of a detailed implementation plan is another element of successful integration efforts. Well-designed implementation plans that assign responsibility, identify risks, and outline mitigation strategies are particularly effective in streamlining the integration process. These types of implementation plans clarify the goals of integration and identify the risks associated with integration, as well as the actions that the organization will need to take to mitigate those risks. We also found that it is critical that the implementation plan assign responsibility and accountability for the various elements of integration. Without such accountability, the integration process can stagnate or atrophy all together. The development of a detailed implementation plan will also ensure that the entire organization will be using the same guidance once a decision about integration is made. Therefore, during the planning phase, it is important to begin to think about which entities will be responsible and accountable for the various elements of the implementation plan.

Establishment of Oversight Mechanisms

Our findings also indicate that gender integration oversight boards have been used elsewhere to conduct oversight and monitoring, but also in setting and defining requirements for longer-term progress. It is critical to keep in mind that the data needed for proper oversight must be identified, and the software modifications must be made to facilitate or enable the collection of the needed data. This element of monitoring may have the longest lead time and may be expensive. As the Marine Corps begins implementation planning, it would be prudent to think about the structure of oversight mechanisms that it could establish to oversee and monitor the integration process. External oversight is also important to building trust, transparency, and accountability both within an organization and externally.

Consideration of Long-Term Career Progression Issues

One of the primary lessons from the experiences of both foreign militaries and civilian organizations is that gender integration is a long process. The evidence from our analysis of civilian organizations indicates that integration challenges evolve over time as women progress through their careers. During the period immediately following integration, challenges tend to focus on issues such as recruiting and hiring, whereas later integration challenges focus on promotion and retention issues. Our analysis of the integration experiences of foreign militaries also found that long-term retention of women in the combat arms occupations is a challenge. This suggests that the Marine Corps should consider these longer-term career progression challenges from the onset of its implementation planning so that it can put the mechanisms in place to mitigate later integration challenges related to promotion and retention.

Development of Customized Integration Strategies Through Experimentation

One of the key observations from both foreign militaries and civilian organizations is that their integration experiences varied widely. While these experiences can provide insights and signposts for the Marine Corps as it embarks on gender integration in the infantry, none of these organizations is a direct analog to the Marine Corps infantry. Therefore, the Marine Corps will ultimately need to develop integration strategies and approaches that best suit it as an organization and its missions.

While moving forward in the implementation planning process, we suggest that the Marine Corps consider experimenting with different integration strategies and options, including

- gender training programs, including content, timing, and delivery

- mentoring programs
- recruiting strategies
- critical mass
- physical training.

Lastly, if the Marine Corps chooses to use experimentation during the integration process, it should link that experimentation to data collection, analysis, and evaluation. This is significant not only because it is valuable for experiential learning, but also because these data, analyses, and evaluations are the building blocks for near- and middle-term monitoring of the integration process, which we discuss below. These data, analyses, and evaluations can also help to refine the implementation plan and associated policies.

Monitoring Integration Progress over Time

Across the findings from our studies, it is apparent that sustained monitoring is a key element to integration success over the long term. A strong monitoring plan relies on robust data systems that facilitate the necessary data collection to measure integration progress. As the Marine Corps plans for implementation, it should consider which data systems are already in place to collect the appropriate data to monitor progress over time and whether any new data systems are necessary.

The monitoring framework presented in Appendix D offers the Marine Corps suggestions on which issues might be included in a monitoring plan, as well as how to measure progress on those issues and what type of data collection methods could be employed. However, in order for a monitoring plan to be effective, it cannot be static. As data are collected and analyzed, new issues and measures may need to be added to or deleted from the monitoring plan. It will also be helpful to identify key metrics that leaders should track over time.

Management of Expectations

Lastly, as the Marine Corps begins the implementation planning process, it will need to manage both internal and external expectations. Both proponents and opponents of integration will have particular expectations about how the Marine Corps should handle the decision to integrate the infantry, as well as how to implement any changes. In order to maximize the chances of integration success, the Marine Corps will need to base its decision and implementation strategy on empirical data. This strategy will enable the Marine Corps to set realistic goals and to counter pressure from both proponents and opponents of integration. Also, as the Marine Corps embarks on setting its integration goals and defining integration "success," it should set realistic goals based on input from the various analytic efforts that it has under way, including our study, as well as other efforts. The experiences of foreign militaries offer cautionary signposts indicating that integration could be a long, slow process, and that the number of women entering combat arms positions is likely to be relatively low.

During this planning process, both near- and long-term issues should be considered, and the mechanisms put into place during the planning process should be flexible enough to accommodate learning and adjustments. Integration will likely be a process of continual, iterative improvements. Putting the systems in place to collect the appropriate data throughout the integration process will help to build the evidence base for those improvements along the way and will facilitate integration success.

Acknowledgments

The authors would like to extend thanks to our United States Marine Corps sponsors for their support for the research.

We also benefited from the contributions of RAND colleagues. Susan Hosek and Michael Decker provided helpful formal peer reviews of this report. Michelle McMullen and Amy McGranahan provided administrative support, Samantha Bennett provided editorial assistance, and Benson Wong and Matthew Byrd provided oversight of the publication process.

Finally, we note that we could not have completed this work without the participation of subject matter experts from the Marine Corps, foreign militaries, and U.S. civilian organizations, who shared their insights with us through confidential interviews.

We thank them all, but we retain full responsibility for the objectivity, accuracy, and analytic integrity of the work presented here.

Abbreviations

ADF	Australian Defence Force
AVF	All-Volunteer Force
CF	Canadian Armed Forces
CREW	Combat Related Employment for Women
DACOWITS	Defense Advisory Committee on Women in the Services
DGCDAR	Direct Ground Combat Definition and Assignment Rule
DMDC	Defense Manpower Data Center
DoD	U.S. Department of Defense
DOTMLPF-P	Doctrine, Organization, Training, Materiel, Leadership, Personnel, Facilities-Policy
EU	European Union
FDNY	Fire Department of New York
GAO	General Accounting Office
HRM	human resources management
IDF	Israeli Defense Forces
IOC	Infantry Officer Course
MCDP	Marine Corps Doctrinal Publications
MOD	Ministry of Defense
MOS	Military Occupational Specialty
NATO	North Atlantic Treaty Organization

NCO	noncommissioned officer
NDAA	National Defense Authorization Act
NZDF	New Zealand Defence Force
PME	Professional Military Education
PTP	predeployment training plan
SOI	School of Infantry
SRB	selective reenlistment bonus
SWINTER	Servicewomen in Non-Traditional Environments and Roles
TBS	The Basic School
UN	United Nations
USMC	United States Marine Corps
USSOCOM	United States Special Operations Command
WAC	Women's Army Corps
WAAC	Women's Army Auxiliary Corps
WAVES	Women Accepted for Volunteer Emergency Service

CHAPTER ONE

Introduction

Background and Study Purpose

On January 24, 2013, the Secretary of Defense and Chairman of the Joint Chiefs of Staff announced the rescission of the 1994 Direct Ground Combat Definition and Assignment Rule (DGCDAR). The 1994 DGCDAR restricted assignments of women to occupational specialties or positions in or collocated with direct ground combat units below the brigade level, in long-range reconnaissance and special operations forces, and in positions including physically demanding tasks the "vast majority" of women cannot do. The rescission of DGCDAR also included the requirement to implement "validated, gender-neutral occupational standards."[1] Section 543 of the 1994 National Defense Authorization Act (NDAA) established the military requirement for gender-neutral standards by requiring that

> In the case of any military occupational career field that is open to both male and female members of the Armed Forces, the Secretary of Defense—

> (1) shall ensure that qualification of members of the Armed Forces for, and continuance of members of the Armed Forces in, that occupational career field is evaluated on the basis of common, relevant performance standards, without differential standards of evaluation on the basis of gender;

> (2) may not use any gender quota, goal, or ceiling except as specifically authorized by law; and

> (3) may not change an occupational performance standard for the purpose of increasing or decreasing the number of women in that occupational career field.[2]

---

[1] U.S. Department of Defense, "Memorandum for Secretaries of the Military Departments; Subject: Elimination of the 1994 Direct Combat Definition and Assignment Rule," January 24, 2013.

[2] Public Law 103-160, Section 543, 1993.

The 2014 NDAA amended section 543 and redefined "gender-neutral occupational standard" to mean that

> all members of the Armed Forces serving in or assigned to the military career designator must meet the same performance outcome–based standards for the successful accomplishment of the necessary and required specific tasks associated with the qualifications and duties performed while serving in or assigned to the military career designator.[3]

It also mandated that, no later than September 2015, "the Services and USSOCOM [U.S. Special Operations Command] should develop, review, and validate individual occupational standards, using validated gender-neutral occupational standards, so as to assess and assign members of the Armed Forces to units, including Special Operations Forces."[4]

The effect of this rescission will be to open previously closed occupational fields—including the United States Marine Corps (USMC) infantry—to women who can meet occupation-specific, gender-neutral standards of performance. This decision to rescind the DGCDAR could open more than 230,000 positions in the U.S. armed forces to women. The services were required to report their implementation plans to the Department of Defense (DoD) by May 2013, and they have until January 2016 to seek exemptions if they want any positions to remain closed to women. It is within this context that the USMC considers the implications of integrating women into its infantry.

In response to this change in policy, the Marine Corps Combat Development Command asked RAND's National Defense Research Institute to assist in identifying the issues that may arise if women are integrated into the Marine Corps infantry, describe efforts that have been successful in addressing these issues in the past, and estimate the potential costs associated with integration.

The successful integration of women into the Marine Corps infantry will require careful advance planning that identifies the following:

- the potential impacts of integration on unit performance, unit cohesion, and unit members' individual interactions
- changes or adaptations that may need to be made to promote successful gender integration
- the costs associated with the changes that may need to be made to promote successful gender integration.

---

[3] Public Law 113-66, Section 523, 2013.

[4] Public Law 113-66, Section 524, 2013.

The successful integration of women into the Marine Corps infantry can be informed by experiences from elsewhere in the U.S. military, physically demanding civilian occupations, and foreign militaries. These experiences are likely to suggest issues that may arise with gender integration of the USMC infantry, as well as ways to make that integration successful.

The Central Role of the Marine Corps Infantry

The infantry is the organizational, operational, and cultural foundation of the Marine Corps. The infantry occupational field is the largest occupational field in the Marine Corps. Infantry tactics are singled out for additional emphasis during initial entry training, through a mandatory short course for all noninfantry enlisted Marines (Marine Combat Training, or MCT) and through a heavy emphasis on infantry rifle platoon tactics for all officers during The Basic School (TBS). Infantrymen are trained to locate, close with, and destroy the enemy by fire and maneuver or to repel his assault by fire and close combat.[5] The foundational series of Marine Corps doctrinal publications (MCDP 1 through MCDP 6) all use historical and hypothetical infantry operations as exemplars to highlight the basic tenets of the Marine Corps' warfighting philosophy.[6]

That centrality also suffuses the Marine Corps' organizational culture. The slogan "every Marine a rifleman" is acknowledged as the cultural touchstone of the Marine Corps by Marine leaders and outside observers alike. In examining the American use of military force in the last century, Adrian Lewis plainly states that "[t]he Marine Corps has traditionally been a light infantry force."[7] Noted national security commentator Tom Ricks writes that "[t]he phrase 'every Marine a rifleman' . . . is more than just a common denominator, it is an ethos encapsulated in a phrase, a way of looking at life and behaving."[8] The centrality of the infantry to the Marine Corps' organizational, operational, and cultural foundation is clear.

The primary infantry Military Occupational Specialty (MOS) is "Rifleman" (MOS 0311). Among enlisted Marines serving in 2012, about 9 percent held the MOS of Rifleman, while another 7 percent held another infantry MOS. Thus, during 2012, about 16 percent of all enlisted Marines were part of the infantry. Other infantry MOSs held by enlisted personnel in our data include "Light Armored Vehicle (LAV) Crewman," "Combat Rubber Raiding Craft (CRRC) Coxswain," "Scout Sniper," "Reconnaissance Man," "Machine Gunner," "Mortarman," "Infantry Assaultman,"

---

[5] See U.S. Department of the Navy, Headquarters U.S. Marine Corps, "Organization of Marine Corps Forces," MCRP 5-12D, October 1998.

[6] This is particularly true for MCDP 1 Warfighting, MCDP 1-0 Marine Corps Operations, MCDP 1-3 Tactics, and MCDP 3 Expeditionary Operations.

[7] Adrian R. Lewis, *The American Culture of War,* New York: Routledge, 2007.

[8] Ricks, Thomas E., *Making the Corps.* New York: Scribner, 1997.

and "Antitank Missleman." Finally, those holding the MOS of "Infantry Unit Leader," as well as some personnel who serve with Marine Corps Forces Special Operations Command (MARSOC), are also part of the infantry.

In some cases, infantry personnel may hold a specific MOS only after achieving a certain promotion. For example, infantry unit leaders have all achieved the rank of at least staff sergeant. These personnel previously held other infantry MOSs (most often "Rifleman") prior to becoming unit leaders. Infantry MOSs are also quite common among Marine Corps officers. In 2012, about 12 percent of Marine Corps officers held an infantry MOS.

Study Approach

This study consisted of four tasks: (1) review the literature on the integration of women in ground combat and other physically demanding occupations, (2) conduct interviews with representatives of organizations that have integrated women into physically demanding occupations, (3) estimate the costs of potential initiatives to promote successful gender integration, and (4) develop an approach for monitoring implementation of gender integration of the infantry.

In order to carry out task one and task two, our review of the literature on the integration of women in ground combat and other physically demanding occupations spanned a number of topics. These included reviews of the following, as well as targeted interviews with key personnel:

Review of the expansion of the role of women in the U.S. military. This historical review provided us context for the most recent change in policy to rescind the DGCDAR. It also helped to identify MOSs that were previously closed to women so that we could derive any relevant lessons learned from those previous integration experiences.

Review of the integration of other U.S. military services and other MOSs. We conducted a broad general review of previous gender integration efforts in other services and then a more focused review of the experiences of a few MOSs (e.g., aviation, combat engineers). We had initially planned to focus on this review quite intensely, but in response to changing needs, we were later directed by our research sponsor to focus more of our efforts on the integration experiences of foreign militaries.

Review of the current literature on cohesion. We surveyed the literature on cohesion to identify the potential implications that gender integration might have on cohesion in the Marine Corps infantry.

Review of the current literature on critical mass (the notion that minorities have different experiences as their numbers in a group increase). We surveyed the literature on critical mass to identify the strengths and weaknesses of this literature, as well as its ability to inform any decisions regarding the "optimal" number of women in a given-sized unit.

Review of the integration experiences of foreign militaries. Our investigation and analysis of the integration experiences of foreign militaries involved three phases: first, a broad sweep of 55 countries (each of which allows women in its military in at least some capacity); second, an in-depth analysis of 21 of those countries;[9] and third, a deep dive into seven countries to pull out key insights. Our seven deep dive cases are Australia, Canada, Israel, New Zealand, Norway, Sweden, and the United Kingdom.

Review of the integration experiences of domestic police and fire departments. We began our review of the experiences of civilian organizations with a broad sweep of physically demanding civilian occupations. We then developed a rubric and a scale that allowed us to compare civilian organizations against the Marine Corps infantry. We ultimately identified police and fire departments as the civilian organizations that could provide the most comparable insights for the Marine Corps. Consequently, we conducted a focused review of the integration experiences of police and fire departments. In addition, we conducted an analysis of post-integration lawsuit data.

Our findings in task one and task two informed our effort in task three to estimate the costs associated with integration. In task three, we focused on personnel data and estimating the number of women likely to enter the Marine Corps, as well as the number likely to enter the infantry in the future. Based on this information, we estimated the representation of women in the infantry and demonstrated how representation is likely to vary based on the number of women who enter the Marine Corps, the proportion who successfully complete infantry training, and the continuation rates of women and men in the infantry over time. Because the services have generally opened positions to women by MOS, we focus our attention on the most common MOS within the infantry, that of "Rifleman" (there are other smaller MOSs that are part of the infantry as well). However, most of our results are quite general in nature. Our estimates of the number of women likely to join the Marine Corps, for example, do not vary based on which MOSs are opened.

Finally, our findings from all three of the previous tasks fed into our last task: the development of a monitoring framework that suggests how the USMC might think about monitoring the integration process.

Organization of This Report

Chapter Two presents a historical overview of the integration of women into the U.S. military. The chapter covers the time period from World War II though the present

---

[9]   With the exception of the United Kingdom, all of the countries selected allow women in combat occupations and are comparable to the USMC in at least some capacity. At the time of this study, the United Kingdom did not allow women in combat occupations, but the UK case was included in the study as a contrasting case.

and offers valuable background and context for the current decisions confronting the USMC. Next, the report turns to the current research on cohesion and *critical mass*. Chapter Three presents an overview of the literature on cohesion, the potential implications of gender integration for cohesion, and steps that can be taken to mitigate those effects. Chapter Four presents an overview of the literature on *critical mass*. The chapter identifies what the literature and the experiences from foreign militaries can and cannot tell us about the concept of critical mass.

Chapter Five presents our analysis of the gender integration experiences of foreign militaries. This chapter provides a broad overview of findings from the full set of 55 countries we reviewed, as well as seven deep-dive case studies that we conducted: Australia, Canada, Israel, New Zealand, Norway, Sweden, and the United Kingdom. The chapter highlights policy implications, key lessons that might be relevant for the USMC, as well as possible areas for additional research. Chapter Six presents our analysis of the gender integration experiences of domestic police and fire departments. The chapter summarizes the method we used to compare and select the most relevant domestic civilian organizations to examine (police and fire departments), as well as lessons learned from civilian organizations and key lessons that the Marine Corps can draw on as it considers plans to integrate women into the infantry occupational field. Chapter Seven presents our assessment of the potential costs associated with integration. The chapter identifies both recurring and one-time costs that may be associated with integration and presents a cost model that focuses on recurring personnel costs.

Lastly, our report focuses on issues related to implementation. Chapter Eight identifies broad strategic monitoring issues for consideration, after presenting a summary of previous monitoring efforts and tools and a description of how we went about developing our monitoring framework. Chapter Nine discusses cross-cutting implications of our findings and recommendations for implementation. Appendix A presents our rubric for evaluating USMC infantry characteristics. This rubric was very valuable in helping us to identify civilian organizations that are most analogous with the USMC infantry. Appendix B summarizes Fire Department of New York postintegration lawsuit data. These lawsuit data highlight the fact that integration can be a long process and that integration challenges and issues evolve over time. Appendix C includes the results of a regression model used as part of our cost analysis. Appendix D presents our monitoring framework. This monitoring framework comprises two phases: (1) the planning phase (the time before a decision regarding integration is made) and (2) Phase One (up to five years after a decision regarding integration has been made). Appendix E presents our approach to developing the monitoring framework.

History of Integrating Women into the U.S. Military

The Expanding Role of Women in the Military

World War II

Women have been present on the battlefield throughout U.S. history, but initially they had very limited roles as volunteers, nurses, and caretakers. During World War II, 350,000 women—an unprecedented number—participated in the war effort, and they began to take on new auxiliary roles so that more men could fight in combat.[1] Shortly after the establishment of the Women's Army Auxiliary Corps (WAAC), Congress established the Women Accepted for Volunteer Emergency Service (WAVES) in June 1942 as a branch of the naval reserve.[2] Unlike the WAAC, which was a temporary auxiliary corps, women in the WAVES were afforded the same rank and ratings as the Regular Navy. However, the following restrictions were placed on the women in the WAVES: the number and rank of officers in the WAVES was limited,[3] the authority of WAVES officers could be exercised only over women in the WAVES, members of the WAVES were restricted to shore duty within the continental United States, and they could not be assigned to duty on board Navy vessels or in combat aircraft.[4]

In 1943, the WAAC was converted to full status as the Women's Army Corps (WAC), but similar restrictions applied:[5]

---

[1] Jeanne Holm, *Women in the Military: An Unfinished Revolution*, revised ed., Novato, Calif: Presidio Press, 1992, p. 100; Public Law 77-554, An Act to Establish a Women's Army Auxiliary Corps for Service with the Army of the United States, May 14, 1942. For a comprehensive history of the WAAC and the WAC, see Mattie E. Treadwell, *The Women's Auxiliary Corps*, Washington, D.C.: Government Printing Office, 1954.

[2] Public Law 689, H.R. 6807 [Chapter 538], Establishment of Women's Reserve, July 20, 1942.

[3] No more than one officer in the grade of lieutenant commander, nor more than 35 officers in the grade of lieutenant, and the number of officers in the grade of lieutenant (junior grade) could not exceed 35 percent of the total number of commissioned officers.

[4] Public Law 689, 1942.

[5] Treadwell, 1954, p. 264.

- WAC units would contain only women and be commanded by WAC officers, just as men's units were composed of and commanded by men.
- WACs could not serve in combat.
- WACs would not be confined in the same building with men, except a hospital.
- WACs would not be used in "restaurants or cafeterias in service clubs, guest houses, officers' clubs or messes."
- WAC officers would not be promoted to the grade of colonel.
- WACs would not command men unless specifically ordered to do so.
- WACs would not be employed as physicians or nurses.
- WAC officers would be appointed only from officer candidate school graduates, and officer candidates would be selected only from women already in the Corps.
- Enlistment standards would differ from men's in the age and citizenship requirements set by Congress, and in a different physical examination; venereal disease was also disqualifying, and women with dependent children were ineligible.
- Discharge was mandatory for minors; authority was included for discharge for pregnancy.

In 1948, the Women's Armed Services Integration Act formally gave all women regular and reserve status in the Armed Forces (as opposed to the temporary, emergency status that most had up to this point). While this act formally mandated the integration of women into the military, it also mandated restrictions on their participation in the military. For example,[6]

- women could constitute no more than 2 percent of each branch
- each service was limited to only one female full colonel or Navy captain
- women were excluded from flag ranks (general and admiral)
- different enlistment standards and dependency entitlements were set for men and women
- women could not be assigned to duty on Navy ships that engaged in combat missions or on aircraft that engaged in combat missions.[7]

Therefore, "while the new law included women as an integral part of the permanent establishment, it failed to give them status equal to that accorded men."[8] From the outset of their formal integration into the military, women were treated differently

---

[6] See Public Law 625, Women's Armed Services Integration Act, June 12, 1948; M. C. Devilbiss, *Women and Military Service*, Maxwell Air Force Base, Ala.: Air University Press, 1990.

[7] Because the WAC already excluded women from combat, there was no need for a separate statute for Army servicewomen.

[8] Bettie Morden, *The Women's Army Corps, 1945–1978*, Washington, D.C.: Government Printing Office, 1990, p. 56.

than men, and restrictions were placed on their integration. These restrictions would remain in place for decades, and some continue to this day.

Korea and Vietnam

In response to the Korean War, the military's overall goal was to mobilize half a million to one million women to join. In spite of active recruiting efforts, the military fell far short of its goals.[9] At its peak, the number of women in the Armed Forces during the Korean conflict was 48,700, declining to about 35,000 by war's end in June 1955.[10] In 1951, Secretary of Defense George C. Marshall created the Defense Advisory Committee on Women in the Services (DACOWITS), a civilian advisory board, to advise on the recruitment and retention of military women for the Korean War. DACOWITS remains in existence today, and its recommendations have greatly impacted the evolution of women's roles in the military.

During the Vietnam War, the DoD had a goal of adding 6,500 women to the military in an attempt to reverse a downward trend after the Korean Conflict.[11] However, women continued to be used in very limited roles. In 1967, the 2-percent ceiling and promotion ceilings established by the Women's Armed Services Integration Act were lifted, partially in response to recommendations made by the DACOWITS. Despite the lifting of these ceilings, large numbers of women did not begin to join the military until the 1970s. Five years after the 2-percent ceiling was lifted, the non-nurse female proportion of the military stood at only 1.7 percent.[12] During this time, the military continued to rationalize the restriction of women due to their gender and physical capabilities. For instance, the Army reported that

> In the military service, the woman finds herself the minority among males; she requires separate facilities and is precluded for social reasons, and for her own safety, from performing duties within the confines of an all-male atmosphere. Physically, the military woman is not well suited for the rigors of field duty or capable of performing fatigue details normally performed by men, and cannot be considered self-sufficient enough in this regard to perform under the conditions experienced by maneuver elements in tactical operations. For this reason, the utilization of women in units below Corps level is not considered feasible.[13]

---

[9] Holm, 1992, p. 157.

[10] Holm, 1992, p. 157.

[11] Holm, 1992, p. 187.

[12] Francine D'Amico and Laurie Weinstein, eds., *Gender Camouflage: Women and the U.S. Military*, New York: New York University Press, 1999, p. 42.

[13] Butler, Jack Sibley, *Provide (U) Project Volunteer in Defense of the Nation*, Vol. II, Washington, D.C.: Directorate of Personnel Studies and Research, Department of the Army, 1969.

From the Advent of the All-Volunteer Force to Operation Desert Storm: 1971–1991

On September 28, 1971, President Richard Nixon signed the bill committing the country to an All-Volunteer Force (AVF),[14] and the draft formally ended on June 30, 1973. With the introduction of the AVF, there was an increased perception that women were needed to fill the ranks of the volunteer force and, subsequently, the services were directed to develop contingency plans to increase the use of women in the military.[15] It was only then that large numbers of women began to join the military.

In 1972, the Central All-Volunteer Force Task Force was created to examine issues related to ending the draft. One of the issues that the task force was charged with studying was "women in the military." When Congress passed the Equal Rights Amendment in April 1972, Assistant Secretary of Defense Roger T. Kelley instructed the services to "take action to eliminate all unnecessary [restrictions] applying to women."[16] At the end of 1972, the task force "conclud[ed] that the potential supply of military women could sustain a substantial increase in accession of military women," and the task force set goals to increase the number of women in all of the services.[17] In anticipation of the ratification of the Equal Rights Amendment, the Army and Navy decided to double the number of women in uniform; the Air Force chose to triple the number of women serving; and the Marines sought to increase the number of female Marines by 20 percent.[18]

In many ways, the role of women in the military during this time mirrored the developments in American society, including the emergence of the women's rights movement and feminism. In 1976, women were allowed to enter the nation's three service academies for the first time. In 1978, President Jimmy Carter signed Public Law 95-485, which: (1) disintegrated the all-female WAC and integrated women into the Regular Army and (2) allowed women in the Navy to be assigned to duty aboard noncombatant ships.[19]

Subsequently, the early 1980s marked a period in which the role of women in the military was reassessed. At this time, claims of "reverse discrimination" in the military also began to emerge. This issue came to a head in 1980, when Bernard Rostker, the director of the Selective Service System, was sued in an attempt to rescind women's exemption for selective service. The case was appealed to the Supreme Court, and in

---

[14] For a comprehensive account of the evolution of the All-Volunteer Force, see Bernard Rostker, *I Want You! The Evolution of the All-Volunteer Force*, Santa Monica, Calif.: RAND Corporation, MG-265-RC, 2006.

[15] Devilbiss, 1990, p. 13.

[16] Central All-Volunteer Task Force, *Utilization of Military Women: A Report of Increased Utilization of Military Women, FYs 1973–1977*, Washington, D.C.: Office of the Assistant Secretary of Defense (M&RA), AD764510, 1972, p. 8.

[17] Central All-Volunteer Task Force, 1972, p. 22.

[18] Rostker, 2006, p. 176.

[19] Public Law 95-485, Department of Defense Appropriation Authorization Act, October 20, 1978.

1981 the Court ruled that women are exempt from selective service because "women as a group . . . are not eligible for combat. The restrictions on the participation of women in combat in the Navy and Air Force are statutory."[20]

When the Reagan administration came into office in 1981, the Army decided to roll back the advances that women had made in the military during the Carter administration.[21] The Army announced its objection to OSD's goal to increase the number of enlisted women in the Active Army and instead voiced its desire to

> level out the number of enlisted women in the Active Army at 65,000. . . . These modifications were prompted by indications from field commanders that combat readiness is being affected by such factors as attrition, pregnancy, sole parenthood, and strength and stamina, which have come to light during the recent rapid increase in the number of women in the Army.[22]

Accordingly, the Army decided to take a "pause" in the recruitment of women in lieu of an examination of their impact on military readiness—a period subsequently termed "Womanpause."[23]

OSD was quick to respond and announced a rapid study of the impacts of women on readiness. When the study concluded, Secretary of Defense Casper Weinberger sent a memo to the Services indicating that

> Qualified women are essential to obtaining the numbers of quality people required to maintain the readiness of our forces. This Administration desires to increase the role of women in the military, and I expect the Service Secretaries actively to support that policy. . . . This Department must aggressively break down those remaining barriers that prevent us from making the fullest use of the capabilities of women in providing for our national defense.[24]

Therefore, the focus of the Reagan administration turned to eliminating institutional barriers for women in the military.[25] However, Lawrence Korb, an assistant secretary of defense, acknowledged that central to the issue of eliminating barriers was

---

[20] Rostker v. Goldberg, 453 U.S. 57, 1981.

[21] Rostker, 2006, p. 565.

[22] William D. Clark, "Women in the Army," memorandum to Acting Assistant Secretary of Defense (MRA&L), Washington, D.C., February 1981.

[23] Holm, 1992, pp. 380–388.

[24] Caspar W. Weinberger, "Women in the Military," Memorandum to Secretaries of the Military Departments, Washington, D.C., 1982.

[25] Rostker, 2006, p. 567.

the question of combat exclusions. If combat exclusions were legitimate, "the barriers that result are neither artificial nor discriminatory."[26]

In 1982, the Army reassessed the coding system it used to assess a woman's risk on the battlefield and, as a result, some jobs were restored to women while others were eliminated altogether. In response, Secretary Weinberger responded:

> It is the policy of this Department that women will be provided full and equal opportunity with men to pursue appropriate careers in the military services for which they can qualify. This means that military women can and should be utilized in all roles except those explicitly prohibited by combat exclusion statutes and related policy. This does *not* mean that the combat exclusion policy can be used to justify closing career opportunities to women. The combat exclusion rules should be interpreted to allow as many as possible career opportunities for women to be kept open.[27]

In 1988, a task force proposed a new "risk rule which excluded women from noncombat units or missions if the risks of exposure to direct combat, hostile fire, or capture were equal to or greater than the risk in the combat units they supported."[28] In less than two years, Assistant Secretary Christopher Jehn reported to Congress that, as a result of the new "at risk" rule, "31,000 new positions were opened to women in both the active and reserve components [and] over 63 percent of all positions in the services are now open to women."[29]

From Desert Storm to Today: 1991–2010

Of the more than half a million U.S. troops deployed to the Persian Gulf during Operations Desert Shield and Desert Storm, approximately 7 percent (about 41,000) were women.[30] This precipitated major changes in policy with regard to the role of women in the military, including a reexamination of exclusionary laws. In 1991, Congress repealed 10 U.S.C. 8549, the combat aviation exclusion and, in a compromise move, established a presidential commission to study the issue of combat exclusions further.[31]

---

[26] Lawrence Korb, "Women in the Military," information memorandum to Secretary of Defense, Washington, D.C., August 16, 1982.

[27] Caspar W. Weinberger, "Women in the Military," Memorandum to Thomas K. Turnage, Washington, D.C., 1983, emphasis in the original.

[28] U.S. General Accounting Office, *Information on DoD's Assignment Policy and Direct Ground Combat Definition*, Washington, D.C.: U.S. General Accounting Office, 1988, p. 2.

[29] Christopher Jehn, Women in the Military, hearing Before the House Armed Service Committee, Subcommittee on Military Personnel and Compensation, 101st Congress, 2nd Session, Washington, D.C., March 20, 1990.

[30] U.S. General Accounting Office, *Women in the Military: Deployment in the Persian Gulf War*, Washington, D.C.: GAO/NSIAD-93-93, July 1993, p. 10.

[31] Rostker, 2006, p. 572; Holm, 1992, pp. 473–510.

The Presidential Commission on the Assignment of Women in the Armed Forces, consisting of nine men and seven women,[32] spent seven months taking testimony from more than 300 witnesses. It also solicited comments from more than 3,000 retired officers, considered 11,000 letters and statements, and visited 22 military installations.[33] While there was division and acrimony within the Commission, as well as external criticism of it, the commission issued a report in 1992 and proposed several recommendations, including the following:[34]

- adoption by the military services of "gender-neutral assignment policies" to ensure that no one is denied access to a post open to both men and women on the basis of gender
- acknowledging the physiological differences between men and women, and calling on services to "retain gender-specific physical fitness tests and standards to promote the highest level of general fitness and wellness"
- the retention of existing policies that did not allow for the assignment of servicewomen to Special Operations Forces apart from service in a medical, linguistic, or civil affairs capacity
- a new law banning women from air combat positions (18 months after Congress repealed an identical law), as well as urging legislation to exclude women from ground combat assignments in the infantry, artillery, and armor, as well as certain assignments in air defense and combat engineers
- opening nonflying positions to women on Navy combat ships while disqualifying women from service on submarines and landing aircraft.

Five commission members were not happy with the conclusions of the report and instead issued an "Alternative View Section."[35] The crux of the alternative view was that "the military, in building fighting units, must be able to choose those most able to fight and win in battle."[36] The alternative view argued that allowing women to serve in combat units would endanger not only women, but also the men serving with

---

[32] Some commission members would later become central figures in the debate on gay rights in the military, including Charlie Moskos—a military sociologist and the architect of Don't Ask Don't Tell; retired Army Colonel Darryl Henderson—former commander of the Army Research Institute and author of *Cohesion: The Human Element in Combat*, who argued that cohesion could not be developed in mixed-gender units; and Elaine Donnelly—president of the Center for Military Readiness and a frequent critic of defense personnel policies.

[33] Rostker, 2006, p. 574.

[34] Presidential Commission on the Assignment of Women in the Armed Forces, *Report to the President*, November 15, 1992, Washington, D.C.: Government Printing Office, 1992a.

[35] Presidential Commission on the Assignment of Women in the Armed Forces, "Section II—Alternative Views: The Case Against Women in Combat," *The Presidential Commission on the Assignment of Women in the Armed Forces: Report to the President*, November 15, 1992, Washington, D.C.: Government Printing Office, 1992b.

[36] The Presidential Commission on the Assignment of Women in the Armed Forces, 1992b, p. 44.

them.[37] In addition, the alternative view noted that the issue of women in combat is not comparable to racial integration in 1948 because "dual standards are not needed to compensate for physical differences between racial groups, but they are needed where men and women are concerned."[38]

It was left to incoming Secretary of Defense Les Aspin to arbitrate the competing views expressed on the Commission.[39] In April 1993, President Bill Clinton ordered the services to open combat aviation to women and to investigate other opportunities for women to serve. In response, Aspin ordered the services to "permit women to compete for assignments in aircraft including aircraft engaged in combat missions."[40] Later that year, Congress repealed 10 U.S.C. 6015 (the combat ship exclusion), opening most Navy combatant ships to women except submarines. In 1994, DoD rescinded its "risk rule" because "the rule no longer applied since, based on experiences during [Operation] DESERT STORM, everyone in the theater of operation was at risk."[41] DoD also announced its new ground combat exclusion:

> Women shall be excluded from assignment to units below the brigade level whose primary mission is to engage in direct combat on the ground . . . with individual or crew served weapons, while being exposed to hostile fire and to a high probability of direct physical contact with hostile force's personnel.[42]

As a result of these and other policy changes, the number of positions open to women increased substantially. For instance, in both the Navy and the Marine Corps, about 30 percent more positions were open to women.[43] Before these policy changes in 1993, 67 percent of positions were available to women in the military; by 1997, 80.2 percent of positions in the military were available to them.[44]

---

[37] The Presidential Commission on the Assignment of Women in the Armed Forces, 1992b, p. 44

[38] The Presidential Commission on the Assignment of Women in the Armed Forces, 1992b, p. 45.

[39] Rostker, 2006, p. 574.

[40] Les Aspin, "Policy on the Assignment of Women in the Armed Forces," Memorandum to Secretaries of the Military Department, Chairman of the Joint Chiefs of Staff, Assistant Secretary of Defense (FM&P) and Assistant Secretary of Defense (RA), Washington, D.C., 1993.

[41] U.S. General Accounting Office, *Information on DoD's Assignment Policy and Direct Ground Combat Definition*, Washington, D.C.: U.S. General Accounting Office, 1988, p. 3.

[42] Aspin, 1993. According to DoD officials from the Office of the Under Secretary of Defense for Personnel and Readiness, "the prohibition on direct ground combat was a long-standing Army policy, and for that reason, no consideration was given to repealing it when DoD adopted the current assignment policy in 1994" (U.S. General Accounting Office, 1988).

[43] Margaret C. Harrell and Laura L. Miller, *New Opportunities for Military Women: Effects Upon Readiness, Cohesion, and Morale*, Santa Monica, Calif.: RAND Corporation, MR-896-OSD, 1997, p. xvii.

[44] Harrell and Miller, 1997, p. 12.

OEF and OIF Blurred the Lines of Direct Combat

The wars in Iraq and Afghanistan proved to be a pivotal watershed in the story of the integration of women into the military. Peter R. Mansoor, a retired Army colonel who served as executive officer to General David H. Petraeus while he was the top American commander in Iraq, noted that "Iraq has advanced the cause of full integration for women in the Army by leaps and bounds. . . . They have earned the confidence and respect of male colleagues."[45] The wars in Afghanistan and Iraq presented a less predictable, nonlinear battlefield with asymmetric threats that could potentially expose female soldiers to combat. This caused some to question the relevance of the ground combat exclusions, since some female soldiers were already experiencing combat.

As the Army developed its new modularity plan in the midst of the wars in Iraq and Afghanistan, concerns grew once again over the potential exposure of women to combat. In May 2005, House Armed Services Committee Chairman Duncan Hunter (R-Calif.), introduced a bill that would have (1) prohibited women from serving in any company-size unit that provided support to combat battalions or their subordinate companies and (2) blocked the assignment of women to thousands of positions previously open to them, and in which they were already serving. The Army opposed this bill, with General Richard A. Cody, the Army's Vice Chief of Staff, noting, "[t]he proposed amendment will cause confusion in the ranks, and will send the wrong signal to the brave young men and women fighting the Global War on Terrorism."[46] The bill was ultimately defeated.

In February 2010, Secretary of Defense Robert Gates notified Congress of the Department of the Navy's desire to reverse the policy of prohibiting women from submarine service. When General George Casey, the U.S. Army's chief of staff, was asked about his view on allowing women to serve in combat roles, he told the Senate Armed Services Committee that it was time to review the policy. "I believe it's time we take a look at what women are actually doing in Iraq and Afghanistan and to look at our policy," Casey said.[47] In 2012, the Army announced that it would open as many as 14,000 combat-related jobs in six MOSs at the battalion level. Brigadier General Barry Price, the director of human resources policy at the time at the Army G-1 (Personnel) said, "The last 11 years of warfare have really revealed to us there are no front lines. There are no rear echelons. Everybody was vulnerable to the influence of the Army." In May 2012, Representative Loretta Sanchez (D-Calif.) and Senator Kirsten Gillibrand (D-N.Y.) introduced legislation in both houses of Congress to encourage the repeal of the ground combat exclusion.[48] These were ultimately defeated. In May 2012,

---

[45] Lizette Alvarez, "Women at Arms: G.I. Jane Breaks the Combat Barrier," *New York Times*, August 15, 2009.

[46] Ann Scott Tyson, "Panel Votes to Ban Women from Combat," *Washington Post*, May 12, 2005.

[47] Gearan, Anne, "Navy Will Soon Let Women Serve on Subs," *Associated Press*, February 23, 2010.

[48] Jena McGregor, "Military Women in Combat: Why Making it Official Matters," *Washington Post*, May 25, 2012.

two Army reservists also filed a lawsuit that sought to overturn the remaining ground combat exclusions, claiming that the exclusions limit "their current and future earnings, their potential for promotion and advancement, and their future retirement."[49]

The latest expansion of the role of women in the military came in January 2013, when Defense Secretary Leon Panetta announced that the ground combat exclusion would be lifted. Panetta said women had already found themselves in "the reality of conflict" in Iraq and Afghanistan, and that not everyone can meet the qualifications to be a combat soldier, but everyone is entitled to that opportunity.[50] This decision overturned the 1994 rule that banned women from being assigned to ground combat units and could open more than 230,000 positions to women. The services were required to report their implementation plans to DoD by May 2013, and they have until January 2016 to seek exemptions if they want any positions to remain closed to women. It is within this context that the USMC considers the implications of integrating women into its infantry.

---

[49]   McGregor, 2012.

[50]   "Military Leaders Lift Ban on Women in Combat Roles," *Fox News,* January 24, 2013.

CHAPTER THREE

Research on Cohesion

One area of potential concern when integrating women into male-dominated professions is the effect that integration might have on group cohesion. This is for good reason: research on group cohesion has demonstrated that cohesion has a direct relationship with important outcomes such as group performance and job satisfaction. It is unclear whether gender integration will impact group cohesion in Marine Corps infantry units, but in specific situations, gender integration has been shown to negatively affect group cohesion. However, as illustrated in this chapter, there are evidence-based actions that the Marine Corps can take to mitigate potential negative impacts of gender integration on group cohesion, and to address any negative consequences should they occur. The following review of the literature draws upon research conducted in both military and civilian settings, with special attention paid to research in a military context.

Definition of Cohesion

In order to understand the current state of the literature on group cohesion, it is necessary to understand the various ways that researchers have defined cohesion and how it has been measured. Research on group cohesion grew out of work done on military competencies during World War II.[1] Early conceptions of cohesion were very broad. For instance, Leon Festinger defined *group cohesion* as

> the resultant of all the forces acting on the members to remain in the group. These forces may depend on the attractiveness or unattractiveness of either the prestige of the group, members in the group, or the activities in which the group engages.[2]

---

[1] Edward A. Shils and Morris Janowitz, "Cohesion and Disintegration in the Wehrmacht in World War II," *Public Opinion Quarterly*, Vol. 12, No. 2, 1948, pp. 280–315.

[2] Leon Festinger, "Informal Social Communication," *Psychological Review*, Vol. 57, No. 5, 1950, p. 271.

Perhaps because cohesion depends on the levels of several different forces that work to keep the group together, subsequent definitions of group cohesion have been inconsistent, often focusing on one aspect of cohesion at the expense of others.[3] Thus, although group cohesion is a concept that has long been used and understood in the military and civilian world, the topic is controversial among behavioral researchers. The controversy is not about whether or not group cohesion is a valid group process, but about the best way to define—and consequently measure—group cohesion. The controversy is not just a matter of theory: How cohesion is defined and measured has implications for the extent to which gender integration can be expected to bear on cohesion and the recommended strategies for mitigating any negative impact. Due to the importance of this controversy, we will spend the next few paragraphs giving an overview of the different definitions of group cohesion and the evidence relating each variation of cohesion with group outcomes important to the Marine Corps.

Task and Social Cohesion

In the military and civilian literature, one distinction between cohesive forces that has considerable backing is the distinction between social and task cohesion.[4] *Task cohesion* is defined as the "shared commitment among members to achieving a goal that requires the collective efforts of the group,"[5] while *social cohesion* is defined as the "nature and quality of the emotional bonds of friendship, liking, caring, and closeness among group members."[6] Task cohesion is important for goal attainment: When groups are cohesive around their group-based tasks, achievement of group goals also allows individuals to meet their personal goals.[7] There is consistent evidence of a positive relationship between task cohesion and group performance.[8] For example, research on group decisionmaking has shown that groups with higher task cohesion perform

---

[3] Peter E. Mudrack, "Defining Group Cohesiveness: A Legacy of Confusion?" *Small Group Research,* Vol. 20, No. 1, February 1, 1989: pp. 37–49.

[4] Robert J. MacCoun and William M. Hix, Unit Cohesion and Military Performance, Santa Monica, Calif.: RAND Corporation, MG-1056-OSD, 2010; Brian Mullen and Carolyn Copper, "The Relation Between Group Cohesiveness and Performance: An Integration," *Psychological Bulletin*, Vol. 115, No. 2, 1994, p. 210; Stephen J. Zaccaro and Charles A Lowe, "Cohesiveness and Performance on an Additive Task: Evidence for Multidimensionality," *Journal of Social Psychology*, Vol. 128, No. 4, 1988:, pp. 547–558.

[5] MacCoun and Hix, 2010, p. 157.

[6] MacCoun and Hix, 2010, p. 157.

[7] Leon Festinger, Kurt W. Back, and Stanley Schachter, *Social Pressures in Informal Groups: A Study of Human Factors in Housing,* Stanford University Press, 1950.

[8] Daniel J. Beal, Robin R. Cohen, Michael J. Burke, and Christy L. McLendon, "Cohesion and Performance in Groups: A Meta-Analytic Clarification of Construct Relations," *Journal of Applied Psychology,* Vol. 88, No. 6, 2003, p. 989; Mullen and Copper, 1994.

better under time pressure than do groups with lower task cohesion.[9] In contrast, social cohesion emphasizes interpersonal liking and social activities. The focus of task cohesion on job-related tasks rather than purely social activities suggests that task cohesion is a more relevant outcome to consider when integrating women into the Marine Corps infantry than is social cohesion. Indeed, there is some evidence that task cohesion better predicts group performance than does social cohesion.[10]

Task cohesion is also a more defined construct to measure than is social cohesion. Task cohesion is assessed by measuring individual and group commitment to group-based goals (e.g., agreement with the statement: "Our team is united in trying to reach its goals for performance"). Social cohesion's focus on liking is more problematic: There are many factors that influence liking between individuals.[11] Research on interpersonal liking considers liking as an outcome to be predicted by different aspects of people's relationships, rather than a predictor of a group process such as cohesion. Importantly, factors that predict liking can also be task related, such as trust, effective communication, and openness to opposing ideas. But factors that predict liking can also be unrelated to group tasks, such as shared activities and preferences, common ideologies, and similar demographic backgrounds (e.g., race, age, socioeconomic status).

The task-related aspects of social cohesion help explain why research has shown that there is substantial overlap in task and social processes, especially in groups where members need effective and efficient interaction to succeed.[12] For instance, research on gender-integrated Air Force units demonstrated that social cohesion in integrated units significantly predicted unit teamwork, as assessed by external observers.[13] Research has also shown that female Marines are susceptible to the same gender stereotypes as women outside the Marine Corps (e.g., they are perceived as having less ability than male Marines).[14] Furthermore, research on the influence of gender stereotypes on

---

[9] Stephen J. Zaccaro, James Gualtieri, and David Minionis, "Task Cohesion as a Facilitator of Team Decision Making Under Temporal Urgency," *Military Psychology*, Vol. 7, No. 2, 1995, p. 77.

[10] For example, see Mullen and Copper, 1994, for a review.

[11] Robert B. Hays, "The Development and Maintenance of Friendship," *Journal of Social and Personal Relationships*, Vol. 1, No. 1, March 1984, pp. 75–98; Roy F. Baumeister and Mark R. Leary, "The Need to Belong: Desire for Interpersonal Attachments as a Fundamental Human Motivation," *Psychological Bulletin*, Vol. 117, No. 3, 1995, p. 497; Jean-Philippe Laurenceau, Lisa Feldman Barrett, and Paula R. Pietromonaco, "Intimacy as an Interpersonal Process: The Importance of Self-Disclosure, Partner Disclosure, and Perceived Partner Responsiveness in Interpersonal Exchanges," *Journal of Personality and Social Psychology*, Vol. 74, No. 5, June 1998, p. 1238.

[12] Stephen J. Zaccaro and M. Catherine McCoy, "The Effects of Task and Interpersonal Cohesiveness on Performance of a Disjunctive Group Task," *Journal of Applied Social Psychology*, Vol. 18, No. 10, 1988, pp. 837–851.

[13] Robert R. Hirschfeld, Mark H. Jordan, Hubert S. Feild, William F. Giles, and Achilles A. Armenakis, "Teams' Female Representation and Perceived Potency as Inputs to Team Outcomes in a Predominantly Male Field Setting," *Personnel Psychology*, Vol. 58, No. 4, December 2005, pp. 893–924.

[14] Emerald M. Archer, "The Power of Gendered Stereotypes in the US Marine Corps," *Armed Forces and Society*, Vol. 39, No. 2, April 1, 2013, pp. 359–391.

marksmanship has shown that making female stereotypes salient to female Marines leads them to perform worse at marksmanship compared to female Marines who did not experience stereotype salience.[15] A recent meta-analysis of cohesion research found that both task and social cohesion predict performance-related behaviors (e.g., "ratings of specific combat behaviors during tactical field problems") and performance efficiency, especially when the tasks involve a high degree of reciprocity and/or collaboration between group members.[16] Thus, we consider findings for both task and social cohesion in the following review of the literature, but important divergences in findings between each type of cohesion will be highlighted where relevant.

Vertical and Horizontal Cohesion

Another body of literature on military cohesion defines cohesion as having both vertical and horizontal dimensions.[17] *Vertical cohesion* is defined as bonding between followers and their leaders, and *horizontal cohesion* is defined as bonding between group members at the same level.[18] Although much research on cohesion in military groups uses these definitions of cohesion, the vertical dimension overlaps with the more precisely defined constructs of leadership and followership,[19] and the horizontal dimension mixes elements of both task and social cohesion among group members. As noted above, the distinction between the task and social aspects of cohesion is important in determining the exact nature of the impact of gender integration on the group and for determining the best policies and procedures for mitigating any negative impact of gender integration. Therefore, in this chapter we will use the more precise definitions of task and social cohesion.

Relationship Between Cohesion and Performance

In general, prior research demonstrates that more cohesive groups perform better than less cohesive groups. Several researchers have analyzed the results of previous studies and found significant relationships between cohesion and various measures of individual and group performance. Some of these meta-analyses have made distinctions

---

[15] Emerald M. Archer, "You Shoot Like a Girl: Stereotype Threat and Marksmanship Performance in the U.S. Marine Corps," *The International Journal of Interdisciplinary Civic and Political Studies*, Vol. 8, No. 1, 2014, pp. 9–21.

[16] Beal et al., 2003. Performance outcomes and measures of the overall effectiveness of the group were not associated with group cohesion, perhaps because group inputs such as preparedness and ability were not taken into account by the research.

[17] Guy L. Siebold, "The Essence of Military Group Cohesion," *Armed Forces and Society*, Vol. 33, No. 2, January 1, 2007, pp. 286–295; Guy L. Siebold, "Key Questions and Challenges to the Standard Model of Military Group Cohesion," *Armed Forces and Society*, Vol. 37, No. 3, July 1, 2011, pp. 448–468.

[18] Siebold, 2007.

[19] Edwin P. Hollander, "Leadership, Followership, Self, and Others," *Leadership Quarterly*, Vol. 3, No. 1, 1992, pp. 43–54.

between research on different types of cohesion—primarily between task and social cohesion—while other meta-analyses have not separated the findings from research on task and social cohesion. For example, an analysis of studies of military units found that unit cohesion was positively associated with unit performance across studies.[20] However, this analysis did not distinguish studies of task cohesion from studies of other types of cohesion. One analysis of the military and civilian literature on the relationship between individual levels of cohesion and performance found that task cohesion, but not social cohesion, was associated with better performance.[21] A recent analysis of 64 research publications examining unit-level cohesion and performance found that both task and social cohesion were related to better unit-level performance.[22] This was particularly true when performance was measured as a process (e.g., group communication, coordination of actions) rather than as an outcome (e.g., successfully accomplishing a task, performance time). Thus, research findings that link social cohesion and performance may be due to the relationship between interpersonal communication and coordination and performance rather than between liking and performance.

Importantly, there is evidence that the link between unit cohesion and performance is bidirectional. Mullen and Copper's (1994) analysis revealed that unit cohesion increases performance, but also that increasing unit performance leads to greater unit cohesion. In fact, the evidence suggests that the effect of performance on cohesion is stronger than the effect of cohesion on performance.[23] Thus, increasing cohesion can increase performance, but performing well can also feed back to increase unit cohesion.

Gender Integration and Cohesion
The expansion of the role of women in the military caused some to warn that "an accumulation of problems will have a devastating impact on combat readiness, unit cohesion and military effectiveness."[24] We found that a number of studies indicated that these concerns about the detrimental impact of women on military readiness and cohesion did not materialize.

The General Accounting Office (GAO) visited ten units, which had both men and women assigned to them, after their return from deployment to the Persian Gulf War. The GAO found that gender was not generally identified as a component or

[20] Laurel W. Oliver, Joan Harman, Elizabeth Hoover, Stephanie M. Hayes, and Nancy A. Pandhi, "A Quantitative Integration of the Military Cohesion Literature," *Military Psychology*, Vol. 11, No. 1, 1999, p. 57.

[21] Mullen and Copper, 1994.

[22] Beal et al., 2003.

[23] Mullen and Copper, 1994.

[24] The Presidential Commission on the Assignment of Women in the Armed Forces, 1992b, p. 48.

determinant of cohesion, and most respondents considered bonding in mixed units to be as good as, and sometimes better than, bonding in single-gender units.[25]

In 1997, RAND was also asked to assess the impact of the watershed policy changes in the early to mid- 1990s on readiness, cohesion, and morale. The RAND study found that the integration of women had not had a major effect on readiness, cohesion, or morale.[26] In the units that RAND studied, neither gender issues nor the presence of women were perceived to have a significant impact on readiness.[27] The study also found that divisions caused by gender were minimal or invisible in units with high cohesion. Gender was an issue only in units characterized as "divided into conflicting groups, and then it took second place to divisions along the lines of work groups or, within work groups, along the lines of rank."[28] Lastly, the study found that "gender is one of many issues that affect morale, but it is not one of the primary factors influencing morale."[29] The studies mentioned above also reinforce the fact that diversity may have some impact on social cohesion (because some members may be uncomfortable with a particular individual or group), but it does not necessarily have a negative impact on task cohesion. People do not necessarily have to like the people that they work with in order to carry out a job well.

The Importance of Unit Culture for Successful Gender Integration

Research has demonstrated that the impact of integrating women on the cohesion of traditionally male groups depends on the culture of the group—groups more hostile to women experience lower cohesion after gender integration than do groups less hostile toward women. Research examining the integration of women into Army units showed that the impact of integration on cohesion varied by the degree of hypermasculine culture exhibited by the unit.[30] *Hypermasculine culture* was defined as one where interactions among group members are "characterized by exaggerated masculine values and interactions."[31] The researchers found that, while hypermasculinity was associated with more cohesion in all-male units, in mixed-gender units, hypermasculinity was associated with less unit cohesion.[32]

---

[25] U.S. General Accounting Office, *Women in the Military: Deployment in the Persian Gulf War*, Washington, D.C., GAO/NSIAD-93-93, July 1993.

[26] Harrell and Miller, 1997.

[27] Harrell and Miller, 1997, p. 34.

[28] Harrell and Miller, 1997, p. 66.

[29] Harrell and Miller, 1997, p. 69.

[30] Leora N. Rosen, Kathryn H. Knudson, and Peggy Fancher, "Cohesion and the Culture of Hypermasculinity in US Army Units," *Armed Forces and Society*, Vol. 29, No. 3, Spring 2003, pp. 325–351.

[31] Rosen, Knudson, and Fancher, 2003.

[32] Rosen, Knudson, and Fancher, 2003.

Sexual harassment against women is another indicator of unit culture, and a recent study found that 21 percent of women in the military reported experiencing workplace sexual harassment in the past year, with 27 percent of female Marines reporting that they experienced harassment in their workplace.[33] Similarly, research on sexual harassment in Army units found that mixed-gender units with more sexual harassment were less cohesive, less accepting of women, and less ready for combat than those units with less sexual harassment.[34] This research also demonstrated that cohesion suffers for both men and women in mixed-gender units with hypermasculine cultures and/or higher levels of sexual harassment. In addition, research on civilian organizations has found that a higher overall level of sexual harassment in a work group is associated with more team social and task conflict[35] and lower organizational commitment by women.[36] Furthermore, research indicates that female service members who experience sexual harassment are more likely than others to leave the military.[37]

In contrast, commentators have argued that the hypermasculine environment engendered in many military units is necessary for cohesion in combat units—that masculinity is an important element in holding the unit together and making it a well-functioning team.[38] Other commentators have argued that masculinity is only one of the forces keeping a group together, and other forces, such as loyalty and task importance, are as central to unit cohesion as masculinity.[39] Masculinity could be defined as a force for social cohesion because it is a way for men to bond with one another, ostensibly unrelated to the unit's task. As such, regardless of whether hypermasculinity increases male social bonding within units, the reduction of hypermasculinity in gender-integrated units should neither affect task cohesion nor be detrimental to unit performance.

In conclusion, where the environment is not hostile toward women, integration is less likely to negatively affect cohesion; indeed integration has been found to increase

---

[33] National Defense Research Institute, *Sexual Assault and Sexual Harassment in the U.S. Military: Top-Line Estimates for Active-Duty Coast Guard Members from the 2014 RAND Military Workplace Study*, Santa Monica, Calif.: RAND Corporation, RR-944-USCG, 2014.

[34] Leora N. Rosen and Lee Martin, "Sexual Harassment, Cohesion, and Combat Readiness in U.S. Army Support Units," *Armed Forces and Society,* Vol. 24, No. 2, Winter 1998, pp. 221–244.

[35] Jana L. Raver and Michele J. Gelfand, "Beyond the Individual Victim: Linking Sexual Harassment, Team Processes, and Team Performance," *Academy of Management Journal,* Vol. 48, No. 3, 2005, pp. 387–400.

[36] Anne M. O'Leary-Kelly, Lynn Bowes-Sperry, Collette Arens Bates, and Emily R. Lean, "Sexual Harassment at Work: A Decade (Plus) of Progress," *Journal of Management*, Vol. 35, No. 3, June 2009, pp. 503–536.

[37] Carra S. Sims, Fritz Drasgow, and Louise F. Fitzgerald, "The Effects of Sexual Harassment on Turnover in the Military: Time-Dependent Modeling," *Journal of Applied Psychology*, Vol. 90, No. 6, 2005, p. 1141.

[38] Kingsley Browne, *Co-Ed Combat: The New Evidence that Women Shouldn't Fight the Nation's Wars*, New York: Penguin, 2007.

[39] Madeline Morris, "By Force of Arms: Rape, War, and Military Culture," *Duke Law Journal*, Vol. 45, 1996, p. 651.

cohesion in some cases. In contrast, when the social context creates a hostile work environment for women, gender integration is more likely to have negative consequences for unit cohesion. This may help explain why some studies of gender integration in the military have found no negative effects of integration on cohesion,[40] while others have found that gender-integrated units are less cohesive than all-male units.[41]

Steps to Lessen the Impact of Gender Integration on Cohesion

Although the military and civilian literature emphasizes the potential negative impact of gender integration on group cohesion, it also demonstrates the steps that organizations can take to prevent any negative impacts of gender integration on cohesion and to mitigate negative effects if they occur. As detailed below, a substantial body of research has revealed that the factors associated with successful integration of women include leadership, cohesion-building activities, and time. .

Good Leadership Is Key

Research has found that leadership styles and practices have considerable impact on cohesion in diverse groups. Research has demonstrated that leadership is important for building unit cohesion among integrated units,[42] and successful bonding with leaders is an important dimension of cohesion.[43] Several studies show that specific leadership practices are associated with higher cohesiveness in diverse groups, including (1) respect and fairness and (2) leadership style and tone.

Respect, Fairness, and a Supportive Environment

Perceptions of respect and fair treatment by leaders are central aspects of group commitment and cohesion.[44] In mixed-gender groups, research has shown that group cohesion is highest in groups where both men and women perceive that they are respected and treated fairly by group leaders.[45] In this research, respect was defined as women

---

[40] For instance, in the Israeli military; see Sasson-Levy, 2003.

[41] For instance, see Leora N. Rosen, Doris B. Durand, Paul D. Bliese, Ronald R. Halverson, Joseph M. Rothberg, and Nancy L. Harrison, "Cohesion and Readiness in Gender-Integrated Combat Service Support Units: The Impact of Acceptance of Women and Gender Ratio," *Armed Forces and Society*, Vol. 22, No. 4, 1996, pp. 537–553.

[42] Guy L. Siebold and Twila J. Lindsay, "The Relation Between Demographic Descriptors and Soldier-Perceived Cohesion and Motivation," *Military Psychology*, Vol. 11, No. 1, 1999, pp. 109–128.

[43] Siebold, 2007.

[44] Heather J. Smith, Tom R. Tyler, and Yuen J. Huo, "Interpersonal Treatment, Social Identity, and Organizational Behavior," *Social Identity at Work: Developing Theory for Organizational Practice*, 2003, pp. 155–171.

[45] Donna Chrobot-Mason, and Nicholas P. Aramovich, "The Psychological Benefits of Creating an Affirming Climate for Workplace Diversity," *Group and Organization Management*, Vol. 38, No. 6, 2013, pp. 659–689.

being fully integrated into the functions and roles of the group. Additional research on women in male-dominated fields has found that women who feel they have been treated fairly and have not been discriminated against perform better and feel more integrated into male-dominated groups.[46] In addition, when unit cohesion is a problem in gender-integrated military units, the complaint is often that women and men are treated differently in the unit (e.g., different standards for men and women, segregated housing).[47] Thus, leaders of gender-integrated units who display fair and equitable treatment of both women and men are likely to encourage group cohesiveness.

Leadership Style and Tone

Leaders differ in their style of leadership and the tone they set for their group. Research has demonstrated that leadership style and tone are associated with differential success for gender integration. The relationship between transformational leadership style and successful gender integration has been examined in research. Transformational leaders are ones who "[move] followers beyond their self-interests for the good of the group, organization, or society."[48] Transformational leadership is associated with greater group cohesion and better performance.[49] Furthermore, one study found that, compared to nontransformational leaders, transformational leaders of diverse teams fostered more team cohesion, which was associated with better team performance.[50]

In the same manner that good leadership can facilitate cohesion between diverse group members, poor leadership can undermine group cohesion. Poor leadership can make gender integration worse by setting a negative tone or by purposefully separating women from men, making it difficult for them to work together.[51] Furthermore, poor leadership can create a hostile work environment, where sexual harassment is tolerated by leadership and other members of the unit, and bonding with leaders is low.[52]

---

[46] Laura Smart Richman, Michelle vanDellen, and Wendy Wood, "How Women Cope: Being a Numerical Minority in a Male-Dominated Profession," *Journal of Social Issues*, Vol. 67, No. 3, September 2011, pp. 492–509.

[47] Harrell and Miller, 1997.

[48] Bernard M. Bass, "Does the Transactional-Transformational Leadership Paradigm Transcend Organizational and National Boundaries?" *American Psychologist*, Vol. 52, No. 2, 1997, pp. 130–139.

[49] Bernard M. Bass, Bruce J. Avolio, Dong I. Jung, and Yair Berson, "Predicting Unit Performance by Assessing Transformational and Transactional Leadership," *Journal of Applied Psychology*, Vol. 88, No. 2, 2003, p. 207; Greg L. Stewart, "A Meta-Analytic Review of Relationships Between Team Design Features and Team Performance," *Journal of Management*, Vol. 32, No. 1, February 1, 2006, pp. 29–55.

[50] Eric Kearney and Diether Gebert, "Managing Diversity and Enhancing Team Outcomes: The Promise of Transformational Leadership," *Journal of Applied Psychology,* Vol. 94, No. 1, January 2009, pp. 77–89.

[51] Harrell and Miller, 1997.

[52] Rosen and Martin, 1998.

Cohesion-Building Activities

One way that gender-integrated units can build cohesion is through structured cohesion-building activities. Research suggests that activities that integrate women and support them in contributing to unit success increase cohesion in mixed-gender units. For example, group success breeds cohesion and vice versa,[53] so successful group-based tasks that involve the participation of all group members, including women, lead to higher group cohesion. It is important that women be allowed to perform roles in these activities that allow them to thrive as part of the group. Research on gender-integrated military teams has found that early group success leads to greater group cohesiveness,[54] and research with Norwegian naval cadets shows that the shared experience of stressful training activities is associated with increased unit cohesiveness.[55] In addition, qualitative research on women in Army units suggests that units where women perform well on group tasks are more cohesive than units where women perform poorly.[56] Marine Corps training creates a good atmosphere in which to provide cohesion-building activities for gender integrated units.

In addition to structured team-building activities, creating an environment where women are not isolated from the men in the unit can foster cohesion. Evidence from qualitative studies of gender integration in the United States,[57] Canada, [58] and Norway[59] suggest that women experience greater cohesion with their unit when housing and facilities for women and men are integrated rather than segregated by gender. For example, gender-segregated accommodations during field operations created the perception of unequal standards for men and women,[60] and separate berthing on ships isolated women from communications with their peers and leadership.[61]

Effects of Time

Although Marine Corps leaders need to be cognizant of potential problems early in the integration process, research suggests that early difficulties with integration do not purport longer-term failure. In general, cohesion within gender-diverse groups improves

---

[53] Mullen and Copper, 1994.

[54] Hirschfeld et al., 2005.

[55] P. T. Bartone, B. H. Johnsen, J. Eid, W. Brun, and J. C. Laberg, "Factors Influencing Small-Unit Cohesion in Norwegian Navy Officer Cadets," *Military Psychology*, Vol. 14, No. 1, 2002, pp. 1–22.

[56] Harrell and Miller, 1997.

[57] Harrell and Miller, 1997.

[58] Chief Review Services, 1998; Vivian, 1998.

[59] *Norwegian Report to Committee on Women in NATO Forces*, March 26, 2002.

[60] Vivian, 1998.

[61] Harrell and Miller, 1997.

over time.[62] For example, Canada's early studies of the integration of women into the Canadian Forces found that women felt isolated from males in their units, but over time the negative effects of integration on cohesion lessened.[63] Therefore, instead of assuming that any early cohesion problems are permanent, leaders should take a longer time frame that allows cohesion to develop more slowly.

In summary, although the integration of women into male-dominated groups can have detrimental effects on group cohesion, these effects can be mitigated through a variety of methods. Good leadership is key to increasing the acceptance of women. Leaders who treat both women and men fairly, provide support for women, and emphasize the good of the group create cohesive groups where women are fully integrated into group life. In addition, women perform better in groups where they are not the only woman in the group;[64] however, the best proportion of women for group cohesion is not clear from the existing research. Finally, there are cohesion-building activities that the Marine Corps can put in place to build cohesion in gender-integrated groups, and it is important to understand that cohesion in integrated groups is likely to increase over time as groups work together and develop a sense of shared group identity.

Implications

Although group cohesion is an important concept in both military and civilian literature on group functioning and performance, cohesion as a construct has been difficult to define[65] and measure.[66] Many different measures of cohesion have been used,[67] and

---

[62] David A. Harrison, Kenneth H. Price, and Myrtle P. Bell, "Beyond Relational Demography: Time and the Effects of Surface- and Deep-Level Diversity on Work Group Cohesion," *Academy of Management Journal,* Vol. 41, No. 1, February 1, 1998, pp. 96–107; Warren E. Watson, Kamalesh Kumar, and Larry K. Michaelsen, "Cultural Diversity's Impact on Interaction Process and Performance: Comparing Homogeneous and Diverse Task Groups," *Academy of Management Journal,* Vol. 36, No. 3, June 1, 1993, pp. 590–602.

[63] Winslow and Dunn, 2001.

[64] Charles G. Lord and Delia S. Saenz, "Memory Deficits and Memory Surfeits: Differential Cognitive Consequences of Tokenism for Tokens and Observers," *Journal of Personality and Social Psychology,* Vol. 49, No. 4, 1985, p. 918; Denise Sekaquaptewa and Mischa Thompson, "Solo Status, Stereotype Threat, and Performance Expectancies: Their Effects on Women's Performance," *Journal of Experimental Social Psychology,* Vol. 39, No. 1, 2003: pp. 68–74.

[65] Leonard Wong, Thomas A. Kolditz, Raymond A. Millen, and Terrence M. Potter, *Why They Fight: Combat Motivation in the Iraq War,* Carlisle Barracks, Pa: Strategic Studies Institute, U.S. Army War College, 2003; Robert J. MacCoun, Elizabeth Kier, and Aaron Belkin, "Does Social Cohesion Determine Motivation in Combat? An Old Question with an Old Answer," *Armed Forces and Society,* Vol. 32, No. 4, July 2006, pp. 646–654; Siebold, 2011.

[66] Milly Casey-Campbell and Martin L. Martens, "Sticking it All Together: A Critical Assessment of the Group Cohesion–Performance Literature," *International Journal of Management Reviews,* Vol. 11, No. 2, 2009, pp. 223–246.

[67] Casey-Campbell and Martens, 2009.

cohesion can be measured at both the individual level (e.g., average ratings of how attached individual Marines are to their unit) and the unit level (e.g., a unit-level rating by leaders or outside observers).

Based on this prior research, we recommend using multiple measures of cohesion at the individual and group level, for men and women, with a focus on task cohesion rather than social cohesion. As noted above, task cohesion measures shared commitment to the group's goals. One commonly used measure of task cohesion comes from the revised Group Environment Questionnaire.[68] This measure contains four items assessing task cohesion: "Our team is united in trying to reach its goals for performance," "I'm unhappy with my team's level of commitment to the task" (reverse scored), "Our team members have conflicting aspirations for the team's performance" (reverse scored), and "This team does not give me enough opportunities to improve my personal performance" (reverse scored). These items are oriented toward group goals and individual achievement through the group rather than social relationships between group members.

It is also important to note that, even though individual men in integrated units may have positive experiences with women in their unit, such positive experiences may be interpreted by these individuals as an exception to the rule. Much research has shown that, for men who endorse traditional gender stereotypes, women who do not fit conventional gender expectations (e.g., who perform well in combat) are often seen as exceptions to the rule rather than confirmation that the stereotype is not accurate for all women.[69] In addition, women who perform better than men on stereotypically male tasks may be subject to backlash and undermining of their future performance.[70] Thus, men in integrated combat units that function well may continue to have negative attitudes toward women in combat, despite their own positive experiences. Indeed, a study of gender integration within ground combat units conducted by the UK Ministry of Defence found that, although males in gender-integrated units perceived that their units had lower team cohesion, an analysis of survey data revealed that "a comparison of cohesion reported by men in mixed-gender teams with those in all-male teams showed no differences for either overall cohesion or any of the cohe-

[68] Sally A. Carless and Caroline De Paola, "The Measurement of Cohesion in Work Teams," *Small Group Research*, Vol. 31, No. 1, February 2000, pp.71–88.

[69] Ziva Kunda and Kathryn C. Oleson, "Maintaining Stereotypes in the Face of Disconfirmation: Constructing Grounds for Subtyping Deviants," *Journal of Personality and Social Psychology*, Vol. 68, No. 4, April 1995, p. 565; Lucy Johnston and Miles Hewstone, "Cognitive Models of Stereotype Change: Subtyping and the Perceived Typicality of Disconfirming Group Members," *Journal of Experimental Social Psychology*, Vol. 28, No. 4, 1992, pp. 360–386.

[70] Laurie A. Rudman and Julie E. Phelan, "Backlash Effects for Disconfirming Gender Stereotypes in Organizations," *Research in Organizational Behavior*, Vol. 28, 2008, pp. 61–79; Laurie A. Rudman and Kimberly Fairchild, "Reactions to Counterstereotypic Behavior: The Role of Backlash in Cultural Stereotype Maintenance," *Journal of Personality and Social Psychology*, Vol. 87, No. 2, 2004, p. 157.

sion subscales."[71] Thus, men in gender-integrated units *perceived* a detrimental impact of women on unit cohesion, but the analysis of survey data found that that perception was inaccurate, and that gender-integrated units displayed similar levels of cohesion as in all male units.

We recommend that levels of sexual harassment should be used as an indicator of a hostile work environment for women. As noted above, in gender-integrated units, the level of sexual harassment is associated with unit cohesion,[72] so reports of sexual harassment could serve as one proxy for a hostile work environment for women and poor unit cohesion. Note that harassment need not be extreme to indicate that unit cohesion is being undermined—even relatively minor reports of harassment should be seen as indicators of a problem.

---

[71] *Study of Women in Combat—Investigation of Quantitative Data*, Berkshire Consultancy, United Kingdom, June 2010, p. 3.

[72] Rosen and Martin, 1998.

CHAPTER FOUR

Insights on Critical Mass

Review of the Literature on Critical Mass

As the Marine Corps analyzes how best to integrate women into infantry units, it should consider whether there is a minimum number of women (a *critical mass*) that should be assigned to a given unit. There are two potential sources of information on the likely effects of considering critical mass as part of the assignment process. First, there is a substantial literature exploring the effects of various levels of critical mass, as well as the effects of solo status (i.e., being the only woman) in civilian groups. Second, there is some existing information from other militaries. We discuss each in turn.

The Literature on Civilian Organizations

Critical mass is a concept that originated in nuclear physics, where it referred to the quantity needed to start a chain reaction. The debate on the role of critical mass in gender dynamics, however, can be traced back to a 1977 sociological study that claimed gender *proportions* influenced patterns of gender interaction. From an analysis of a then-recently integrated sales force within an American *Fortune 500* company, Rosabeth Moss Kanter argued that in *skewed* group types (or groups in which there were "a large preponderance of one type over another"[1]), women were subject to "the dynamics of tokenism."[2] Tokenism, according to Kanter and others writing in this vein, is viewed as bringing on a variety of issues, including sexual harassment, performance pressures, role entrapment, and self-distortion; these factors collectively put women at a competitive disadvantage within the organization, decreasing their performance and asserting dominant-group solidarity.[3] The study concluded by saying,

> merely adding a few women at a time to an organization is likely to give rise to the consequences of token status. . . . Women (or members of any other underrepre-

---

[1] Rosabeth Kanter, "Some Effects of Proportions on Group Life: Skewed Sex Ratios and Responses to Token Women," *American Journal of Sociology*, Vol. 82, No. 5, March 1977, p. 966.

[2] Kanter, 1977, p. 970.

[3] Kanter, 1977, pp. 969–977.

sented category) need to be added to total group or organization membership in sufficient proportion to counteract the effects of tokenism.[4]

Kanter's study assumed that *skewed* groups transitioned to *tilted* groups[5] when the minority group comprised 15 to 35 percent of total group population. However, it stated specifically that further research was needed to help determine the "tipping points" at which: (1) a person's status changed from "token" to full group member and (2) group types shifted from *skewed* to *tilted*.[6]

The next major social science study to examine critical mass extended Kanter's analysis to the study of women in politics. Conducted by Drude Dahlerup, this study examined how women were able to influence political culture and policy outcomes as their minority status grew in proportion. Using five Scandinavian countries as case studies, Dahlerup identified 30 percent as the tipping point for gauging the impact of women in Scandinavian politics.[7] However, she concluded her study by stating that the available empirical evidence simply did not support a relationship between *specific* percentages of women and changes in political culture and/or policy outcomes: "it is not possible to conclude that these changes follow from any fixed number of women, e.g., 30 percent."[8] In fact, she suggested that factors beyond numbers, particularly "generational change in attitudes towards women in public roles," better explained changes in the political landscape following the influx of women into the male-dominated profession.[9] She also stated "the example of just a few successful women in top positions (e.g., as prime minister or president) may have contributed substantially to the change in the perception of women as politicians."[10] With that in mind, Dahlerup stated: "we should look for *critical acts, not for a critical mass.*"[11]

A considerable amount of research has examined the effects of one extreme—being the only woman in a traditionally male group. The majority of research indicates that women in solo-status positions in groups draw more attention from the rest of the group, which is associated with decreases in performance.[12] Research with civilians

---

[4]   Kanter, 1977, p. 988.

[5]   *Tilted* groups have "less extreme distributions and less exaggerated effects . . . with a ratio perhaps 65:35." Kanter, 1977, p. 966.

[6]   Kanter, 1977, p. 986.

[7]   Drude Dahlerup, "From a Small to a Large Minority: Women in Scandinavian Politics," *Scandinavian Political Studies*, Vol. 11, No. 4, December 1988, pp. 280–281.

[8]   Dahlerup, 1988, p. 287.

[9]   Dahlerup, 1988, pp. 286–287.

[10]   Dahlerup, 1988, pp. 286–287.

[11]   Dahlerup, 1988, p. 290, emphasis in original.

[12]   Lord and Saenz, 1985, p. 918; Sekaquaptewa and Thompson, 2003, pp. 68–74.

suggests that the presence of other women in the group reduces this effect and provides social support that can increase performance and resilience.[13]

A 1990 report by the Women's Research and Education Institute concurred more generally with Kanter and stated, "as long as women constitute small numbers in non-traditional employment contexts, substantial obstacles will remain. The presence of a few token women may do little to alter underlying stereotypes, and the pressure placed on such individuals makes successful performance less likely."[14] Konrad et al.'s 2008 study of corporate boards reinforced Kanter's findings and stated that "lone women," or *solos*, reported feeling invisible or overly visible, having to play catch-up, having to break stereotypes, and difficulties in having their voices heard—all of which reduced their capacity to contribute.[15] The adverse effects of skewed groups were also present in the construction professions, wherein women made up less than 5 percent of the total workforce (including the managerial levels of the industry) and faced occupational isolation and limited promotion prospects.[16]

At the same time, some critical mass scholars reject Kanter's theory of "tokenism" altogether. As stated by Lynn Zimmer, a sociology professor from the State University of New York, Geneseo,

> Tokenism alone, without attention to sexism, offers little insight into the organizational behavior of women. . . . [I]t does not seem that scarcity alone explains the reaction of men to women co-workers; nor is there any evidence to suggest that women's occupational problems can be alleviated by achieving numerical equality. The problem is not just that tokenism is an inadequate explanation for women's occupational difficulties; the bigger problem is that a focus on tokenism diverts attention away from sexism—not only away from the sexist behavior of individual males in the workplace, but away from the sexist society in which the workplace itself is embedded.[17]

Others, such as Janice Yoder, a professor at the Center for Women's Studies at the University of Wisconsin, Milwaukee, rejected Kanter's theory of tokenism because her theory, "which identified numbers as the primary cause of the negative effects, did not

---

[13] Richman, vanDellen, and Wood, 2011.

[14] Sarah E. Rix, ed., *The American Woman 1990–1991: A Status Report*, for The Women's Research and Education Institute, New York: W. W. Norton and Company, 1990, p. 185.

[15] Alison Konrad, Vicki Kramer, and Sumru Erkut, "Critical Mass: The Impact of Three or More Women on Corporate Boards," *Organizational Dynamics*, Vol. 37, No. 2, April 2008, pp. 145–151.

[16] Clara Greed, "Women in the Construction Professions: Achieving Critical Mass," *Gender, Work, and Organization*, Vol. 7, No. 3, July 2000.

[17] Lynn Zimmer, "Tokenism and Women in the Workplace: The Limits of Gender-Neutral Theory," *Social Problems*, Vol. 35, No. 1, 1988, p. 72.

reflect the complexities of gender discrimination in the workplace."[18] Though Yoder's study acknowledged that minority women faced discrimination in male-dominated professions, other, more recent studies counter the notion that skewed groups or even solo status adversely affect female performance. For instance, in a 2011 study of American corporate board members, the narrative of the detrimental stresses of being the first and only woman was at odds with many female board members' embrace of their "pathbreaker" status and the benefits they perceived accompanying this status.[19] Some research also indicates that women who have more masculine gender role identification[20] or lower female gender identity[21] demonstrate fewer performance deficits on tasks than do women who have higher levels of feminine gender identity.[22]

The literature on critical mass does not agree on specific (or even general) thresholds for what substantiates or constitutes a critical mass. As Kanter's study of one *Fortune 500* company suggested, critical mass tipping points existed when the minority group comprised 15 to 35 percent of total group population. Twenty percentage points is a relatively wide margin, and the findings from other studies support the gap in agreed-upon tipping points. For example, one 2008 study of women on select *Fortune 1000* company corporate boards stated that 30-percent representation on corporate boards (or three out of ten board members) was the "magic number" that allowed for women's perspectives to impact boardroom decisions.[23] A 2013 study of 151 corporate

---

[18] Janice Yoder, "Rethinking Tokenism: Looking Beyond Numbers," *Gender and Society*, Vol. 5, No. 2, June 1991, p. 178.

[19] Lissa Broome, John Conley, and Kimberly Krawiec, "Does Critical Mass Matter? Views from the Boardroom," *Seattle University Law Review*, Vol. 34, 2011, p. 1051.

[20] Diane M. Bergeron, Caryn J. Block, and Alan Echtenkamp, "Disabling the Able: Stereotype Threat and Women's Work Performance," *Human Performance*, Vol. 19, No. 2, 2006, pp. 133–158.

[21] Toni Schmader, "Gender Identification Moderates Stereotype Threat Effects on Women's Math Performance," *Journal of Experimental Social Psychology*, Vol. 38, No. 2, 2002, pp. 194–201. Gender identity refers to "one's sense of oneself as male, female, or transgender" (American Psychological Association, 2006).

[22] Social identity theory maintains that individuals possess two sources of identity: their personal identities as unique individuals and social identities as members of social groups; see Schmader (2002, p. 195). While some researchers construe social identity in categorical terms, other researchers maintain that any given social identity might be a more important source of identity for some members of a group than for others; see Turner et al., 1987; M. B. Brewer and M. D. Silver, "Group Distinctiveness, Social Identification, and Collective Mobilization," in S. Stryker, T. J. Owens and R. W. White, eds., *Self, Identity and Social Movements,* Minneapolis, Minn.: University of Minnesota Press, 2000; and N. Ellemers, R. Spears, and B. Doosje, "Sticking Together or Falling Apart: In-Group Identification as a Psychological Determinant of Group Commitment Versus Individual Mobility" *Journal of Personality and Social Psychology*, Vol. 72, No. 3, 1997. With respect to gender, Schmader, 2002, p. 195, maintains that while some women recognize their membership in the social category of "women," there is considerable variation on the extent to which individual women consider gender to be a central or important part of their self-identity. This variation, moreover, influences performance and behaviors, as noted in the text.

[23] Konrad, Kramer, and Erkut, 2008, p. 148.

boards in Germany between the years 2000 and 2005 confirmed this number.[24] However, a 2001 study on women in the New Zealand Parliament between 1975 and 1999 (a period in which the proportion of women in the New Zealand Parliament grew from 4 to 29 percent) stated that at 15 percent of the parliamentary population, female politicians were more actively involved in debates on childcare and parental leave, but even at 30 percent of the parliamentary population, women proved unable to significantly alter parliamentary culture or policy decisions.[25]

Despite a substantial literature asserting and examining the benefits of critical masses of women within groups,[26] critical mass theory is "increasingly rejected as an explanatory theory of women's substantive representation."[27] In fact, a reoccurring theme within the critical mass literature is the complete rejection of the idea that gender proportions, in and of themselves, influence patterns of gender interactions. In most cases, these authors point out that the mechanisms by which critical mass produces a change in the status or employment conditions of women are not specified.[28]

The Literature on Critical Mass in Militaries

Existing military personnel policies provide very little in terms of specific guidance on using or assuring critical mass in assignment policies. Indeed, a survey of the following 14 Air Force, Army, Marine Corps, and Navy regulations relating to the assignment of female personnel reveals a dearth of critical mass concepts:

---

[24] Jasmin Joecks, Kerstin Pull, and Karin Vetter, "Gender Diversity in the Boardroom and Firm Performance: What Exactly Constitutes a 'Critical Mass,'" *Journal of Business Ethics*, Vol. 118, No. 1, November 2013, pp. 435–451.

[25] Sandra Grey, "Women and Parliamentary Politics: Does Size Matter? Critical Mass and Women MPs in the New Zealand House of Representatives," paper written for the 51st Political Studies Association Conference in Manchester, United Kingdom, April 10–12, 2001, p. 15.

[26] Studies on the benefits of critical mass include Kanter, 1977; Sarah Childs and Mona Lena Krook, "Critical Mass Theory and Women's Political Representation," *Political Studies*, Vol. 56, No. 3, 2008; Konrad, Kramer, and Erkut, 2008; Joeks et al., 2013; Rosen and Martin, 1998; Linda Hagedorn, Winny Chi, Rita Cepeda, and Melissa McLain, "An Investigation of Critical Mass: The Role of Latino Representation in the Success of Urban Community College Students," *Research in Higher Education*, Vol. 48, No. 1, February 2007; and Torchia, 2011.

[27] Quote from Sarah Childs, Paul Webb, and Sally Marthaler, "Constituting and Substantively Representing Women: Applying New Approaches to a UK Case Study," *Politics and Gender*, Vol. 6, No. 2, June 2010, p. 199.

[28] See Patricia Martin, Dianne Harrison, and Diana Dinitto, "Advancement for Women in Hierarchical Organizations: A Multilevel Analysis of Problems and Prospects," *Journal of Applied Behavior Science*, Vol. 19, No. 1, March 1983; Zimmer, 1988; Yoder, 1991; Grey, 2001; Karen Beckwith and Kimberly Cowell-Meyers, "Sheer Numbers: Critical Representation Thresholds and Women's Political Representation," *Perspectives on Politics*, Vol. 5, No. 3. September 2007; Amy Caiazza, "Does Women's Representation in Elected Office Lead to Women-Friendly Policy? Analysis of State-Level Data," *Women and Politics*, Vol. 26, No. 1, 2004; Sarah Poggione, "Exploring Gender Differences in State Legislators' Policy Preferences," *Political Research Quarterly*, Vol. 57, No. 2, June 2004; Childs and Krook, 2009; and Paul Chaney, "Critical Mass, Deliberation and the Substantive Representation of Women: Evidence from the UK's Devolution Programme," *Political Studies*, Vol. 54, No. 4, December 2006.

- Air Force Regulations
  - AFI 36-2110: Assignments (2005, with update in 2014)
  - AFI 32-6005: Unaccompanied Housing Management (2010, with changes in 2013)

- Army Regulations
  - AR 600-13: Army Policy for Assignment of Female Soldiers (1992, with changes, 2012)
  - AR 614-100: Officer Assignment Policies (2006)
  - AR 614-200: Enlisted Assignment and Utilization Management (2009)
  - AR 420-1: Army Facilities Management (2006)
  - Army Pamphlet 420-1-1: Housing Management (2009)

- USMC Regulations
  - MCO P1300.8R: Marine Corps Personnel Assignment Policy (1994)
  - MCO 5000.12: Pregnancy and Parenthood (2004)
  - MCO P1100.22: Marine Corps Housing Management Manual (1991)

- Navy Regulations
  - OPNAVINST 1300.17B: Assignment of Women in the Navy (27 May 2011)
  - OPNAVINST 6000.1C: Navy Guidelines Concerning Pregnancy and Parenthood (14 June 2007)
  - MILPERSMAN 1300-1000: Military Couple and Single Parent Assignment Policy (with changes, 2009)
  - MILPERSMAN 1320-180: Temporary Duty Assignment of Women to Ships and Squadrons (2002).

In fact, the only service regulation stating *minimum* numbers of women assigned to particular units is a 2011 Navy regulation stating that a minimum of one female officer and one female chief petty officer will be assigned to all gender-integrated ships and squadrons.[29]

A few studies have examined critical mass in the U.S. military. Early research on critical mass found that Army work groups with a higher percentage of women were less cohesive than those with fewer women.[30] However, later research found that a higher proportion of women in Army work groups was associated with higher levels

---

[29] See U.S. Department of the Navy, Office of the Chief of Naval Operations, OPNAV Instruction 1300.17B: Assignment of Women in the Navy, Washington, D.C., May 27, 2011, p. 5. At the same time, however, this regulation rejected thresholds by stating the "gender mix of any given work center will *not* be a consideration in the assignment of women," (p. 5), emphasis added.

[30] Rosen et al., 1996. The percentage of women in the groups ranged from less than 1 percent to 59 percent.

of perceived acceptance by those women.[31] It is worth noting that the former research was conducted using data collected in 1988, and the latter research was conducted with data from 1998, after Desert Storm. Rosen and Martin (1998) comment that the difference between studies "could be an indication of progress in the integration of women into Army units" (p. 239) between study years. Given the changes in the roles for women in the Army over the past 13 years, the relationship between gender proportion and cohesion in present-day Army units is unclear.

The critical mass approach is used by foreign militaries when integrating women into the armed forces generally and into combat units in particular. Countries such as Canada, Norway, Sweden, and Australia have all used a critical mass approach to assignment, particularly in occupations that tend to attract fewer women. The logic behind this approach, according to military leaders and researchers from these countries, is that women are more likely to be successful in new occupations when they have adequate support from colleagues and supervisors.[32]

Several studies suggest that solo status for women in the military has negative effects. For instance, the Norwegian military has found that women assigned as solos are less satisfied with their jobs and tend to leave their units quickly (within a year) because they feel isolated and that they do not fit in.[33] A study of female officers in gender-integrated Israeli Defense Force units found that solo-status female officers in the unit had lower performance ratings than male officers in the unit, whereas women in units with higher proportions of women had better performance ratings than men in the unit.[34]

There is even less information available about the number or proportion that actually constitutes a *critical mass*, and different countries have pursued different strategies on this issue. The Norwegian military, for example, has a target that the military will be 20 percent women, but they did not conduct any formal analysis to establish that target, and this target has not been reached.[35] In Canada, the use of a critical

---

[31] Rosen and Martin, 1998. In this study, the percentage of women in each group ranged from 2 percent to 48 percent.

[32] See Hannah Evans, "Steyrs and Sheilas: The Modern Role of Women in the Australian Army," *Australian Army Journal,* Culture edition, Volume X, No. 3, 2013; R. Egnell, P. Hojem, and H. Berts, *Implementing a Gender Perspective in Military Organisations and Operations: The Swedish Armed Forces Model,* Department of Peace and Conflict Research, Uppsala University, 2012. We were not able to find any data indicating whether or not a critical mass approach has been successful in the foreign militaries in our analysis.

[33] Author interview with Norwegian military analyst, August 6, 2014.

[34] Asya Pazy and Israela Oron, "Sex Proportion and Performance Evaluation Among High-Ranking Military Officers," *Journal of Organizational Behavior,* Vol. 22, No. 6, September 2001, pp. 689–702.

[35] Norwegian military researchers note that if the percentage of women in the military is below this number, women tend to be isolated. Norway also recognizes that it may take as much as 40 to 60 percent women to fully achieve integration and to avoid many of the challenges faced by women when they make up a smaller percentage of the force (interview with Norwegian military analyst).

mass approach to assigning women was one outcome of the CREW (Combat Related Employment for Women) trials, used to assess the likely effects of integrating women into some occupations in 1987 (prior to their full integration). Initially, the critical mass approach meant that women could not be assigned in groups smaller than ten to training programs and operational units.[36] Later, this threshold was revised so that the target for women in the army in general, and in combat arms training courses and units specifically, was 25 percent. A strategic plan published in 1998 noted that "the establishment of a critical mass of women in designated mixed-gender combat arms units will create confidence in the abilities of mixed-gender teams."[37] Similarly, in Sweden, the critical mass approach used small groups of women to trigger cultural changes within the military and to ensure that women had the support structure that they needed to be successful.[38] Finally, in Australia, the critical mass approach has been balanced against a desire to spread women evenly throughout the force. It is worth noting that small numbers of women have meant that critical mass thresholds often had to be modified in practice.

Implications

The Marine Corps should consider the degree to which the literature on critical mass in other professions is relevant to unit cohesion, unit/individual readiness, and unit/individual proficiency associated with warfighting. The literature's focus on critical mass in legislatures and boardrooms suggests that the desired outcomes addressed in this body of literature are not uniquely relevant to the Marine Corps. Also, an understanding of how contextual factors, such as training, education, and leadership, affect work environments and the gender dynamics therein is missing from this literature. This seems especially pertinent for the Marine Corps and suggests that some of the literature may have only limited relevance for the Marine Corps.

However, the Marine Corps can learn from the experience of foreign militaries in using critical mass to guide the assignment of women. The experiences from foreign militaries suggest that attention to critical mass and to the numbers of women assigned to integrated combat units is likely to be important. Assigning women in groups of a sufficient size does seem to increase their satisfaction and success, particularly in occupations in which there are a small number of women. That said, the experiences of foreign militaries do not recommend a precise threshold or standard for what constitutes a critical mass. Indeed, their experiences suggest that setting a single, rigid standard or

---

[36] See Davis, 2014.

[37] Canadian Army, "Leadership in a Diverse Army—the Challenge, the Promise, the Plan," Army backgrounder, Ottawa, 1998.

[38] See Egnell, Hojem, and Berts, 2012; Gustafsson, 2006.

proportion may be difficult and counterproductive, given the small number of women likely to be both attracted to combat occupations and able to meet the physical requirements. Instead, military leaders may need to set critical mass standards on an ad hoc basis, considering the needs of the force and the number of women available.

The Marine Corps should consider the implications of solo status. Indeed, "tokenism" and its purported adverse effects are cause for concern, especially in the context of the sharp increases in reported sexual assaults against women in the U.S. military.[39] However, the evidence described above also indicates that the adverse effects do not exclusively derive from the proportional scarcity of the minority. It may very well be that the self-selecting nature of the women who volunteer for Marine Corps infantry assignments will produce female infantrywomen akin to Broome et al.'s "pathbreaker" or Kanter's "iron-maiden,"[40] rather than Konrad et al.'s "solos." If the "United States Marine" (the byproduct of the socialization process that exists in Marine Corps entry-level training) is the most powerful social category with which Marines identify, then the adverse effects of skewed groups may not affect the Marine Corps to the extent that the literature on critical mass suggests.

However, even if the Marine Corps determines a specific critical mass policy, there may be cases where solo status cannot be avoided. In such cases, additional mentoring mechanisms should be put into place. For instance, research has found that having a female rather than a male leader to serve as a role model is associated with greater cohesion among women in diverse groups. A study of military cadets found that, for female cadets, having a female rather than a male leader increased bonding/cohesion with the leader.[41] Other research has shown that, even if women do not have a female leader, having successful female role models improves performance of women in male-dominated fields.[42]

Particularly in the early years of women joining the infantry, there is potential for very small numbers of women to be assigned to an infantry battalion with no female infantry noncommissioned officers (NCOs) as mentors. However, Marine Corps infantry battalions include noninfantry personnel, and female NCOs from combat

---

[39] United States Commission on Civil Rights (USCCR), *Sexual Assault in the Military*, September 2013; Jamie Crawford, "Reports of Military Sex Assault up Sharply," *CNN.com*, May 1, 2014. See, also, National Defense Research Institute, *Sexual Assault and Sexual Harassment in the U.S. Military: Top-Line Estimates for Active-Duty Service Members from the 2014 RAND Military Workplace Study*, Santa Monica, Calif.: RAND Corporation, RR-870-OSD, 2014.

[40] Kanter stated that tokenism can produce "iron-maidens" who are "tougher" and "more militant" women (Kanter, 1997, p. 984).

[41] Robert P. Vecchio and Donna M. Brazil, "Leadership and Sex-Similarity: A Comparison in a Military Setting," *Personnel Psychology*, Vol. 60, No. 2, 2007, pp. 303–335.

[42] David M. Marx and Jasmin S. Roman, "Female Role Models: Protecting Women's Math Test Performance," *Personality and Social Psychology Bulletin*, Vol. 28, No. 9, September 2002, pp. 1183–1193.

support or combat service support MOSs could provide some mentoring to young female Marines serving in the infantry.

Finally, when considering the utility of critical mass, the Marine Corps should experiment and collect data to allow comparison of performance of units with various gender mixes. This information will allow the Marine Corps to make an assessment of what constitutes critical mass. As described above, the academic literature on critical mass does not provide the Marine Corps with a defensible critical mass threshold, nor does it provide conclusive evidence on the validity of critical mass. Despite this lack of empirical evidence, the *potential* benefits of employing critical mass concepts to guide the assignment of women into infantry units are such that it may be worth it to experiment with critical mass thresholds to determine if there are optimal gender proportions in certain types of units. To do so, the Marine Corps could frame experimentation around the following types of questions:

1. In what numbers, in what ranks, in what sequences, and on what timelines should female infantry Marines be assigned to an infantry battalion or infantry battalions?
2. Given the relatively slow matriculation of female Marines from the School of Infantry (SOI) and Infantry Officer Course (IOC), will the Marine Corps have to deviate from its "quality spread" assignment policies to achieve target critical mass thresholds?
3. Given the relatively slow matriculation of female Marines from SOI and IOC, will the Marine Corps have to use horizontal transfer policies to assign more senior enlisted and officer women to infantry units?
4. Should the Marine Corps designate a specific battalion to receive the first cohort of female infantry Marines? If so, should the Marine Corps give the battalion commander the authority to assign women within the battalion as he/she desires, or should the Marine Corps designate subbattalion assignments (at company, platoon, squad, or fire-team levels) to test critical mass thresholds?
5. Should the Marine Corps consider assigning women to infantry battalions earmarked to deploy on Marine Expeditionary Units versus those battalions earmarked to perform other kinds of deployments?
6. Given the lack of female infantry leaders available in the first years of integration, should female officers, staff NCOs, or NCOs from other MOSs be assigned to USMC infantry battalions as female junior enlisted (E3 and below) Marines are assigned to infantry battalions? If so, what are the desired (and realistic) female officer–NCO–enlisted ratios? What types of training, screening, and career experiences would best prepare female officers, staff NCOs, or NCOs for these roles?
7. Would gender adviser billets improve unit-level functionality?

In summary, the literature suggests that assigning women in a way that creates solo status is likely to be problematic. However, the literature offers no specific guidance to the Marine Corps in terms of what would constitute an appropriate critical mass target. Given the low representation of women in the Marine Corps today, achieving specific critical mass targets may not be possible in the near term anyway. This suggests that the Marine Corps should approach the question of critical mass from an analytic perspective; assignment policies that create variation in terms of the density of men and women are likely to yield useful information for setting future assignment policies. At the same time, focusing on tracking and eliminating sexual harassment and other potential negative outcomes from skewed groups should play an important role in the Marine Corps' integration efforts.

CHAPTER FIVE

Lessons Learned from the Experiences
of Foreign Militaries

Introduction

The challenge currently faced by the USMC is to clearly and accurately assess the implications of integrating women into USMC infantry units, including implications on unit effectiveness, unit readiness, training, recruiting and retention, and cohesion. However, the USMC is not the first military organization to face the question of whether and how to integrate women into infantry units. In fact, militaries around the world have been grappling with this question since the 1980s, when the first among them began allowing women to serve in combat occupations. As a result, the experiences of foreign militaries are important because they provide some insight into challenges and uncertainties faced by the USMC regarding the effects of integrating women into combat units. For example, USMC leaders can study how the decision to allow women into combat units has affected cohesion and performance in foreign militaries. They can also identify common integration strategies while also learning about mistakes and missteps.

However, there are limits to what the USMC can learn from foreign military examples. First, militaries are designed to serve national security functions, which vary from country to country. These variations include the degree to which a particular country's military may be domestically versus internationally focused. Some countries, for example, develop and use their militaries to maintain internal order; other countries develop and use their militaries primarily to defend their borders; while other countries develop and use their militaries to operate in an expeditionary capacity around the globe. Second, personnel policies that govern the ingress of a country's people into its military also vary from country to country. These policies can produce an all-volunteer military at one end of the spectrum or a conscripted military at the other. There may also be variation in more specific personnel policies, such as criteria for eligibility, terms of service, enlistment and training procedures, and retention incentives. Foreign militaries will also draw from different civilian populations—there may be demographic and socioeconomic factors that influence who joins the military and where and how they serve. Importantly, the varying social composition of disparate militaries also means that different militaries have varying levels of professionalization and specializa-

43

tion. While all militaries have similar warfighting functions and mixes of offensive and defensive capabilities, country-specific national security orientations shape the philosophy behind military design, as do the personnel policies that provide manpower to enable military functions. In reality, the USMC is qualitatively different from many foreign militaries due to its amphibious heritage; its combined-arms capabilities for the operational and tactical levels of war; its size; its crisis response capabilities for employment in austere, expeditionary environments; its operational tempo; and its all-volunteer composition.[1]

The lessons that can be extracted from foreign military experience are also curtailed by the limited amount of publicly available data on the outcomes and success of the integration of women into combat positions, as well as the fact that most countries that have allowed women into combat occupations have not actually been tested in true combat situations and have had only limited success in getting women into combat positions. This means that rigorous data on the implications for unit effectiveness, unit readiness, training, recruiting and retention, and cohesion of having women in combat occupations during close combat situations do not exist. Furthermore, we also do not have detailed information on specific programs used by countries to integrate women into combat units, or systematic data on how many women have qualified for combat occupations and how successful they have been in these positions. Instead, what is known is based on anecdotal information from peacetime assessments and peacekeeping missions, such as those in Bosnia and more recently in Afghanistan. The vast majority of statements in this chapter assessing the effectiveness of various integration policies and initiatives are based on the perceptions, observations, and opinions of senior leaders and key officials. Where we were able to find systematic and rigorous evidence of the effectiveness of a given strategy, we have provided as much detail as possible.

Another limitation of available data has to do with specificity. In many cases, we only have very general descriptions of the strategies and policies used by foreign militaries to support integration. For example, in many cases, we know that foreign militaries have used targeted recruiting and retention strategies, but we do not have details on what these policies entailed. We have provided as much detail as possible on the strategies and programs described in this report. However, in many cases, we are able to provide only these more-general descriptions. Even with these limitations, foreign military experience can still provide a number of valuable insights for the USMC, including identifying particularly successful (or unsuccessful) strategies and innova-

---

[1] Of course, there will also be similarities between the U.S. military and foreign militaries. For example, most foreign militaries' infantry missions are similar to the USMC's (e.g., to "close with and destroy the enemy by fire and maneuver"). Second, the USMC and foreign militaries will face similar equipment issues related to the integration of women into combat missions. Finally, while the USMC may have a higher operational tempo and unusual mission set, many foreign military infantry divisions share an environmental context with the USMC, for example having to live in the field, walk long distances, and receive fire from the enemy.

tions, highlighting key lessons learned, and providing some information about possible implications of policy changes in this area.

In this chapter, we pull out these key insights, innovations, strategies, and cross-cutting themes by conducting a broad sweep and exploratory analysis of foreign militaries and their policies toward women in combat occupations. This will be supplemented by a deep dive into seven countries, most of which have allowed women into combat occupations or have at least spent a significant amount of time studying the issue and its implications for cohesion and military performance. In each case study, we consider the status of women in combat occupations, the apparent progress achieved in integrating them into these occupations, the strategies used to accomplish the integration, institutional commitment to integration, challenges remaining, and lessons learned thus far. In addition to focusing on the seven deep dives, we also consider lessons and insights from about 14 other in-depth country analyses and our initial sweep of 55 foreign militaries.

The remainder of this chapter is organized as follows: first, we provide an overview of the integration experiences of foreign militaries. We discuss our approach and methodology, as well as the definition of key terms such as *institutional commitment to integration* that were central to our case study analysis. The second section of the chapter includes the seven deep-dive case studies that we conducted. Then, we provide a broad overview of findings from the full set of countries we reviewed. Finally, the fourth section highlights policy implications, key lessons that might be relevant for the USMC as it moves ahead on this issue, and possible areas for additional research.

Approach and Methodology

Our investigation and analysis of the integration experiences of foreign militaries involved three phases: first, a broad sweep of 55 countries, each of which includes women in its military in at least some capacity; second, an in-depth analysis of 21 countries selected because they allow women in combat occupations and are comparable to the USMC in at least some capacity; and third, a deep dive into seven countries to pull out key insights. At each phase, we focused on a number of attributes and dimensions of the countries under investigation. These included

- number of occupations open to women
- percent of women in the military
- institutional commitment to integration of women into combat units (see below)
- progress of integrating women into combat units (and evidence of success, see below)
- rationales for integration (focus on countries that *choose* to integrate)
- strategies for integration

- continued challenges
- lessons learned.

Among these dimensions, several warrant additional discussion and definition. First, when considering rationales for integration, we focused on countries that choose to integrate, rather than those that are forced to integrate due to manpower shortages or legal rulings and mandates. Legal considerations and manpower concerns affected the decisions of most countries we looked at, but we tended to exclude countries that allowed women into combat occupations only during war (e.g., Russia during World War II) before forcing them out once the conflict ended.

Second, to assess institutional commitment to integration, we looked for the following types of evidence:

- policy or legal changes to support the integration of women into combat positions (including addressing sexual harassment)
- clear evidence of strong leadership commitment or involvement (manifested in statements or speeches or policy documents)
- national plans that included strategies for the integration of women into combat positions and that assigned accountability for integration
- force-wide training programs to facilitate integration and ensure its success
- postimplementation assessments.

When countries had all or many of these types of policies, strategies, or programs, we classified them as having high commitment (see Table 5.1). Countries that had one or two of these types of programs or strategies but were missing key elements (e.g., they had made some policy changes and had training programs, but leaders remained more disengaged, or they had no clear strategy) were categorized as moderate on this dimension. Countries that had none of these things and those with policies that worked against integration were categorized as having low commitment. To make these deter-

Table 5.1
Assessment of Integration Success and Institutional Commitment in Foreign Militaries

Integration Success	Institutional Commitment		
	High	Moderate	Low
High	Australia Canada Denmark Norway Sweden Israel		
Moderate	Germany Netherlands New Zealand South Africa	Albania Belgium Finland Hungary Italy Romania Slovenia Spain	France
Low		Croatia Greece Latvia Lithuania Mexico Russia	Poland Portugal Slovakia Ukraine

minations, we relied on policy documents, implementation plans, news articles, news releases by government and defense agencies, reports made by independent organizations and to the United Nations and other bodies, and academic journal articles. Table 5.1 presents a summary of our findings.

Third, to assess integration progress (or success), we looked for evidence that the country was actually getting women into some of the more combat-oriented occupations (few countries have a large number of women in these occupations, and simply looking at the numbers of women in combat arms occupations is a limited way to measure success), that women were deploying and participating in operational ways in combat-like settings (Iraq and Afghanistan), and that steady progress was being made in integrating women into combat arms positions (including jobs in infantry, armor, and artillery occupations). We also considered whether or not there were problems associated with the integration of women (e.g., reports of sexual harassment, reports of obstacles to promotion, evidence that women were not actually entering combat occupations, evidence of high attrition rates among women in these occupations, evidence of continued male prejudice, difficulty recruiting women, difficulties setting appropriate physical standards). To make these determinations, we relied on several types of information, including policy documents, country self-assessments, news reports, and statements by women themselves in news/journal articles. We loosely binned countries based on their level of progress or success, but because we were dealing with very different types of information from different sources, we could not develop a single set of criteria or a rigorous typology. However, the breakdown between progress "categories" was fairly clear. There were countries that had more substantial evidence of progress, countries with very limited evidence (positions open, but only a few women and continued problems), and there were cases where there was no real evidence of any integration.

Finally, as we gathered information on strategies, lessons learned, and remaining challenges, we looked at some of the same sources of information: policy documents, country self-assessments, news reports, and statements by women themselves in news/journal articles, reports made by independent organizations and to the United Nations and other bodies, and academic journal articles, implementation plans, and almost any other document that we could find on the topic. The amount and type of information available on each country varied significantly, and we tried to be as comprehensive in our review and assessment as possible.

Although we collected a large amount of information from diverse sources, there were several types of information completely missing from our analysis. Most significantly, there was extremely limited information on the number of women who have actually been integrated into combat occupations. We attempted to assess the level of integration progress using numbers and statistics provided in news reports, but these rarely gave us the direct and objective data on numbers of women in combat occupations that we ideally would have liked. For a few of our case studies, specifically

Norway, Canada, and Australia, we were able to speak with researchers and military personnel involved in the integration of women into combat arms positions. In these cases, we were able to gather more specific statistics and some data assessing integration progress. Even in these cases, the specific information on programs and strategies used and the detailed data on integration outcomes and success that we were able to collect were limited. This means that we often do not know the specific types of tests or pilot studies a country used prior to integrating women into combat occupations or the full range of policies and specific programs used to integrate women into these new positions. Reports by objective third parties somewhat address this limitation, but these are rare and often narrowly focused, meaning that they still do not give us a clear and complete view of the policies on women in combat in foreign countries. For the cases where we did complete limited interviews, we are able to provide some additional specifics, but even here, much of the information remains rather general.

A final important note is that having occupations open to women does not equal success at integrating women into these occupations. Some countries have been forced to open occupations due to legal requirements, but then made no effort to actually integrate women into these positions. Other countries have all occupations open to women, but no women in those occupations, either due to their inability to meet requirements or the lack of interest in those jobs among women. None of the countries we looked at forces women to serve in combat occupations.

Case Studies

In this section, we describe the findings of our seven deep dive case studies: Australia, Canada, Israel, New Zealand, Norway, Sweden, and the United Kingdom. The seven cases were selected to include primarily countries that have high institutional commitment and at least some success in integrating women into combat-oriented occupations. Our rationale for focusing on these cases was to maximize the lessons that we can glean from our analysis. However, we also include the United Kingdom (which initially decided not to integrate) in order to understand why it made this decision, what data it has collected, and how it interprets that data. Although the types of information and detail presented in each case are different, we touch on the same key issues in each case: status of integration, progress of integration, strategies, challenges, and lessons learned.

Australia

Australia is the most recent integrator, starting the process of opening combat operations in 2013 with the intention of completing integration by 2016.[2] The decision to open all positions to women was a response to several different factors, including pressures from society, social norms, the general expansion of the role played by women in society, manpower needs caused by lower than normal recruiting and retention among men, the desire to tap into high-quality female recruit pools, and the recognition that with the proper training, some women can meet the physical standards for combat occupations.[3] As of 2012, the Australian Defence Force (ADF) was 14 percent female, and women made up about 9 percent of personnel deployed on overseas operations.[4] Women seem well integrated into the military overall, according to the opinions of senior leaders, but integration into combat operations is just beginning (the first women were accepted into training in early 2014), so it is too early to assess progress on this dimension. Thus far, however, there have been few reports of negative outcomes, and women seem to perform as effectively as men in operational situations and in training.[5]

The institutional commitment to integration in Australia is evidenced in a number of ways. First, ADF and the Australian Department of Defence (DOD) began the process with several well-developed institutional implementation plans, one for each service and one for the DOD overall. These plans not only outlined initiative timing, but also key stakeholders, those with accountability, and important risks and mitigation strategies.[6] The ADF has also established centrally administered (jointly for all services) recruiting, retention, and integration strategies, as well as a set of training programs to ensure women are prepared to enter combat occupations.[7] This includes preenlistment training for women to help promote readiness. Senior leaders have also been involved in discussions about manning, distribution of women, and building female leadership.[8]

[2] Annemarie Randazzo-Matsel, Jennifer Schulte, and Jennifer Yopp, *Assessing the Implications of Possible Changes to Women in Service Restrictions: Practices of Foreign Militaries and Other Organizations*, Alexandria, Va.: Center for Naval Analyses, DIM-2012-U-000689-Final, July 2012.

[3] Hugh Smith, "The Dynamics of Social Change and the Australian Defence Force," *Armed Forces and Society*, Vol. 21, No. 4, 1995; Hugh Smith and Ian McAllister, "The Changing Military Profession: Integrating Women in the Australian Defence Force," *Journal of Sociology*, Vol. 27, No. 3, 1991.

[4] Evans, 2013.

[5] Smith and McAllister, 1991; Clare Burton, *Women in the Australian Defence Force: Two Studies*, Canberra: Director Publishing and Visual Communications, Defence Centre, December 1996.

[6] Australian Government, Department of Defence, *Removal of Gender Restrictions from ADF Combat Roles: Implementation Plan*, August 2013a.

[7] "Increasing Women in Army," January 2013.

[8] "Increasing Women in Army," January 2013; Burton, 1996.

The ADF has employed a number of strategies as it has embarked on its integration of women into combat occupations. First, as noted above, it developed a detailed implementation plan that outlines key steps, risk mitigation, and accountability, even for the most senior leaders.[9] Second, the ADF appointed women to senior positions in their occupations to serve as role models and mentors for new female recruits.[10] Third, it used a phased implementation that first allowed lateral transfers, which enabled women to move from noncombat occupations into combat occupations (if they met physical qualifications), and gradually recruited new personnel into opened positions.[11] Fourth, the ADF has sought to strike a balance between the desire to have a critical mass of women in specific units/occupations and an interest in spreading women throughout the force, although specific details on how this balance will be implemented were not provided. Fifth, the ADF has used gender awareness training, along with physical training, to smooth the integration process. As noted above, the ADF's training program for new recruits includes preenlistment training for recruits of both genders to support achievement of physical requirements.[12] It has also made use of the service academies as a means of institutional and cultural change by adding classroom instruction on gender sensitivity and related issues (although the content of this training is not publicly available).[13] Finally, it has conducted integration alongside an extensive effort to establish new gender-neutral physical standards for all occupations, a process that is still ongoing. This process has involved identifying relevant physical tasks and key capabilities needed to complete these tasks, observing task completion and collecting measures of performance, and then designating benchmark tasks for each physical task, along with assessments to test these physical capabilities. These new standards establish a baseline level of qualification for men and women that can ensure readiness, support operational effectiveness, and help reduce barriers and discrimination based on perceived physical qualifications.[14]

Although integration is new, the ADF has already had to confront a number of different challenges in its integration process. First, external observers note that there is continued resistance from men, particularly those with 20 to 30 years of service, as well as men in traditionally "masculine" occupations that will be opening.[15] Second, sexual

---

[9]   Australian Government, Department of Defence, 2013a.

[10] Burton, 1996.

[11] Randazzo-Matsel, Schulte, and Yopp, 2012; Australian Government, Department of Defence, 2013a.

[12] Randazzo-Matsel, Schulte, and Yopp, 2012.

[13] Australian Human Rights Commission, *Audit Report: Review into the Treatment of Women at the Australian Defence Force Academy*, Sydney: Australian Human Rights Commission, 2013.

[14] Randazzo-Matsel, Schulte, and Yopp, 2012; Anne Summers, "The Lady Killers: Women in the Military," *The Monthly*, December 2011.

[15] Burton, 1996; Australian Government, Department of Defence, *Removal of Gender Restrictions on Australian Defence Force Combat Role Employment Categories: Risk Management Plan*, 2013b.

harassment has been a concern, although revisions to sexual harassment policies have helped mitigate some of these issues.[16] [17] Other issues relate to human resource management (HRM) policies, such as recruiting, retention, career track assignment, and promotion.[18] Early, subjective reports from senior leaders and military researchers suggest that additional attention to these issues may help smooth integration even further.

While they have not yet led to challenges, the ADF has also identified a number of risks that could lead to challenges down the road. These include risk of high injury rates, media attention and associated pressure, internal resistance, and inconsistent messaging across the force. Their mitigation strategies for these risks include developing clear and well-enforced entry requirements, gender awareness training, strong leadership, discipline for violations, a media strategy, a communication strategy, and an implementation plan.[19]

It is likely too early to draw many lessons from the Australia case. However, several observations do emerge. First, as in other countries, key stakeholders in the integration process have noted the importance of leadership commitment and accountability. Second, the case suggests the perceived value (according to military commanders and leaders) of having a clear implementation plan that includes possible risks and mitigation strategies. Third, military commanders have reported that their experience thus far suggests the value of diversity and gender-specific training programs.[20]

Canada

The Canadian Armed Forces (CF) was one of the first to allow women into combat occupations and began the process in 1989 after the Canadian Human Rights Tribunal ruled that limitations on where women could serve violated equal opportunity laws. The decision to integrate in 1989 not only followed the court ruling, but also responded to societal pressure and norms, which increasingly favored equal opportunities for women, and manpower shortages that made increasing emphasis on recruiting women necessary.[21] However, even today, the number of women in combat occupations is low, and women have not served in elite Joint Task Force occupations, as they have not been able to meet the physical requirements.[22] According to a 2014 estimate, 15 percent of the CF is made up of women (16.8 percent of officers and 13.2 percent of

---

[16] Burton, 1996; Australian Government, Department of Defence, 2013b.

[17] We do not have specifics on the types of policy changes made.

[18] Burton, 1996; Australian Government, Department of Defence, 2013b.

[19] Australian Government, Department of Defence, 2013b.

[20] Burton, 1996.

[21] Chief Review Services, "Evaluation—Gender Integration in the CF," June 1998 (revised November 1998) 5000-1 (CRS).

[22] Paul Cawkill, Alison Rogers, Sarah Knight, and Laura Spear, *Women in Ground Close Combat Roles: The Experiences of Other Nations and a Review of the Academic Literature*, Defence Science and Technology Laboratory,

noncommissioned officers), but women constitute only 4 percent of the combat arms (artillery, infantry, and armor career fields) officer corps and 1.5 percent of soldiers in the combat arms occupations.[23] Furthermore, despite institutional commitment and interest in increasing the number of women in combat arms occupations, the representation of women in these occupations has been reasonably constant over the past five years without a marked increase.[24] The representation of women in the highest ranks among commissioned and noncommissioned members across occupations also remains low. For example, women make up only about 2 percent of generals, 4 percent of colonels, and 5 percent of chief warrant officers.[25]

The initial integration of women into combat arms positions consisted of many different initiatives without a central guiding framework and did not follow a clear integration plan.[26] Several reviews of the integration process conducted in the 1990s highlighted this lack of a clear and coherent plan as a shortcoming of early integration efforts, providing more emphatic evidence for the benefits of having an implementation plan. A 1998 review, for example, noted that while there had been progress and some important initiatives, the integration process was impeded by the lack of a guiding framework for integration, insufficient leadership attention, incomplete training, poor monitoring mechanisms, continuing institutional barriers, resistance to the integration of women (particularly into combat roles), and a need for cultural change. The review criticized the training programs that had been implemented thus far and recommended training that would address communication, leadership issues, and common stereotypes. The report also noted that the monitoring mechanisms put in place during integration lacked accountability and did not include the type of data collection and trend analysis needed to support a successful integration process.[27]

After 1998, however, renewed attention to integration led to several new initiatives and the development of more rigorous implementation plans by each of the services. New initiatives included added billets in training programs reserved specifically for women; the allocation of significant resources explicitly targeted for the recruitment of women; revision of fitness standards to ensure equity; the development of new

---

British Ministry of Defence, DSTL/CR37770 V3-0, September 2009; Randazzo-Matsel, Schulte, and Yopp, 2012.

[23] Cawkill et al., 2009; Randazzo-Matsel, Schulte, and Yopp, 2012; Kristen Davis, "The Integration of Women into the Combat Arms in Canada," remarks made for ADF visit, 2014; Canadian Ministry of Defence, *Canadian Armed Forces Employment Equity Report*, 2012–2013.

[24] Canadian Ministry of Defence, *Annual Report on Regular Force Personnel*, 2010–2011.

[25] Canadian Ministry of Defence, 2010–2011.

[26] Chief Review Services, 1998.

[27] Chief Review Services, 1998; Kristen Davis, *Chief Land Staff Gender Integration Study: The Regular Force Training and Employment Environment*, Sponsor Research Report 97-2, Personnel Research Team, National Defence Headquarters, Ottawa, September 1997.

clothing and equipment geared toward women; the implementation of new policies on harassment, maternity leaves, and childcare; and the development of additional integration-focused training programs.[28] [29]

Each of the services also developed more detailed integration plans intended to guide the integration process. These plans included targets and benchmarks, along with a timeline for achieving those goals.[30] Some additional discussion of these plans is useful, as it highlights some of the key elements and areas of focus that should be included in a comprehensive and successful integration plan. As an example, the air force's five-year plan, released in 1998, focused on increasing the representation and integration of women throughout the air force. The plan included targets for recruitment, data-gathering efforts to track progress on integration and identify barriers, a goal to increase the representation of women in leadership roles, the development of women's advisory groups, attention to physical standards and ensuring they were fair to both genders, initiatives to identify and address issues of relevance to women in training and military service, the development of gender awareness training force-wide and for senior leaders, and efforts to revise harassment and other policies to ensure that they supported equity throughout the force.[31] For each goal and initiative identified, the plan also noted the office that would lead that effort within the air force.[32]

The army's plan had as its goal to "eliminate the systemic and attitudinal barriers against women."[33] The plan discussed changes to fitness standards and the approach to physical training to promote the success of women (specifically placing more emphasis on physical fitness in the training course provided to new recruits to increase the percentage of recruits of both genders able to achieve physical requirements), recruiting targets, use of a critical mass approach to assigning women in combat units,[34] diversity training focused on gender-integration issues, and modifications to clothing and equipment to better accommodate female soldiers (specifically the uniforms and rucksack). The plan also outlined the intention to develop clearer policies and training courses on issues related to harassment, targeted recruiting to increase the number of women in combat arms, the development of monitoring procedures to track progress on integration, and modification to existing facilities (bases, washrooms, show-

---

[28] Chief Review Services, 1998.

[29] Once again, we do not have specifics on the initiatives launched at this time.

[30] Canadian Air Force, *Gender Integration Strategy*, 1998; Canadian Navy, Navy VISION 2010, April 1998; Canadian Army, 1998.

[31] Canadian Air Force, 1998.

[32] Canadian Air Force, 1998.

[33] Canadian Army, 1998.

[34] Details on what constituted a critical mass or how recruiting targets would be set were not provided in these documents.

ers, and field accommodations) to ensure equity and privacy for women.[35] One of the most significant pieces of this new plan was a directed recruiting campaign targeted at very specific audiences. The campaign included new material developed following interviews with women already serving in the military and tested on focus groups in major population centers. The effort emphasized the wide range of positions open to women in the military and in combat arms occupations specifically and used a media campaign and recruiting presentations at schools and other locations to reach as many potential female recruits as possible.[36]

The navy's plan, known as VISION 2010–The Integrated Navy, aimed at advancing integration of women within the navy and listed a number of areas of focus, including identifying and eliminating attitudinal barriers, promoting cultural change, developing a communication plan to disseminate policy and other information relevant to gender integration throughout the force, and revisiting existing policy on issues such as pregnancy, harassment, clothing and equipment, bunking, fraternization, and family issues.[37] The plan also outlined recruiting targets and a research agenda intended to support the integration process and monitor progress. This agenda included studies of why men and women leave the service and analysis of attitudes toward integration. Like the Air Force Gender Integration Strategy, VISION 2010 includes a breakdown of these specific initiatives with benchmarks, a timeline, and identification of individuals with the Canadian Navy's leadership accountable for reaching the goals of VISION 2010.[38]

The renewed focus on integration contributed to additional progress in the recruitment and retention of women into the force, including into combat arms occupations, as the representation of women across ranks of the CF grew after 1999.[39] In 2014, women made up 5.6 percent of artillery–air defense occupations (noncommissioned), 6 percent of artillery-field (noncommissioned), 0.4 percent of infantry positions (noncommissioned), 6.8 percent of artillery officers, 4.3 percent of armor officers, 2 percent of infantry officers, and 7 percent of combat engineer officers.[40] Women have also made up an increasing percentage of new recruits to the CF since 1999, another factor that has contributed to greater representation within the force. Promotion rates among women in all occupations have also been improving, albeit slowly and somewhat inconsistently. Furthermore, attitudes among women toward a military career

---

[35] Canadian Army, 1998.

[36] Lieutenant Commander Kevin R. Vivian, "From the Past and into the Future: Gender Integration in the Canadian Armed Forces," Ottawa: Directorate of Military Gender Integration and Employment Equity, 1998.

[37] Canadian Navy, 1998.

[38] Canadian Navy, 1998.

[39] Kristen Davis, "The Integration of Women into the Combat Arms in Canada," remarks made for ADF visit, 2014; Canadian Ministry of Defence, 2012–2013; Canadian Ministry of Defence, 2010–2011.

[40] Davis, 2014.

may be improving. A retention study conducted in 2010 shows that women and men score nearly the same on measures such as institutional commitment, intention to stay (men are actually more likely to state an intention to leave, although the size of the effect is small), job satisfaction, satisfaction with deployments, and satisfaction with career development. Women also score the same as men on dimensions such as burnout, depression, and anxiety.[41] These results suggest that women who join the military do seem to be satisfied with their positions, one measure of successful integration.

However, there are a number of factors contributing to relatively slow progress in increasing the representation of women in combat occupations. First, the low number of women entering the combat arms field is partly because the number of women able to meet the physical standards (which are gender neutral) remains low.[42] Interestingly, this experience differs from the belief among ADF leadership that some women will be able to meet the physical requirements of combat jobs. Another reason is the low level of interest among women in taking on combat arms occupations. In addition, retention rates among women in these occupations are lower than those of their male colleagues.[43] Finally, women who have entered the combat arms field find that they still face institutional barriers and discrimination, are excluded by their male colleagues, and have fewer opportunities, particularly for leadership positions, than men in similar occupations. These factors limit the entrance and advancement of women in combat arms occupations. However, some reports suggest that these barriers are dissipating.[44]

The CF pursued a number of different strategies as it worked to integrate women into combat occupations. First, integration followed a number of pilot studies in the 1980s. For example, the Servicewomen in Non-Traditional Environments and Roles (SWINTER) trials assessed the feasibility of integrating women into some combat positions as early as the early 1980s. The SWINTER trials were intended to compare the performance of men and women and of mixed-and single-gender units. They were also intended to assess the tolerance of the public for using women in combat occupations and to explore the resource and cost implications of expanding the roles

---

[41] Natasha Parfyonova and Andrea Butler, "The 2012 CF Retention Survey: Descriptive Results," Human Resource Systems Group, Ottawa; Nikki Holden, "Retention of Air Force Officers in the Canadian Forces," briefing, International Military Testing Association, Defense Research and Development, 2010.

[42] Chief Review Services, 1998; Randazzo-Matsel, Schulte, and Yopp, 2012; Mary Sue Hay and Charles G. Middlestead, *Women in Combat: An Overview of the Implications for Recruiting*, U.S. Army Research Institute for the Behavioral and Social Sciences, Research Report 1568, July 1990; Donna Winslow and Jason Dunn, "Women in the Canadian Forces," in *The Challenging Continuity of Change and the Military: Female Soldiers—Conflict Resolution—South America*, Gerhard Kummel, ed., Proceedings of the Interim Conference 2000 of ISA RC 01, 2001.

[43] Chief Review Services, 1998; Randazzo-Matsel, Schulte, and Yopp, 2012; Hay and Middlestead, 1990; Winslow and Dunn, 2001.

[44] Chief Review Services, 1998; Randazzo-Matsel, Schulte, and Yopp, 2012; Hay and Middlestead, 1990; Winslow and Dunn, 2001.

available for women.[45] In these trials, performance was assessed along two dimensions: the ability of women to complete specific military tasks, and the psychological and emotional impact of having women in nontraditional roles, as assessed by surveys and interviews.[46] Overall, in the air, sea, and land trials, women performed effectively but felt excluded and often were not accepted by their male colleagues. Researchers reported that cohesion and integration of women were low, and that exclusion by male colleagues was one of the most serious challenges faced by women trying to enter land and sea combat occupations.[47]

A subsequent 1987 trial known as the CREW trial evaluated the performance and cohesion of integrated units in the army and navy compared with all-male units in the same occupations. These studies generally found that women performed effectively in combat units but often struggled to meet the physical requirements of combat occupations and were not all that interested in joining the combat arms field. The failure rate in infantry training was particularly high, partly due to poor candidate screening and negative group dynamics. In addition, there was no pretraining to prepare women for the infantry training program. The women selected for infantry occupations, however, were nearly identical to men in these occupations on several dimensions, including aptitude tests and years of schooling.[48] Some women in land and sea occupations during these trials were able to meet physical standards and perform their jobs effectively but reported feeling excluded by their male colleagues. Posttrial analysis suggested this might reflect poor initial training of men in preparation for the integration.[49] One result of the CREW trials was the implementation of a critical mass criterion for assigning women to training courses. Specifically, this new policy prohibited women from being assigned to infantry training programs in groups of smaller than ten, so that women would have stronger support networks while completing these training programs. This policy limited the initial integration of women into combat arms occupations, as this threshold of ten women was not easily reached.[50]

Second, the CF has relied on gender-neutral physical standards for combat occupations, meaning that men and women must meet the same requirements to qualify, and have several times revisited and revised existing physical standards to ensure they are selective without being discriminatory.[51] These standards have also limited the number of women who qualify for combat occupations, as many women are screened

---

[45] Vivian, 1998.

[46] Vivian, 1998.

[47] Winslow and Dunn, 2001; Vivian, 1998; Davis, 1997.

[48] Davis, 2014.

[49] Hay and Middlestead, 1990.

[50] Davis, 2014.

[51] Randazzo-Matsel, Schulte, and Yopp, 2012.

out by stringent requirements intended to exclude unqualified male candidates.[52] As integration has proceeded, the CF has worked to revise and update these standards to ensure that they continue to promote rather than impede the equitable integration of women.[53] [54] The standards were updated first in 1998, as part of the army's updated integration strategy implemented in that year.

More recently, in 2014, the CF implemented a new set of fitness standards developed as part of a three-year research project. These new standards were intended to ensure the physical standards used in evaluating candidates for the CF generally and for specific positions accurately reflect the requirements of current and future military activities and requirements.[55] Known as the FORCE Evaluation, the new standards were developed to rationalize physical standards for all occupations.[56] The development of these standards was a carefully controlled and implemented process. The first step was to update the list of common military tasks associated with each occupation. This evaluation resulted in a set of 13 core tasks for all occupations, which were then validated by technical subject matter experts from each service. The experts provided information on when the task had been performed, along with expected weights, distances, work rates, and performance standards. Some tasks were further validated with field simulations using CF personnel, both men and women. This process resulted in a smaller set of six core tasks common to all CF personnel, which then served as the basis for the new physical fitness standards. In the final phases, a set of simplified simulations were developed that could predict performance and measure aptitude on the core tasks. The final fitness test consists of four components designed to measure physical capabilities: sandbag lift, intermittent loaded shuttles, 20-meter rushes, and sandbag drag. One minimum standard applies to all members, across genders and age groups. Importantly, the FORCE Evaluation is not meant to capture the higher physical fitness standards required by some occupations, but rather the minimum requirements for entry into the force. The standards used in specific occupations were also revisited in 2014, although we do not have additional details on the standards for specific occupations. Standards for combat occupations remain gender neutral.

Third, the CF has used a phased implementation, in which women were gradually integrated into combat occupations over a period of ten years. As a first step, even before women were placed in combat occupations, women from combat service–support occupations were placed in combat units to acclimatize members of combat units to the presence of women. This occurred alongside the implementation of new mixed-

---

[52] Chief Review Services, 1998; Canadian Army, 1998.

[53] Chief Review Services, 1998; Canadian Army, 1998.

[54] We do not have data on the specific standards used in these instances.

[55] Canadian Military, 2014.

[56] Randazzo-Matsel, Schulte, and Yopp, 2012.

gender training (training had been separate for each gender prior to the start of integration in 1989). When integration began in earnest, women were assigned in small groups in combat arms positions (infantry, armor, artillery, anti–air warfare jobs), first in select units and later more broadly.[57] Although the goal was to assign women in groups of no fewer than ten, this was not always possible, given the small number of women interested in and qualified to enter the newly opened jobs. As integration has occurred, the CF has also focused on increasing representation of women in leadership roles and on deployments to address cultural challenges associated with integration and to give younger women role models and mentors.[58] The CF has also emphasized building a critical mass of women who serve together in combat occupations, rather than spreading them throughout the combat arms field.[59] This critical mass approach was a response to the initial results of the CREW trials, outlined above. The CF has used other policies to increase the representation of women in the force as well. To attract more women into these occupations, the CF has developed targeted recruiting and retention programs. This has included using female recruiters to attract female candidates, developing recruiting targets, and allocating sufficient funds to recruiting efforts to support gender-focused programs.[60] They have also reserved training billets for women in specialized schools and leader training programs, hoping to support their ability to meet necessary requirements and enter new occupations.[61]

Fourth, the CF has used monitoring and diversity audits to periodically assess their progress in integrating women (and other minorities) into the force and into combat arms positions specifically. An early review conducted in 1994, known as OP MINERVA, focused primarily on cultural change, rather than other aspects of integration.[62] OP MINERVA also recommended additional leadership support, gender awareness training, greater support for family obligations, recruiting policies that targeted women for nontraditional occupations, and the use of trend analysis to monitor progress on the integration of women. A more substantial audit occurred in the late 1990s (commissioned in 1996, released in 1998), just before the tenth anniversary of the court decision that mandated integration. The assessment considered all aspects of integration, including objective measures, such as the number of women in the force

---

[57] Vivian, 1998.

[58] Grazia Scoppio, "Diversity Best Practices in Military Organizations in Canada, Australia, the United Kingdom, and the United States," *Canadian Military Journal*, Vol. 9, No. 3, 2009; Donna Winslow and Jason Dunn, "Women in the Canadian Forces," in *The Challenging Continuity of Change and the Military: Female Soldiers— Conflict Resolution—South America*, Gerhard Kummel, ed., Proceedings of the Interim Conference 2000 of ISA RC 01, 2001; Randazzo-Matsel, Schulte, and Yopp, 2012; Chief Review Services, 1998.

[59] Chief Review Services, 1998

[60] Chief Review Services, 1998.

[61] Chief Review Services, 1998.

[62] Chief Review Services, 1998.

and their representation in combat occupations, and more subjective measures, such as the work environment, attitudes toward women, and the existence of a framework to guide further integration.[63] It was organized around four pillars: the integration framework, leadership, opportunities for women, and the employment environment more generally. The review also considered the issue of monitoring in the future, recommending additional monitoring of the gender integration process, including reviews by external organizations, which would provide outside perspective and possibly additional objectivity. In addition to this review, the Canadian Human Rights Council reviewed progress on integration each year during the first ten years after its ruling that the CF had to integrate. Currently, the annual CF Equity Report continues to track progress on the integration of women. For example, the 2012–2013 report documented a number of steps taken within the CF to facilitate the integration of women. These included a number of consultations with the Defence Women's Advisory Organization (chaired by an elected civilian representative and a military member) on issues such as sexual harassment policies, strategies to promote a healthier work-life balance for women, issues associated with pregnancy, and introduction of genderless physical fitness standards across occupations. The report also tracks objective benchmarks, including number of women recruited, released, and promoted, over time.

Canada has also demonstrated reasonably high institutional support for the integration of women into combat arms positions. It has modified personnel policies for recruiting and retention as well as training programs (again, we do not have detail on the specific changes made) in order to attract and prepare women for these kinds of occupations.[64] It has also relied on significant commitment and support from senior leaders and commanders, although some sources suggest that it has lacked the accountability mechanisms needed to encourage these leaders to make integration of women into these combat occupations a true priority.[65]

Other policies have aimed to create a culture that supports the broader use of women in combat occupations—for example, a communication plan to diffuse integration as a goal throughout military culture, diversity training plans, and revised sexual harassment policies. While women were initially given separate accommodations and facilities (e.g., barracks, showers, restrooms), they now share facilitates with men, after the divided facilities were found to only further reduce cohesion and complicate the integration of women into these occupations.[66]

As the CF has integrated women, it has faced a number of challenges. As mentioned above, spurring the cultural change needed to support integration and elimi-

---

[63] Chief Review Services, 1998.

[64] Scoppio, 2009; Cawkill et al., 2009; Randazzo-Matsel, Schulte, and Yopp, 2012.

[65] Cawkill et al., 2009; Randazzo-Matsel, Schulte, and Yopp, 2012.

[66] Chief Review Services, 1998; Winslow and Dunn, 2001; Scoppio, 2009.

nating attitudinal barriers to integration were two significant challenges.[67] In addition, in the early years of integration, military commanders were often hesitant to integrate women into their units, doubting their commitment and aptitude for military careers and combat occupations especially. This impeded effective integration and did little to create a more favorable work environment to support integration.[68] Even as women were integrated, double standards, inequitable leadership, favoritism, fraternization, isolation, and segregation continued to be issues raised by men and women surveyed as part of diversity audits and reviews of integration. For example, in the early days of integration, on mixed-gender ships, there was often a separate chain of command for "women's issues," which kept the concerns of women separate from those of men and prevented women from feeling fully integrated in the force or welcomed by their male colleagues.[69]

A second challenge has been simply getting sufficient numbers of women into the military and into combat arms occupations especially. The discussion above has outlined the causes for this challenge, including difficulty in recruiting and retention. Another contributing factor has been physical fitness standards and requirements that, before they were revised and rationalized, were sometimes confusing and inconsistently applied.[70] However, subsequent diversity audits have suggested that targeted recruiting and attention to workplace policies have improved both recruitment and the retention of female recruits, and new physical standards have eliminated some of the confusion and perceived double standards.[71] Related to this second challenge is the lack of female role models and the small number of female soldiers in senior positions, also noted above. Although this is also improving, the slower rate of promotion among women (in 2011, promotion rates among women were between 1 and 4 percent lower than among male counterparts for each rank, and the difference was largest among noncommissioned personnel and at the highest ranks) and the small number of women in leadership positions is another barrier to full integration which must be overcome.[72]

The Canadian example provides a number of important lessons learned from almost 25 years of experience. First among these, according to the reports of diversity audits, is the importance of leadership commitment and having a visible advocate in support of a wider and expanded role for women. At points when senior leadership support has flagged, integration within CF has stalled. To be successful, integration must

[67] Chief Review Services, 1998; Canadian Ministry of Defence, 2012–2013.

[68] Davis, 2014.

[69] Davis, 2014.

[70] Chief Review Services, 1998.

[71] Winslow and Dunn, 2001.

[72] Canadian Ministry of Defence, 2010–2011; Chief Review Services, 1998.

be a priority for leaders.[73] The second lesson, which also emerged during past audits of integration progress, has to do with the necessity of an adequate communication and training plan implemented force-wide to support the integration of women into these roles.[74] Following the 1998 evaluation, each of the services made implementing this type of training program, for both leaders and average soldiers, a priority. The Canadian example recommends the value of explaining the "business imperative," or the operational effectiveness gains, that can be achieved by allowing a wider employment of women.[75] A third lesson that emerged in past assessments of integration relates to the need for adequate personnel and workplace policies that support and protect women as they take on a larger role in combat occupations. This might include policies that promote workplace flexibility, and well-defined and well-communicated fraternization and harassment policies.[76] Another important lesson, reported by military commanders and those involved in integration, is the value of developing a clear set of metrics that can be monitored to assess and track the progress of integration. Clear data monitoring and frequent assessments have helped reaffirm commitment to integration and identify areas of strength and weakness during the integration process.[77] This has included tracking the number of female recruits, releases, and promotions across occupations over time, as well as collecting data on any problems or complaints that emerge.[78] According to the 1998 audit, the Canadian experience also recommends against the use of quotas and fixed proportion goals to achieve or encourage integration.[79] While quotas triggered resentment and harmed cohesion, the use of recruiting targets has been far more successful in increasing the number of women in the military service.[80] In fact, targeted recruiting and retention programs appear to have been important to integration in the Canadian case. Finally, the Canadian experience suggests the importance of developing clear strategies for introducing women into new training programs and occupations, including consideration of the distribution and grouping of these women together in units.

Israel

Israel has opened most but not all combat positions to women. Specifically, women do not serve in close combat positions but do serve in a large number of other combat

---

[73] Chief Review Services, 1998.

[74] Chief Review Services, 1998.

[75] Chief Review Services, 1998.

[76] Chief Review Services, 1998.

[77] Chief Review Services, 1998.

[78] Canadian Ministry of Defence, 2010–2011; Canadian Ministry of Defence, 2012–2013.

[79] Chief Review Services, 1998.

[80] Chief Review Services, 1998.

occupations. Within combat arms, positions filled by women include those in light infantry; nuclear, biological, and chemical weapons occupations; shallow-water diving; dog handling; artillery; aviation; and border patrol.[81] Women make up about a third of conscripts and 20 percent of the professional military.[82] Integration of women into combat arms occupations in the Israeli case, which occurred around 2000,[83] was driven partly by necessity and manpower needs, partly by legal considerations, and partly by a desire to promote equal rights and responsibilities for men and women. There was also pressure from senior leaders and military commanders who sought the ability to use women more flexibly within the force, arguing that this would increase operational effectiveness.[84]

Israel has achieved some real progress in integrating women into combat units, and in 2013, about 2.5 percent of women in the Israeli military occupied open combat positions. For example, women make up about 16 percent of artillery jobs; 15 percent of field intelligence; 21 percent of nuclear, biological, and chemical (NBC) occupations; 14 percent in the Commando K9 Oketz (Israeli special forces canine) unit; and 68 percent of light infantry.[85] However, positions remain gendered, meaning that, unofficially, women are not assigned to certain types of occupations (specifically those that involve high risk of close combat) and face limited opportunities for advancement.[86] In addition, women face institutional obstacles to entering combat occupations (largely in the form of discrimination from senior male leadership) and stereotypes from men.[87] Where women have been integrated (such as in the Caracal Battalion, Israel's only gender-integrated combat unit), experience and the assessments of commanders suggest few adverse effects on performance or unit cohesion.[88] Commanders note that female combatants often exhibit superior skills in areas such as discipline and motivation, maintaining alertness, shooting abilities, managing tasks in an organized manner, and displaying knowledge and professionalism in the use of weapons.[89] In

---

[81] "Women in the IDF," Israeli Defense Forces website, March 7, 2011.

[82] Cawkill et al., 2009.

[83] Women actually served with combat units as early as 1948 due to manpower shortages but were largely kept out of combat units until 2000.

[84] Randazzo-Matsel, Schulte, and Yopp, 2012; Cawkill et al., 2009.

[85] Cawkill et al., 2009, Sasson-Levy, 2003; Randazzo-Matsel, Schulte, and Yopp, 2012.

[86] Sasson-Levy and Amram-Katz, 2007.

[87] Tami Amanda Jacoby, "Fighting in the Feminine: The Dilemmas of Combat Women in Israel," in Laura Sjoberg and Sandra Via, eds., *Gender, War and Militarism: Feminist Perspectives*, Santa Barbara, Calif.: Praeger Security International, 2010.

[88] Sasson-Levy, 2003.

[89] Randazzo-Matsel, Schulte, and Yopp, 2012; Cawkill et al., 2009; Amos Harel, "Is the IDF Ready for Women in Combat?" *Haaretz*, April 29, 2007; Orlee Hauser, "We Rule the Base Because We're Few: 'Lone Girls' in Israel's Military," *Journal of Contemporary Ethnography*, Vol. 40, No. 6, 2011, pp. 623–651.

training, however, women seem to have slightly higher injury rates and higher burnout rates.[90] Specifically, in one 2010 study, 18 percent of women visited the doctor during combat training, compared to 10 percent of men.[91] In another study in 2008, 27 out of 227 women suffered stress fractures during gender-integrated basic training, while none of the 83 men suffered stress fractures.[92] In terms of burnout, women scored slightly higher on burnout scales compared to men.[93] Studies have also shown that women can close the physical gap with men through additional training.[94] To that end, officer training was integrated to include both men and women in 2003, an important step because it allows women to experience more demanding training and increases their chances for advancing to more senior positions.[95]

Institutional commitment to integration has been relatively high in the Israeli case, coming from both political and military leaders. At the same time, some senior leaders remain ambivalent, and there is tension between the pressure for equality and the modesty concerns of religious conservatives.[96]

The Israeli Defense Forces (IDF) has pursued several strategies while working to integrate women into combat occupations. First, it has relied on a mix of gender-neutral and gender-proportional physical standards.[97][98] It has also used a phased integration process, although it did not use a clearly laid-out integration plan, which ultimately hindered integration.[99] The IDF started with all-male and all-female units before gradually moving to integrated units more recently. It has also made necessary modifications to equipment and combat gear to address differences between the bodies and requirements of men and women.[100] The IDF has used quotas as part of integra-

---

[90] Here, *burnout* is defined using the Shirom Melamed Burnout Measure, which asks questions about tiredness, physical/emotional energy, whether respondent is "physically drained" or "fed up," has difficulty concentrating, has slow thinking process, is unfocused, has difficulty thinking about complex issues, is not able to be sensitive to the needs of coworkers and customers, or feels unable to invest emotionally in coworkers and customers (Sasson-Levy and Amram-Katz, 2007).

[91] Randazzo-Matsel, Schulte, and Yopp, 2012

[92] D. S. Moran et al., "Prediction Model for Stress Fracture in Young Female Recruits During Basic Training," *Medicine and Science in Sports and Exercise,* Vol. 40, No. 11 Suppl., November 2008, pp. S636–644.

[93] Randazzo-Matsel, Schulte, and Yopp, 2012.

[94] Randazzo-Matsel, Schulte, and Yopp, 2012; Sasson-Levy and Amram-Katz, 2007, pp. 105–133.

[95] Sasson-Levy and Amram-Katz, 2007; Sasson-Levy, 2003.

[96] Randazzo-Matsel, Schulte, and Yopp, 2012; Harel, 2007.

[97] Sasson-Levy and Amram-Katz, 2007; Sasson-Levy, 2003.

[98] We do not have details here on which occupations use which standards.

[99] Sasson-Levy and Amram-Katz, 2007; Sasson-Levy, 2003.

[100] Sasson-Levy and Amram-Katz, 2007.

tion, something other countries have intentionally avoided.[101] Women are able to volunteer for combat occupations, but there are unofficial limits on how many women will be accepted based on the needs of the force.[102] As has been the case elsewhere, the IDF instituted a number of legal and policy changes to support integration, including revised procedures for dealing with sexual harassment. It also has a Women's Affairs division, whose job it is to address challenging issues faced by women, including sexual harassment, discrimination, and other obstacles.[103] Finally, it has also established "cohesion days," which include women from across units and attempt to build a network to support female soldiers.[104]

Despite some success at getting women into combat occupations, the IDF continues to face some challenges to full integration. First, according to female soldiers, the military culture retains a masculine orientation, leading to stereotypes and discrimination.[105] Second, institutional limitations that stem primarily from the attitudes of some military commanders and religious conservatives continue to thwart the progress of women who have the motivation to enter combat occupations. In fact, some sources suggest that, given high motivation to participate in these occupations, the small percentage of combat occupations filled by women in Israel is somewhat surprising. There is resistance from military commanders as well as religious conservatives and even some female soldiers.[106] Finally, sexual harassment remains a challenge, as does cultural pressure, which keeps women from joining the military in the first place.[107]

The Israeli case does suggest some valuable lessons, even if all occupations are not fully opened to women. First, the Israeli experience has shown that women can perform most tasks that men are able to perform, given the appropriate training.[108] In fact, the importance of using training to ensure the physical readiness of women is one of the key lessons to emerge from the Israeli case. Second, based on the assessment of commanders and female soldiers themselves, the Israeli example suggests that integrated training is most effective at improving the physical performance of women, and that integrated accommodations promote unit cohesion.[109] Finally, the Israeli example

---

[101] Quotas imply a requirement to bring in a certain number of women regardless of the skills and qualifications of these women.

[102] Jacoby, 2010.

[103] Sasson-Levy and Amram-Katz, 2007.

[104] Sasson-Levy and Amram-Katz, 2007.

[105] Sasson-Levy and Amram-Katz; Sasson-Levy, 2003; Jacoby, 2010.

[106] Randazzo-Matsel, Schulte, and Yopp, 2012; Harel, 2007.

[107] Sasson-Levy and Amram-Katz, 2007; Sasson-Levy, 2003; Jacoby, 2010.

[108] Randazzo-Matsel, Schulte, and Yopp, 2012; Sasson-Levy and Amram-Katz, 2007, pp. 105–133.

[109] Randazzo-Matsel, Schulte, and Yopp, 2012; Sasson-Levy and Amram-Katz, 2007.

suggests the importance of having leadership support and of getting women into leadership roles, where they can act as mentors and role models.[110]

New Zealand

Women began entering combat occupations in the New Zealand Defence Force (NZDF) in 2005. Since then, following a concerted effort in 2005 to recruit women into positions in combat arms occupations, such as artillery, infantry, and armor positions, as well as to build a culture that would support the integration of women (including the development of more equitable HRM processes that treat men and women as equals and better procedures to address sexual harassment and other gender-related complaints), there has been progress in recruiting women into combat-oriented occupations. However, even with this progress, the number of women in combat occupations remains low, women generally have not qualified for Special Forces occupations, and the NZDF continues to struggle with the recruiting and retention of women in combat occupations. In 2009, women made up about 17 percent of the NZDF, but the fraction in combat arms occupations was much lower.[111]

Originally, the motive for allowing women to serve in combat occupations was partly social pressure for equality, partly pressure from military leaders who felt a wider recruiting pool would improve operational effectiveness, and partly changes in funding and demographics that necessitated an increasingly large role for women in military occupations.[112] Institutional commitment to integrating women into combat occupations in New Zealand appears to be fairly strong. First, there is strong support at the senior leadership level, with military commanders and defense officials consistently reiterating their strong commitment to increasing the number of women in the military overall and in combat occupations in particular.[113] This commitment is also revealed through organizational audits to assess progress on integration of women. These audits have been conducted at several points, including in 1998 and 2005, just before combat occupations were opened, by independent organizations to ensure their objectivity.[114] [115] There have also been policy changes to support the integration of women.

---

[110] Sasson-Levy and Amram-Katz, 2007; Sasson-Levy, 2003; Jacoby, 2010.

[111] Sarah Selenich, *Women In Combat: A Plan To Implement The Repeal of Combat Exclusion Policies*, master's thesis, Sandford School of Public Policy, Duke University, 2012; John G. S. Rogers, Maj, RNZIR, *Gender Integration in the New Zealand Infantry*, thesis presented as part of completion of Master of Military Art and Science degree, Fort Leavenworth, Kan., 2001.

[112] Rogers, 2001.

[113] Rogers, 2001; Selenich, 2012; "Defence Force Launches Women's Development Steering Group," New Zealand Defence Force, press release, March 8, 2013.

[114] Megan Bastick, "Gender Self-Assessment Guide for the Police, Armed Forces, and Justice Sector," Geneva: Centre for the Democratic Control of Armed Forces, 2011.

[115] For more information on the NZDF audit, see Appendix E in this report.

These have included new recruiting, retention, and flexible workplace policies, as well as policies to address sexual harassment.[116] Finally, the NZDF has established a Women's Development Steering Group to ensure that the NZDF has an inclusive workforce that supports and promotes women and opportunities for women.[117]

As it has pursued the integration of women into combat-oriented occupations, the NZDF has employed a number of specific strategies. First, it has used gender-normed standards (rather than gender-neutral) for all occupations except special operations.[118] Gender-normed standards are designed to differ for men and women but are set based on the performance distribution of women generally. For example, a timed run standard might be set at the 70th percentile of men and women, even if this time differs by gender. There is only one standard for special operations occupations (and as noted above, women do not often meet this standard, but we do not have details on the specific standards used). Second, the NZDF has pursued a more decentralized approach to integration than some countries, giving significant autonomy and responsibility to the services themselves to ensure that women are treated equitably and recruited into all open occupations.[119] In the NZDF, the actual integration of women into combat occupations was conducted in phases. Internal recruits or lateral transfers were integrated first, and then the NZDF began seeking new recruits for these occupations.[120] It has also relied on extensive gender training aimed at making the military culture friendlier to women.[121] The NZDF has also used recruiting, retention, assignment, and promotion processes and procedures to support the integration of women into combat occupations with targeted recruiting and retention initiatives, a focus on increasing the number of women in leadership roles, and new sexual harassment policies to ease obstacles to integration.[122] [123]

Integration of women into combat occupations in the NZDF continues to face some significant challenges, including continued discrimination by male colleagues, low retention rates among female recruits, and continued lack of women in senior positions where they can serve as role models. The NZDF leadership also continues to struggle with some difficult questions related to integration of women into combat occupations, including whether quotas should be used, whether participation in combat occupations should be mandatory, and whether women should serve together

---

[116] Rogers, 2001; Selenich, 2012.

[117] "Defence Force Launches Women's Development Steering Group," 2013.

[118] Selenich, 2012.

[119] Selenich, 2012.

[120] Selenich, 2012.

[121] Selenich, 2012

[122] Selenich, 2012.

[123] We do not have details on the specific programs used.

in a single unit or be spread more evenly throughout relevant units.[124] Finally, while the NZDF has been using gender-normed standards that are different for men and women, there is an increasing interest in developing specific gender-neutral standards for each occupation.

The New Zealand case provides some valuable lessons learned for integration of women into combat-oriented occupations. The first is the need to focus explicitly on recruitment and retention policies as a way to attract women into these occupations and then keep them there once they enter. The NZDF has been able to achieve more success in integration, according to senior and military leaders, since focusing on these HRM policies more explicitly. This may include flexible work schedules, childcare programs, and other similar initiatives intended to appeal directly to women.[125] Second, the NZDF has relied heavily on training programs to promote cultural change in attitudes toward and acceptance of women in nontraditional roles.[126] Third, observations of military commanders, researchers, and women within the NZDF recommend the importance of having women in leadership roles, where they can serve as role models and mentors to younger women just entering these occupations.[127]

Norway

Norway was an early integrator, one of the first to allow women into combat occupations in 1983, but after this early start, the Norwegian Armed Forces has had only halting progress at actually getting women into combat occupations and keeping them there.[128] Initially, the decision to open occupations to women reflected a desire to integrate the female perspective into international operations and a response to manpower demands. It was also a reflection of increasing social pressure within Norway more generally for equality between men and women.[129] In 1979, to prepare for integration, the Norwegian military conducted studies on the requirements for integration, including changes to infrastructure and standards, as well as the expectations of the force. However, when integration began in earnest, it did not follow a carefully laid out integration plan or any kind of phased schedule as occurred in other countries. Instead, all positions were opened to women at once. Norway also did not make use of any pilot studies prior to integration, as were conducted elsewhere.[130]

---

[124]Rogers, 2001.

[125]Selenich, 2012.

[126]Selenich, 2012.

[127]Selenich, 2012.

[128]Schjølset, Anita, "NATO and the Women: Exploring the Gender Gap in the Armed Forces," PRIO paper, Peace Research Institute, Oslo, July 2010.

[129]Schjølset, 2010.

[130]Interview with Norwegian military analyst, 2014.

Currently, women make up about 9 percent of the military in Norway but fill only 2 to 3 percent of combat occupations (including infantry, armor, artillery, and anti–air warfare positions).[131] According to a report published in 2010, no women had served in close combat situations, and few women had served in leadership roles (although they have similar opportunities, based on policy documents and HRM processes, as men).[132] Military researchers report that women work primarily in support functions rather than combat occupations. In the special forces, they work in personnel and logistics occupations, rather than as operatives. Women are playing a larger role in international operations. Even here, however, the absolute numbers of women on these deployments have remained the same in recent years.[133]

There are several reasons for the low representation of women in combat occupations, according to the observations and the work of military analysts. First, women do not often select into these occupations, due to the nature of the work, the necessity of a lot of training and a lot of time away from home, and the very small number of women in these occupations, which is seen as isolating. A second·reason for the low number of women in these occupations is that women still do not feel accepted by their male colleagues and often choose to leave combat occupations after facing significant exclusion by men in their units. Finally, women are often unable to meet the high physical standards set for these occupations.[134]

Thus far, studies of the Norwegian military have found no negative effects of integration on unit cohesion, although studies have found that women often feel isolated and excluded. Women report adopting a number of coping mechanisms to increase the extent of their inclusion, including adopting more masculine behaviors during the first three months after entry into boot camp, such as rougher language.[135] Studies of men in the force suggest that men who have served with women are typically more open to serving with women than men who have never worked closely with women during a military task.[136]

Institutional commitment to integration of women into combat occupations in Norway has been strong. Most notably, there has been significant and public support at the senior leadership level. There have also been policy changes, specifically related to the use of HRM policies that promote integration, including training and recruiting

---

[131] Interview with Norwegian military analyst, 2014.

[132] Schjølset, 2010.

[133] Schjølset, 2010.

[134] Interview with Norwegian military analyst, 2014.

[135] Interview with Norwegian military analyst, 2014.

[136] Interview with Norwegian military analyst, 2014.

policies that increase opportunities for women, as well as incentives that support retention and employment of women in specific occupations.[137]

Norway has pursued a number of different strategies over the past 30 years as it has tried to integrate women into combat occupations. First, the Norwegian strategy has focused on equal treatment of men and women in personnel processes, such as recruitment and promotion. Military leaders have explicitly avoided the use of quotas or policies that give women priority over men in things such as access to training courses or assignment to positions. That said, they do have certain target percentages in mind. For example, although they have not achieved it, military leaders set a goal of having 20 percent women in the military and 25 percent of seats in military school filled by women.[138] They have also used targeted recruiting and retention programs to increase the representation of women specifically in combat-related occupations. At the same time, leaders have placed special emphasis on increasing representation of women in leadership roles.[139] Currently, there are three women in leadership positions. These women are in education, logistics, and the home guard.

The Norwegian military has also used training programs that promote a gendered perspective to develop a climate that supports the integration of women in nontraditional roles. Mentoring programs for female recruits and personnel have also played a key role in the integration process thus far and are intended to support retention of women in combat occupations.[140] Norway has also been an active participant in "gender force" initiatives, funded by the European Union (EU). These programs include gender coaches and advisers, deployed throughout the organization, who train senior leaders and commanders while serving as a resource for women throughout the military.[141]

In terms of physical standards and training, the Norwegian military has used gender differentiated training standards, but certain units have more stringent standards that are gender-neutral.[142] Under current training standards and requirements, men and women complete the same basic tasks (for example, running or a strength exercise), but the minimum requirements are different for men and women (e.g., finishing a run in 14 minutes for men and 15 for women). Military leaders chose this approach because they felt using gender-neutral standards favored men and would severely restrict the number of women able to enter the force. They set the different standards so that the requirements seemed equally challenging for both men and

[137] Schjølset, 2010.

[138] Norwegian Report to Committee on Women in NATO Forces, March 26, 2002.

[139] Norwegian Report to Committee on Women in NATO Forces, 2002; Schjølset, 2010.

[140] Norwegian Report to Committee on Women in NATO Forces, 2002.

[141] Norwegian Report to Committee on Women in NATO Forces, 2002.

[142] Schjølset, 2010; Office on Women in the NATO Forces, *Women in the NATO Armed Forces, Year-In-Review, 1999–2000*, Brussels, Belgium: NATO Headquarters, 2000.

women. However, while these basic physical requirements are gender differentiated, many occupations have more stringent requirements that are not gender differentiated, but rather are based on the specific occupation.[143] [144]

The Norwegian military has also used integrated training and accommodations to minimize gender differences after finding that segregation only worsened cohesion problems as integration occurred.[145] The integration of accommodations followed complaints by women that they were isolated and excluded by their male colleagues and did not feel a part of the force, feelings exacerbated by the fact that their rooms were removed from the rooms of other soldiers. Now, men and women can be put in the same rooms and barracks. There are typically six people in a room, usually three women and three men (and never only one woman alone). Studies of the integration found subsequently that men and women who were in the mixed-gender rooms were happier than those in the single-sex rooms.[146]

The military uses a critical mass approach to assign women to units, but there is no clear standard of exactly what percentage of women constitutes a critical mass. As noted previously, the military overall aims at having 20 percent women but has not been able to achieve this number of women, in any occupation, let alone combat arms occupations. Studies have shown, however, that singletons, women assigned to units on their own, are less satisfied with their military career and leave their units quickly because they do not feel welcome.[147] Importantly, although the Norwegian military uses this 20-percent target, it did not conduct any formal analysis to arrive at that target. Norwegian military researchers note that, if the percentage of women in the military is below this number, women tend to be isolated. Norway also recognizes that it may take as much as 40 to 60 percent women to fully achieve integration and to avoid many of the challenges faced by women when they make up a smaller percentage of the force.[148]

Finally, the Norwegian military continues to study issues related to integration to increase its understanding of the effect of integration on readiness and to identify ways to increase the number of women in the military, particularly in occupations that have small numbers of women in them. For example, in 2014 the Norwegian special forces conducted an experiment in which 400 women went through basic training for special operations forces occupations. In August 2014, the experiment had reached

---

[143] Interview with Norwegian military analyst, 2014.

[144] In the United States, gender-normed standards are used to ensure overall health and fitness but are not considered to be appropriate for qualification into physically demanding occupations. It is not clear whether Norway also makes this distinction.

[145] Interview with Norwegian military analyst, 2014.

[146] Interview with Norwegian military analyst, 2014.

[147] Interview with Norwegian military analyst, 2014.

[148] Interview with Norwegian military analyst, 2014.

the equivalent of what is known in U.S. Special Forces training as Hell Week. Fifty of the original 400 applicants remained at the start of this phase of training.[149] After the completion of the training, the women all returned to the conventional forces.

Despite this array of strategies, however, and its commitment to integrating women into combat positions, Norway continues to face challenges in this area. The first challenge, highlighted above, is simply continuing to increase the number of women who enter and stay in the military generally and in combat arms occupations specifically.[150] The Norwegian military has never reached its goal of 20 percent women and has had difficulty getting and keeping women in some of the more difficult occupations. For example, a study of the numbers of women in submarines found that the percentage of positions filled by women tends to rise and fall, rather than expanding consistently.[151] Norwegian military leaders suggest that more sophisticated recruitment plans are needed to ensure a sufficient number of women are integrated into these occupations.

However, even more than recruitment of women, retention of women has been an obstacle to increasing the number of women in the military. Studies of why women leave conducted between 2007 and 2010 show that about 40 percent of women who leave use the military as a stepping stone to entering the Norwegian police. The next most common reason for leaving was to enter medical studies/nursing school. About 30 percent leave for individual reasons, such as moving, leaving for school, getting married, or having children. Finally, about 20 percent left because of bullying and sexual harassment, most of which was verbal in nature.[152] Studies like these can be used to support policy changes and improvements to amenities, incentives, and benefits that might encourage women to stay in the military longer.

Getting women into senior leadership positions, also essential to the effective integration of women into combat occupations, is another challenge faced by the Norwegian military.[153] While there are no intentional barriers to the promotion of women, researchers in Norway note that men in the military tend to use their informal networks of connections to speed their promotion more than do women in the military.[154] Researchers note that serving in combat positions also speeds promotion, so that low

---

[149] Interview with Norwegian military analyst, 2014.

[150] Olivera Simić, *Moving Beyond the Numbers: Integrating Women into Peacekeeping Operations*, executive summary, Norwegian Peacebuilding Resource Center, March 2013; Norwegian Committee on Women in NATO Forces, 2002; Gustavsen, Elin, "Equal Treatment or Equal Opportunity? Male Attitudes Towards Women in the Norwegian and US Armed Forces," *Acta Sociologica*, Vol. 56, No. 4, November 2013; Schjølset, 2010.

[151] Interview with Norwegian military analyst, 2014.

[152] Interview with Norwegian military analyst, 2014.

[153] Gustavsen, 2013.

[154] Interview with Norwegian military analyst, 2014.

rate of participation by women in these types of occupations may act as another type of obstacle to the advancement of women in the military.[155]

The military's record on modifications to clothing and equipment to accommodate women has also been mixed. The Norwegian military has made some modifications to clothing to accommodate women in the force. This has included modifications to the "armed jackets" (armored vests) used by soldiers and some talk of modifying infantry pants (although nothing has been done on this issue). However, there are other equipment issues that have been raised and not yet addressed. These include modifications to handguns and joysticks.[156]

Finally, although the military has implemented diversity training and has established a set of rules governing work relations intended to prevent discrimination, these rules are not always followed on the ground, sometimes leading to situations where women do feel discriminated against or face bullying and harassment. Studies of sexual harassment find that most incidents involve the use of alcohol and occur on weekends. As a result, alcohol has been banned from the barracks, and extra measures to protect women have been put into place, especially on weekends.[157]

The Norwegian case suggests a number of specific lessons for the integration of women into combat occupations. The Norwegian experience and the opinions of military researchers suggest the need to focus on retention in addition to recruitment and the use of training programs as a way to integrate women throughout the force.[158] This includes not only gender awareness training and mentorship programs aimed specifically at new female recruits, but also training for commanders, male soldiers, and physical training.[159] Studies of women who serve in combat occupations in Norway suggest further that physical strength is not a good predictor of performance in combat occupations. Instead, the Norwegian experience suggests that factors such as teamwork, focus, mental and physical endurance, leadership, and competence are more predictive of performance by women in these occupations.[160] Another lesson that emerges from the Norwegian case is that, according to the opinions of senior leaders and military researchers, having integrated training and accommodations can promote cohesion within a mixed-gender unit and reduce stereotypes.[161] The Norwegian experience and the opinions of senior leaders and military researchers also suggest that having a criti-

---

[155] Interview with Norwegian military analyst, 2014.

[156] Interview with Norwegian military analyst, 2014.

[157] Interview with Norwegian military analyst, 2014.

[158] Schjølset, 2010.

[159] However, we do not have details on the specific content of this training.

[160] Ellen Haring, "Insights from the Women in Combat Symposium," *Joint Forces Quarterly*, Vol. 70, February 2013.

[161] Norwegian Report to Committee on Women in NATO Forces, 2002.

cal mass of women can improve the experience of women in combat arms occupations (due to the support this critical mass can provide) and the success of integration. At the same time, however, the lack of rigorous research on this topic somewhat weakens the power of this recommendation.[162] Finally, the Norwegian case suggests the importance of having engaged commanders and leadership. Norwegian military researchers note that if commanders don't understand why integration is happening, they are unlikely to make the changes needed to support it. One way to promote this understanding is to explain to commanders and soldiers why women are important to their unit and to their local community context.[163]

Norwegian military researchers also suggest a number of guidelines for an effective monitoring plan that can be used to track institutional progress on the integration of women. These recommendations are based largely on the Norwegian experience, rather than comparative analysis of different monitoring approaches. First, they suggest using a mix of qualitative and quantitative methods and metrics. This may include in-depth interviews and other techniques, such as behavioral economics. Following each age cohort after it enters basic training and then following up with it each year can also facilitate effective monitoring and data collection. This type of systematic study can also be supplemented with random questionnaires administered across cohorts to find out about the types of expectations that they have and how they really feel about integration. Another aspect of a good monitoring plan is the use of exit interviews with women leaving. These standardized conversations might look at topics such as workforce issues that contribute to the decision to leave, individual reasons to separate, future plans, and changes to the military culture that might have convinced them to stay. Researchers recommend periodically checking in with those women who have left to get additional insight into why women leave and what happens to them when they do.[164]

Sweden

Sweden was another early integrator, opening combat occupations to women in 1989. However, like Norway, Sweden has achieved relatively little progress in actually integrating women into combat occupations (infantry, armor, artillery, anti-air defense), and no women have, as of yet, qualified for special operations occupations because they have not met the physical standards. Sweden is an example where the desire to have women in combat occupations exceeds the ability to actually recruit women into these positions.[165] In addition, despite having all occupations and positions open to

---

[162] Haring, 2013.

[163] Interview with Norwegian military analyst, 2014.

[164] Interview with Norwegian military analyst, 2014.

[165] Egnell, Hojem, and Berts, 2012.

women, there are few women in leadership positions.[166] However, where women do serve in combat-oriented occupations, their performance has been generally effective, according to the reports of commanders and senior leaders.[167] Reports given by soldiers deployed in mixed-gender units in Afghanistan suggest that having women involved had direct benefits for operational effectiveness and that the physical strength of women did not determine their success.[168] Recent surveys have also suggested some recent shift in attitudes of men toward women (particularly among younger men and more highly educated men), and an overall higher tolerance of women in occupations that have small numbers of women in them, including those in infantry, artillery, and armor positions.[169] At the same time, women continue to report discrimination, stereotypes, and harassment. Women currently make up 11 percent of the Swedish Armed Forces.[170]

When combat occupations were initially opened, the decision responded to a number of factors, including an interest in tapping into the unique capabilities and strengths of women, particularly in peacekeeping operations. For example, supporters of integration noted that female soldiers can make contact with women in postconflict situations and have negotiation and other interpersonal skills that can be advantageous in these types of environments.[171] However, the policy change was also forced, to some extent, following a legal ruling that no justifiable rationale existed for keeping women out of these occupations. The actual opening of combat positions occurred as the final stage in a three-stage process (with each stage opening another set of occupations) that integrated women force-wide over a period starting in the early 1980s.[172]

Despite the legal impetus, the institutional commitment in Sweden to integrating women into combat arms occupations has been strong. For example, to support the recruitment and integration of women into new occupations, the Swedish Armed Forces has implemented new recruiting and retention strategies as well as flexible workplace policies. There has also been significant support at the senior level.[173] In addition,

---

[166] D. M. S. Gustafsson, *Gender Integration and the Swedish Armed Forces: The Case of Sexual Harassment and Prostitution*, Aalborg: FREIA – Center for Kønsforskning, Institut for Historie, Internationale Studier og Samfundsforhold, Aalborg Universitet, 2006; Egnell, Hojem, and Berts, 2012.

[167] Sophia Ivarsson, Armando Estrada, and Anders Berggren, "Understanding Men's Attitudes Toward Women in the Swedish Armed Forces," *Military Psychology*, Vol. 17, No. 4, 2005, pp. 269–282.

[168] Ivarsson, Estrada, and Berggren, 2011.

[169] Ivarsson, Estrada, and Berggren, 2011.

[170] Janina Pfalzer, "Swedish Army Turned Professional Tempts More Female Recruits," Bloomberg, August 21, 2013.

[171] Egnell, Hojem, and Berts, 2012.

[172] Gwyn Harries-Jenkins, "Women in Extended Roles in the Military: Legal Issues," *Current Sociology*, Vol. 50, 2002, p. 745.

[173] Egnell, Hojem, and Berts, 2012; Selenich, 2012.

Sweden was a leader in the implementation of the gender force initiatives, referenced previously in this report, which were intended to promote gender equality and empowerment in all occupations, operations, and training programs.[174]

The gender force initiatives have been a central pillar of Sweden's integration strategy, used to integrate women into combat arms occupations, supporting recruitment, mentoring, and force-wide gender-awareness education to support the integration of women into new occupations. As in other countries, Sweden has relied on gender coaches and advisers to promote equality and integration of women with training and education targeted at senior leaders. While gender coaches act force-wide and often target senior leaders and key persons within the Swedish Armed Forces, gender field advisers are located with individual units and advise commanders and personnel on gender-equity issues while on international missions and during routine operations.[175] In addition to gender force policies, Sweden has relied on targeted recruiting and retention programs (but not quotas) and assignment policies that support the advancement of women.[176][177] For example, female officers receive preferential assignment when they meet the minimum physical and other requirements.[178] Sweden has also pursued the critical mass approach, assigning women in small groups and using these groups to trigger cultural changes within the military and to ensure that women have a robust support structure.[179] Finally, Sweden, like other countries, has updated its sexual harassment policies to help facilitate integration.[180] As an example, each unit now has a special administrator in charge of handling gender issues and cases of sexual harassment.[181]

Sweden continues to face some challenges in its integration of women into combat occupations. As in the case of Norway, the biggest challenge is simply getting women into combat occupations and retaining them there.[182]

Another challenge is continued sexual harassment and discrimination by men against women. A 2005 study showed that 35.9 percent of female officers and officer cadets had experienced sexual harassment, along with 35.7 percent of female con-

---

[174] Egnell, Hojem, and Berts, 2012.

[175] Egnell, Hojem, and Berts, 2012.

[176] The difference between quotas and targets is an important one. A quota is a requirement to bring in or promote a certain number of women and suggests a willingness to disregard qualifications if necessary. Targets are goals and objectives, but ones that do not imply this willingness to compromise standards, qualifications, or quality.

[177] Gustafsson, 2006.

[178] Gustafsson, 2006.

[179] Egnell, Hojem, and Berts, 2012; Gustafsson, 2006.

[180] Gustafsson, 2006.

[181] Gustafsson, 2006.

[182] Gustafsson, 2006.

scripts.[183] This includes assignment of women to gender-stereotyped roles and other forms of exclusion. Finally, Sweden has faced some challenges related to equipment and clothing provided to female soldiers in combat arms occupations. In many instances, equipment and clothing provided to men is not sufficient for women, which has led to the development of gender-specific equipment and combat-tested clothing for women.[184]

As in other cases, a number of lessons emerge from the Swedish case. First, according to military commanders and senior leaders involved in integration, the Swedish example suggests the value of having advocates, such as gender force advisors, focused on issues of integration at all levels of the organization.[185] The case also emphasizes the benefits of having women in leadership positions to serve as mentors and role models.[186] According to military commanders, the Swedish case also suggests the benefits of mixed-gender combat units and of having a critical mass of women in units, occupations, and force-wide as a way to encourage the success of integration.[187] Postintegration reports in Sweden also suggest the value of a communication strategy that emphasizes the value of integration not only as a way to achieve equality but also as a way to access the capabilities and strengths unique to women that enhance operational effectiveness.[188] Finally, according to the assessments of female soldiers and military commanders, the Swedish case confirms that strength is not the sole determinant of success of women in combat arms occupations and on contingency deployments.[189] However, it is worth noting that Swedish combat units have not operated in intense combat situations or combat situations in urban or other challenging environments.

United Kingdom

The United Kingdom is slightly different from the other cases considered here, in that it has not opened combat occupations to women. Instead, after two extensive studies, one in 2002 and one in 2009, the British Ministry of Defence (MOD) has elected to keep combat arms positions, such as infantry, artillery, and armor positions, closed to women for the time being. This case study will review what the British studies looked at and found and why the MOD came to the decision that it did.

Both the 2002 and 2009 studies responded to an EU mandate that the British MOD periodically review the status of all positions closed to women, with an eye

---

[183] Gustafsson, 2006.

[184] "Swedish Women Troops Want 'Combat' Bra," *Australian Associated Press*, September 23, 2009.

[185] Egnell, Hojem, and Berts, 2012.

[186] Egnell, Hojem, and Berts, 2012; Gustafsson, 2006.

[187] Egnell, Hojem, and Berts, 2012.

[188] Haring, 2013.

[189] Haring, 2013.

toward hopefully opening all occupations in the near future. This review was necessary after the British MOD declined to open all occupations to women as ordered by an EU court in 2001. The 2001–2002 assessment focused on physical performance and found that some women could meet the physical standards for combat occupations, although overall, women are slower and have a higher failure rate than men on strength and endurance tasks.[190] Based on this assessment, British military leaders decided to keep combat arms occupations (infantry, artillery, armor, anti-air defense) closed to women.[191]

The 2009 study focused not on physical standards, but instead on the effects of women on cohesion and operational performance where they have been integrated into formerly all-male units.[192] While the 2009 study did not conduct physical standard tests or trials, it did report that women in combat roles in Iraq and Afghanistan do perform effectively.[193] The study used surveys and interviews administered to men and women. The men in the survey and interview samples had combat experience in all-male and mixed-gender units, while the women had combat experience (in Iraq or Afghanistan). The survey questions asked of the men and women focused on small-team cohesion during ground combat and asked about issues such as peer bonding, teamwork, leader competence, values, and norms. The survey was also interested in perceptions of the impact of a mixed-gender team. The survey results suggested that, overall, women reported lower cohesion than men and that men in mixed-gender units did not report different levels of cohesion than those in all-male units. It also found that overall ratings of cohesion were high. The study's administrators offered several possible explanations for the findings, including the fact that cohesion is likely to be higher for those who serve together longer (which was less likely to be true for women) and those with longer terms of service and senior positions. They argued, then, that differences in reported cohesion were not clearly due to gender.[194]

Interview findings were consistent with these results. The majority of men reported no effect of having women in mixed-gender teams, and men and women from mixed-

---

[190] We could not locate more specific details on this 2001–2002 evaluation.

[191] James Clark, "Women Soldiers Judged Too Weak to Join Front Line," *Electronic Daily Telegraph*, March 26, 2001.

[192] The measure of cohesion used was based on that used in the Armed Forces Cohesion Questionnaire. It incorporates affective and task-related bonding with peers, leaders, subordinates, and between group members overall into a single summary measure.

[193] *Study of Women in Combat—Investigation of Quantitative Data*, Berkshire Consultancy, United Kingdom, June 2010; *Qualitative Report for the Study of Women in Combat*, Berkshire Consultancy, United Kingdom, November 2009; *Report on the Review of the Exclusion of Women from Ground Close-Combat Roles*, British Ministry of Defence, United Kingdom, November 2010.

[194] *Qualitative Report for the Study of Women in Combat*, 2009; *Study of Women in Combat—Investigation of Quantitative Data*, 2010; Berkshire Consultancy, 2009.

gender teams in Iraq and Afghanistan report high cohesion.[195] In general, the study's authors argued that cohesion is not affected by gender but by the fact that women are newer members of many small teams (and so know others less well). Interviews did find a small number of men who report that women did have a negative effect on performance due to lower levels of competence (perhaps because they have not been doing it as long, but there is no evidence to support this hypothesis). Some leaders also reported a need to "protect" women, which limits flexibility of use. Finally, some men continue to fear that women will be a distraction or will lack necessary stamina and strength despite the fact that these fears do not materialize.[196]

Overall, the 2009 study reported that the results were inconclusive. It made three points. First, women are important to operational effectiveness of the armed forces. Second, women were able to perform in combat roles in Iraq and Afghanistan, and their experience suggests that some women can meet physical requirements of combat situations.[197] And finally, the effects of integration on cohesion remain uncertain. With these results, the British MOD decided that close-combat occupations should remain closed to ensure continued combat effectiveness and to guard against the risks to cohesion of mixed-gender teams. The study did not explicitly reference physical ability as a reason to keep combat occupations closed.[198]

The public reaction to this decision was mixed. Parts of the populace agreed that women should not be in combat roles, while others called their exclusion "bogus" and advocated for equality. The same split exists within the military at both senior and junior levels. However, there is no clear evidence that the decision to keep these occupations closed had any effect on the British military's recruitment or retention.

Although the United Kingdom was not required to review the issue of women in combat occupations again until 2016, the British Army made the decision in 2014 to bring the issue up for another review early because of the attention being paid to the issue in places like the United States and Australia.[199] The results of the six-month review were published in December 2014. The study was overseen by the head of the army and found that there was no evidence that integrating women into combat units would disrupt the effectiveness or morale of these units. The study said that additional research would be needed on the psychological strains that women in combat jobs

---

[195] *Qualitative Report for the Study of Women in Combat*, 2009; *Study of Women in Combat—Investigation of Quantitative Data*, 2010; Berkshire Consultancy, 2009.

[196] *Qualitative Report for the Study of Women in Combat*, 2009; *Study of Women in Combat—Investigation of Quantitative Data*, 2010; Berkshire Consultancy, 2009.

[197] This assessment was based on experience in Afghanistan and Iraq, rather than any formal laboratory testing, and no official statistics or analysis was included.

[198] *Qualitative Report for the Study of Women in Combat*, 2009; *Study of Women in Combat—Investigation of Quantitative Data*, 2010; Berkshire Consultancy, 2009.

[199] Interview with representative of UK Ministry of Defense, April 29, 2014.

would face. As a result of the study's findings, UK Defence Minister Michael Fallon reported that the current ban preventing women from serving in combat units could be lifted as soon as 2016. In his announcement of the results, Fallon stated that if a change were made, physical standards would not be lowered but that positions would be open to anyone who could meet the requirements.[200]

Cross-Cutting Insights

Our seven deep-dive case studies, along with our in-depth analyses of 14 additional countries, reveal a number of cross-cutting observations and insights about motivations and challenges of integrating women into combat units; strategies that are particularly effective, common, or innovative; and key lessons learned that can inform the approach taken by the USMC on the issue of integrating women into combat occupations. In this section, we outline these cross-cutting insights and provide examples from not only the deep-dive cases, but also the broader set of cases that we explored.

Rationales for Integration
The most common rationales for integration included social pressures for equality, legal requirements for equal employment opportunity and treatment (especially true for EU countries), manpower shortfalls, and a recognition that integration of women could improve operational effectiveness, both through their unique skills and capabilities (e.g., ability to search for and interact with women during peacekeeping operations) and because recruiting more women meant tapping into a new pool of recruits. In general, countries that recognized the operational effectiveness gains that could be achieved by integrating women into the force tended to have higher institutional commitment to integration of women into combat occupations and to implement more policy changes to support integration.

Common Strategies: Physical Standards and Training
In the area of physical standards, many but not all countries use gender-neutral standards, requiring men and women to meet a single standard to qualify for all or most occupations. In many cases, these standards have been monitored and updated in recent years to more realistically reflect operational requirements. These standards also, in most cases, limit the number of women who can qualify for combat-oriented occupations. Countries that do not use gender-neutral standards tend to use gender-normed

---

[200] Matthew Weaver, "Women Could Get Combat Roles in British Army by 2016," *The Guardian*, December 19, 2014.

or proportional standards (e.g., Israel and New Zealand). However, even these countries rely on a single standard for some occupations, including special operations.[201]

On the issue of physical training, countries vary on whether they promote integrated or single-sex training programs. A number of countries, including Norway and South Africa, use integrated training programs and argue that these programs better prepare women to meet the requirements of physically demanding occupations.[202] Other countries use preenlistment physical training programs to improve female fitness (e.g., Netherlands, Australia).[203]

Common Strategies: Implementation

The countries in our analyses also relied on a common set of implementation strategies. First, several of the cases that we looked at had fairly detailed implementation plans that defined key activities and assigned accountability. Australia is one good example. Its implementation plan is extensive and clearly identifies key stakeholders and those with responsibility for pushing integration forward.[204] Second, a number of countries, including Australia, Sweden, and New Zealand, relied on phased implementation, integrating occupations more gradually or opening occupations to lateral transfer before permitting external recruits.[205]

Almost all countries also relied on targeted recruiting and retention strategies, hoping to increase the number of female recruits into combat occupations and the percentage willing to stay, not only to gradually increase the representation of women in these occupations, but also to build up a cadre of female leaders in these occupations. While we do not have specifics on the details of these recruiting and retention initiatives, the emphasis on getting women into senior leader and mentorship positions was another common strategy, employed across our cases.

Along these same lines, in addition to physical training, most countries employ gender-awareness training targeted at all levels of the force. While we do not have

---

[201] Orna Sasson-Levy, and Sarit Amram-Katz, "Gender Integration in Israeli Officer Training: Degendering and Regendering the Military," *Signs*, Vol. 33, No. 1, 2007, pp. 105–133; Jacoby, 2010.

[202] Norwegian Report to Committee on Women in NATO Forces, 2002; Hopewell Radebe, "Defence Force 'Struggling' to Meet Gender Equity Targets," *BusinessDay Live*, August 13, 2013; Cheryl Hendricks and Kristin Valasek, "Gender and Security Sector Transformation—From Theory to South African Practice," in Alan Bryden, 'Funmi Olonisakin, eds., *Security Sector Transformation in Africa*, Geneva: Geneva Centre for the Democratic Control of Armed Forces (DCAF), 2010, pp. 69–88.

[203] "Increasing Women in Army," Army News and Media, Australian Army website, January 2013; René Moelker, and Jolanda Bosch, *Hidden Women: Women in the Netherlands Armed Forces*, Netherlands Defence Academy Publications of the Faculty of Military Sciences No. 2008/01, 2008.

[204] Australian Government, Department of Defence, 2013a.

[205] Hay and Middlestead, 1990; Harries-Jenkins, 2002, p. 745; Australian Integration Plan, 2013; Moelker and Bosch, 2008; Rogers, 2001; Michelle Sandhoff, Mady Wechsler Segal, and David R. Segal, "Gender Issues in the Transformation to an All-Volunteer Force: A Transnational Perspective," University of Maryland, working paper, 2010.

detail on the content of this training, it is typically intended to smooth some of the obstacles to integration, including the often masculine culture and resistance from male soldiers. The "gender force" training initiatives funded by the EU and employed by Sweden and Norway (among others) are examples of this type of training. Gender force includes gender coaches who work with senior leaders, field advisers who deploy with commanders, and training programs aimed at all levels of the force.[206]

Finally, a significant portion of the cases that we considered revised and updated their sexual harassment policies and procedures as part of their integration strategy. These changes were another attempt to smooth the integration of women into combat occupations by eliminating a possible obstacle or challenge to the effective integration of women.

Common Experiences and Challenges

The countries we analyzed also have shared some common integration experiences. First, countries that have demonstrated institutional commitment to integration, through policy statements, policy revisions, and senior leader involvement, have generally achieved some slow progress on integrating women into combat occupations. However, even with this slow progress, the number of women in combat-oriented occupations remains low and the number in special operations occupations even lower (and often zero). Where women have been able to integrate into combat occupations, there have been no reports of negative implications for operational effectiveness or unit cohesion. Of course, there have also been few opportunities to test mixed-gender combat units in real close combat situations. The closest experiences have been those in Iraq and Afghanistan, which, while intensive, have involved relatively little direct combat and relatively more reconstruction and stabilization activities. Finally, in all of the cases we examined, women continued to face institutional obstacles to promotion (typically policies that put them at a disadvantage for getting access to key training spots) and discrimination and exclusion from their male counterparts.

Our analysis also revealed a set of common challenges that the countries pursuing integration continue to face. As noted throughout, chief among these was the difficulty of actually recruiting women into combat occupations, even once all occupations were open, and then retaining women in these positions once they got them there. This challenge appeared to result not only from women's frequent inability to meet the physical standards set by integrating countries for entrance into combat occupations,[207] but also from their frequent lack of interest in entering into combat arms occupations. Relatedly, reports from several countries underscore the difficulty of setting appropriate and gender-neutral physical standards that screen out the unqualified but are not

---

[206]Egnell, Hojem, and Berts, 2012.

[207]These standards vary by country. Some details on standards are provided in the cases studies in this chapter. In many cases, we do not have details on the standards set by foreign militaries for entrance into combat jobs.

so hard that even few men will be able to achieve them. A third challenge is the lack of women in senior leadership positions, where they can serve as mentors and role models for new recruits. While this is a challenge facing combat and noncombat occupations, it is particularly acute in the combat arms field. The fourth challenge is that of changing the masculine-oriented military culture in a way that would facilitate the integration of women and the elimination of barriers to their equal employment. This includes addressing their lack of access to important assignments, training, and education, as well as sexual harassment and prejudice from male leaders and colleagues.

Innovating for Integration

In addition to looking for cross-cutting insights, we also looked for innovations that seemed to promote integration according to military commanders, senior leaders involved in integration, female soldiers, and military researchers, as well as policies and programs that were less effective according to these same sources. In this section, we discuss these innovations and the countries that used them.

- **Preimplementation pilot studies:** Several countries conducted pilot studies prior to launching into full integration. These included Canada, Denmark, and Australia. In each case, pilot studies sought to assess either the cohesion and effectiveness implications of integration or to evaluate the physical capabilities of women placed into combat occupations (or both). In Canada and Australia, these pilot studies were later used to set appropriate and gender-neutral physical standards going forward.[208]
- **Preenlistment fitness support:** This strategy was used by Australia and the Netherlands and was intended to increase the physical fitness of women before they entered into the military, specifically into combat occupations. The hope was that this extra training would improve their success rate and their ability to meet physical requirements.[209]
- **Development of new physical standards:** This strategy was pursued by Canada and Australia. To develop appropriate gender-neutral standards that could guide integration, both countries conducted trials that sought to identify key tasks and requirements of specific jobs and then link those tasks with physical requirements and assessments.[210]

---

[208]Hay and Middlestead, 1990; Ella Van den Heuvel and Marten Meijer, *Gender Force in the Netherlands Armed Forces*, Ministry of Defence of the Netherlands and Netherlands Defence Academy, undated; Australian Government, Department of Defence, 2013a; Randazzo-Matsel, Schulte, and Yopp, 2012; Cawkill et al., 2009; Ellen Symons, "Under Fire: Canadian Women in Combat," *Canadian Journal of Women and the Law*, Vol. 4, 1990–1991, p. 477.

[209]"Increasing Women in Army," 2013; Moelker and Bosch, 2008.

[210]Randazzo-Matsel, Schulte, and Yopp, 2012.

- **Critical mass approach:** While there is still some debate and little objective research on whether a critical mass[211] of women is needed to support effective integration, several countries report more success with an approach that assigns small groups of women together than one that assigns women as singletons throughout the force. Countries such as Norway and Sweden as well as Australia have all used this strategy. The logic behind this approach is that women are more likely to be successful in new occupations when they have adequate support from colleagues and supervisors.[212]
- **Gender advisers:** Several countries made use of *gender advisers*, or individuals tasked with advising on, championing, and addressing issues related to gender integration. Gender advisers typically operate at all levels of the organization and are used by Norway, Sweden, Bulgaria, and South Africa, among others.
- **Mentorship:** Many countries make use of mentoring programs designed to allow senior women in leadership roles to advise and consult with more junior personnel and new recruits to support their success and retention. This approach was used by Sweden, Netherlands, and Australia, among others.[213]
- **Information campaigns:** Spain and South Africa relied heavily on information campaigns during their integration process, although other countries also used this strategy. These campaigns focused both inward and outward, addressing the force and the public at large, to socialize them to changes associated with integration and their implications. In South Africa, for instance, there was a whole magazine devoted to women's issues.[214]
- **Organizations dedicated to the integration of women:** Several countries also had organizations (within the military) devoted to women's issues, particularly those related to integration. These organizations were intended to promote women's rights and serve as advocates and sources of support for women in all occupations. Countries using this strategy included South Africa, Spain, Sweden, Norway, and Hungary.[215]

---

[211] There is an ongoing debate about whether women should be integrated in small groups or whether they should be spread as singletons, distributed more broadly across the force. Most countries do seem to lean toward the critical mass approach, as it seems more effective at providing women necessary support and facilitating their longer-term success.

[212] Evans, 2013; Egnell, Hojem, and Berts, 2012.

[213] Egnell, Hojem, and Berts, 2012; Burton, 1996; Norwegian Report to Committee on Women in NATO Forces, 2002; Hay and Middlestead, 1990.

[214] Hendricks and Valasek, 2010, pp. 69–88; M. Bastick and D. de Torres, "Implementing the Women, Peace and Security Resolutions in Security Sector Reform (Tool 13)," Geneva: Centre for the Democratic Control of Armed Forces, 2010; Gustafsson, 2006.

[215] Hendricks and Valasek, 2010; Bastick and Torres, 2010; Gustafsson, 2006; "Promoting Women's Roles in Peace and Security," Government Office of Sweden, 2014.

- **Preferential assignments (favors women):** This approach was used by Norway, Denmark, Canada, and South Africa, while other countries explicitly avoided this approach. The intention of the strategy was to offset the initial barriers and discrimination faced by women by ensuring that they got preferential treatment to boost them to success.[216]
- **Revisions to policy and law to support integration:** Finally, almost all countries have instituted revisions to their policies and law to support integration. These legal and policy changes address basic HRM procedures, such as recruiting and retention, as well as sexual harassment. Germany, Canada, and Norway, among many others, employed this strategy.[217][218]
- **Gender audits (and data collection):** The active collection and analysis of data was employed by New Zealand, Albania, and Canada, each of which used gender audits to assess and monitor their own progress on integration.[219][220]

Common Lessons Learned

Finally, our cases suggest a set of key insights and cross-cutting observations that span cases and that may inform the USMC as it considers how best to integrate women into combat occupations without harming operational effectiveness and unit cohesion. The first set of lessons has to do with implementation. Phased integration, which occurs when integration occurs within only a specific set of occupations or units at first before being gradually expanded to all units and occupations, often appears to support progress, as it allows integration to occur gradually alongside training. This observation stems from the observations of military commanders and senior leaders involved in integration as well as the audits conducted in several countries we studied for this review. Phased implementation also facilitates frequent status checks and course corrections, according to these sources. Although some countries have opened combat occupations without one, a comparison suggests that having a plan appears to facilitate a smoother transition, based on the reports of commanders and scholars, and ensures that integration occurs alongside necessary training and with proper mentorship and institutional support. Third, most countries in our analysis preferred a critical mass

---

[216] Gustafsson, 2006; Sasson-Levy, Orna, "Feminism and Military Gender Practices: Israeli Women Soldiers in 'Masculine' Roles," *Sociological Inquiry*, Vol. 73, No. 3, 2003.

[217] Sandhoff, et al., 2010; Winslow and Dunn, 2001, Ch. Three; German Federal Minister of Defense, "Joint Service Regulation ZDv 10/1: Leadership Development and Civic Education (Innere Führung)," DSK FF140100255, January 2008; Gustavsen, 2013.

[218] We do not have details in most cases on the specific policy changes made.

[219] Scoppio, 2009; Selenich, 2012; Lee Berthiaume, "Canadian Forces to Reduce 'Unattainable' Targets for Recruitment of Women, Visible Minorities," *National Post* (Canada), August 18, 2013; Australian Human Rights Commission, 2013.

[220] See Chapter Eight and Appendix E for additional information on these audits.

approach, in which women were integrated in small groups into combat arms occupations rather than being distributed as singletons throughout the force. According to some commanders, having a critical mass approach encourages more effective integration because women have a proper support system from other women in their unit. However, it is worth noting that there is little systematic research proving that having a critical mass approach to assignments is necessarily better than assigning women as singletons. Finally, mixed-gender units and accommodations are preferred to segregated ones and seem to increase unit cohesion rather than harm it, according to female soldiers and military commanders.[221]

A second lesson has to do with the importance of leadership commitment and accountability. This is another lesson supported by the observations of military commanders and senior leaders involved in integration, as well as audits conducted in our case study countries. The audits argue, as noted above, that without this commitment from key stakeholders and without visible involvement by senior leaders, progress on integration is difficult or impossible to achieve. Integration needs to be supported by legal and policy changes, and senior leaders are uniquely positioned to implement and enforce these types of changes. In addition, it is valuable to place women in leadership roles within combat occupations, where they can serve as mentors to younger service members and new recruits.

Another key lesson is the need for a true cultural change within the military in order to support the integration of women into new occupations. Strategies for achieving this cultural change include the use of gender-integration training aimed at all levels of the organization, information campaigns, and organizations whose focus is identifying opportunities for women. This type of training can help shape military culture and smooth obstacles and concerns about integration, according to the opinions and reports of military commanders and female soldiers.

Our cases also suggest the need for HRM policies that support integration, specifically targeted recruitment and retention policies that attract women into combat arms occupations and keep them there. The value of these programs is emphasized by defense and political leaders involved in integration. Some programs implemented abroad include flexible workplace policies and childcare resources, procedures to ensure that women receive training and promotion opportunities, and updated harassment policies to protect women as they take on nontraditional roles. Notably, however, while there are anecdotal reports that these types of programs support the recruitment and retention of women, there is little hard data to prove that they work. While targeted recruiting and retention programs are associated with progress, according to the reports of foreign military commanders, quotas are not.

---

[221] It is worth noting that the explanations for why each of these factors matters to integration success are based on the reports of commanders and the qualitative assessments of observing analysts.

Conclusion

As stated at the outset, foreign military experience related to the integration of women in combat occupations is valuable to USMC leaders because it provides some insight into common practices, common challenges, and lessons learned in this area as the USMC faces decisions about how best to integrate women into infantry and other combat arms occupations. USMC leaders can use the cross-cutting observations and specific insights discussed in this report to study how the decision to allow women into combat units has affected cohesion and performance in foreign militaries. They can also identify integration strategies that are highly effective, while learning about mistakes and missteps.

Our case studies and broader analysis suggest that, where countries have made a real commitment to integrating women into combat occupations, they have been able to achieve some success in expanding the role of women in these nontraditional occupations, including combat occupations. However, this progress has been slow and has faced numerous challenges, including difficulties in recruiting and retaining women in combat occupations, the limited number of women who choose to pursue these occupations and are able to meet the physical requirements, and continued institutional obstacles and discrimination from male colleagues. Table 5.2 and Table 5.3 present a summary of our findings.

Table 5.2
Gender Integration in Foreign Militaries: Australia, Canada, and Israel

Country	Percentage Occupations Open to Women	Percentage Women in the Military	Percentage Women in Ground Combat Occupations	Physical Requirements for Ground Combat	Preintegration Planning/Pilot Studies	Identified Key Components of Integration Strategy	Challenges Encountered
Australia	All positions opened as of 2013; integration completed by 2016.	As of 2014, 14% female. Air Force: 17.1%. Army: 10.3%. Navy: 18.5%.	Women are in combat occupations only in an "on the job training" capacity. Only 63 women have applied for combat occupations since January 2013.	New gender-neutral standards have been developed.	Detailed implementation plan	Preenlistment physical training. Phased implementation. Gender integration training. Rationalized physical requirements. Media strategy. Critical mass assignment policy. Modification to weapons systems and combat gear. Policy revisions as needed.	Apparent low interest among women. Many women cannot meet physical standards.
Canada	All positions open	As of 2014, 14.8% female	As of 2014: Infantry: 1.76%. Armor: 3.52%. Artillery: 6.77%. *About 3% of combat jobs overall*	Gender-neutral standards	Pilot studies	Phased implementation. Rationalized physical requirements. Gender integration training. Targeted recruiting. Critical mass assignment policy. Monitoring and assessment. Modification to combat gear. Policy revisions as needed.	Stereotypes and discrimination. Few female leaders. Sexual harassment. Recruiting and retention difficulty. Limited interest among women in combat jobs. Many women cannot meet physical standards.
Israel	88% of positions open. Women serve in combat jobs, but not close combat.	As of 2014 20% of professional military, 33% of conscripts are female.	16% of artillery jobs, 15% of field intelligence, 21% of NBC jobs, 14% in the Commando K9 Oketz unit, and 68% of light infantry	Mix of gender-neutral and gender-normed standards	Limited preintegration planning	Mixed-gender training and units. Phased implementation. Women's Affairs Division focused on women's issues. Modifications to weapons systems and combat gear.	Continued stereotypes and gendered assignments. Women suffer high injury rates in training. Few women in leadership roles.

NOTE: "Percentage Occupations Open to Women" column identifies the percentage of total spaces open to women, rather than the percentage of units or MOS.

Table 5.3
Gender Integration in Foreign Militaries: New Zealand, Norway, Sweden, and the United Kingdom

Country	Percentage Occupations Open to Women	Percentage Women in the Military	Percentage Women in Ground Combat Occupations	Physical Requirements for Ground Combat	Preintegration Planning/Pilot Studies	Identified Key Components of Integration Strategy	Challenges Encountered
New Zealand	All positions open	As of 2014: 16.2% female	There are women in combat positions, but numbers remain low (no specifics available).	Gender-normed standards; special ops uses gender-neutral standards.	Limited preintegration planning. No pilot studies.	Targeted recruiting and retention. Phased implementation. Periodic audits of integration. New sexual harassment policies. Women's Development Steering Group to study women's issues. Gender-integrated training.	Recruiting and retention difficulties. Discrimination and stereotypes. Few female leaders. Privacy issues.
Norway	All positions open	As of 2014: 10% female	Between 1% and 5% of combat positions	Gender-neutral standards	Detailed implementation plan	Phased implementation. Targeted recruiting and retention. Gender-integration training. Mixed-gender units, accommodations, training. Mentorship for junior personnel. Critical mass assignment policy.	Recruiting and retention difficulties. Few female leaders. Sexual harassment claims.
Sweden	All positions open	As of 2013: 11% female	Numbers are low (no specifics).	Gender-neutral standards	Limited preimplementation planning	Phased implementation. Gender-integration training. Targeted recruiting, retention. Revised sexual harassment policy. Critical mass assignment policy. Mixed-gender combat units. Modification to combat gear. Policy revision as needed.	
United Kingdom	Open as of 2014: AF 96%, Navy 71%, Army 67%. Planned review 2014–2015.	As of 2013: 9.8% female AF 13.9%, Army 9.1%, Navy 9.3%	Not applicable: Combat occupations closed.	Not applicable: Combat occupations closed.	Pilot study, interviews, focus groups but kept occupations closed	Not applicable: Combat occupations closed.	Not applicable: Combat occupations closed.

NOTE: "Percentage Occupations Open" column identifies the percentage of total spaces open to women, rather than the percentage of units or MOS.

Remaining Questions

While the case studies and our broader analysis do suggest a number of key lessons learned, they also raise a few issues related to integration and implementation that they do not finally answer. First, there is the question of phased implementation and whether a gradual approach is more or less effective than one that integrates all occupations at one time. On one hand, a gradual approach allows for course correction and may spread out any negative implications of integration over time, allowing for necessary adaptation. On the other, a phased approach may be too slow and runs the risk of starting a process that gets sidetracked or never completed. In either case, however, our cases suggest that integration can be a long-term process and that it can (but may not have to) take some time to get some minimum percentage of women into combat occupations.

Second, there is a question about the benefits and costs of integrated training and accommodation versus single-sex training and accommodation. Most countries report that an integrated approach is more effective, but there has been little systematic research comparing the two approaches. Integrated training is, according to the reports of some commanders and female soldiers, able to improve the physical performance of women, while integrated accommodations seem to increase cohesion. However, there are those who still argue that training and accommodations should be segregated due to privacy issues or to address the different physical limitations of men and women (as well as to remove women as a source of distraction).

Third, there is the issue of whether integration should rely on building a critical mass of women who enter a specific unit or occupation together or an approach that spreads women across the force as singletons. There is little systematic evidence on which approach is best, and most assessments are based solely on the observations and opinions of military commanders or researchers. Although most countries report that women are more successful when the critical mass approach is used, in some instances the small numbers of women willing and able to enter an occupation preclude this strategy. Those who support a more distributed approach suggest that the lack of a critical mass should not be an obstacle to integration. More rigorous analysis of this issue is needed to make a final determination.

While the experiences of foreign militaries cannot provide the USMC with simple answers regarding what will and will not lead to successful integration, the experiences of foreign militaries do offer signposts for the Marine Corps as it potentially embarks on the integration processes. Importantly, the experiences of foreign militaries offer potential strategies that the USMC could experiment with to identify which ones work best within the context of the USMC. The integration experiences of foreign militaries suggest that integration will likely be a long, slow process. In order to maximize the potential for integration success, the Marine Corps will need to create customized strategies to fit the unique mission and character of the Marine Corps in general and the infantry specifically.

CHAPTER SIX

Lessons Learned from the Experiences of Domestic Police and Fire Departments

This chapter explores how the gender-integration experiences of domestic civilian organizations can inform the Marine Corps' efforts to integrate the infantry occupational field. While the Marine Corps (and the infantry occupational field in particular) is unique and has no identical civilian analog, there are still limited but important lessons to be learned from similar organizations that pursued gender integration. First, we examine the method we used to compare and select the most relevant domestic civilian organizations to examine. Then we discuss how we examined the selected organizations (police and fire departments) and key lessons that the Marine Corps can draw on as it plans to integrate women into the infantry occupational field.

Identifying Relevant Physically Demanding Civilian Occupations and Organizations

In order to extract applicable gender-integration lessons from domestic civilian organizations, we first identified for study the organizations most similar to the Marine Corps. The initial group of candidate organizations was culled from sponsor input, a review of previous gender-integration research, and previous RAND research. This initial group consisted of

- police departments
- fire departments
- civilian merchant mariners
- construction firms
- private military security companies
- astronauts
- energy and oilfield services firms.

Next, we developed a rubric that summarizes the characteristics of the infantry occupational field.[1] We developed the rubric so that it provided enough detail to differentiate the candidate organizations, but not so much detail that *all* organizations would be excluded. We reviewed the infantry Mission Essential Task Lists and numerous Marine Corps doctrinal publications and used subject matter expertise to summarize infantry characteristics into the following categories:[2]

- **organizational:** characteristics that describe how members are organized and trained to accomplish their mission(s). Examples include the organizational structure and hierarchy and promotion practices.
- **technical:** characteristics that describe how members use materiel resources and skill training to accomplish their mission(s). Examples include individual-use and collective-use equipment.
- **environmental:** characteristics that describe the conditions that members work in. Examples include austerity of the environment and duration of operations.

We also created a scale to rate the comparability of a given organization within each category. The scale categorized organizations as ones that were *most similar*, had *some similarities*, or were *not similar* to the infantry occupational field. We described each characteristic in those terms. For example, the diversity of environments that an organization typically operates in is described in Table 6.1.

The rubric serves as a way of systematically evaluating organizations but does not exhaustively characterize the infantry occupational specialty. Rather, the rubric provides a manageable set of characteristics to help narrow down the organizations from our initial group without eliminating all of them from consideration.

Table 6.1
Comparison of Operational Environments

Scale	Description
Most similar	Expected to operate in all environments, to include physically challenging jungle, mountain, urban, and desert terrain.
Some similarities	Expected to operate in one or more physically challenging environments, but not all.
Not similar	Not expected to operate in physically challenging environments.

---

[1]   See rubric in Appendix A.

[2]   We consulted the following references: U.S. Marine Corps, *MCWP 3-11.2: Marine Rifle Squad,* November 27, 2002; U.S. Marine Corps, *MCIP 3-15.5: MAGTF Anti-Armor Operations,* November 27, 2002; U.S. Marine Corps, *MCIP 3-11.01: Combat Hunter,* February 4, 2011; U.S. Marine Corps, *MCIP 3-11.01A: Infantry Company Operations,* December 5, 2013; U.S. Marine Corps, *MCO 1200.17E Military Occupational Specialities Manual* (Short Title: MOS Manual), August 8, 2013.

Finally, we generalized the characteristics of the candidate organizations. We reviewed documents and publications from candidate organizations where available, as well as other literature, and consulted with subject matter experts to develop an approximate understanding of the typical organizational, technical, and environmental characteristics of the candidate organizations.[3]

Using the rubric, we found that fire departments are most similar to the Marine Corps infantry and have the greatest potential to provide insights to infantry gender integration. Of the organizations we evaluated, fire departments (particularly rural or forestry service fire departments) operate in the most diverse terrain conditions under the greatest austerity. Group dynamics also resemble those of small units (at the platoon level and below). Finally, the role of individual and collective equipment plays the largest role in the ability of a firefighter or fire department to accomplish its mission. In 2010, the United States Department of Labor reported that among the 342,000 career firefighters in the United States, slightly more than 12,000 (3.6 percent) were women.[4]

Police departments are also similar, but less so. Police departments confront the most adversarial environment, but the diversity of terrain, duration of operations, and the level of austerity are not similar. Organizationally, police departments share some similarities to the infantry occupational field in promotion practices, but group dynamics are not similar. Finally, while police officers do use military-like equipment, that equipment plays less of a role in the ability of a police officer or police department to accomplish its mission. In 2013, the Department of Justice reported that female police officers constituted approximately 13 percent of police officers in the country.[5]

The other organizations that we investigated are mostly dissimilar and were eliminated from consideration. While the organizations in the original candidate group were initially attractive, systematic evaluation of these organizations found that they are not suitable for comparison to the infantry occupational field.

Caveats to Comparing Organizations to the USMC Infantry

Although police and fire departments are the most similar and useful organizations to derive integration lessons from, there are major differences to keep in mind between

---

[3] The resources we used to characterize the candidate organizations were less well defined than the Marine Corps resources but still offered enough detail to be useful. Documents we reviewed included Penny E. Harrington, *Recruiting and Retaining Women: A Self-Assessment Guide for Law Enforcement*, National Center for Women and Policing, *Equality Denied: The Status of Women in Policing: 2001*, April 2002; Denise M. Hulett, Marc Bendick, Jr., Sheila Y. Thomas, and Francine Moccio, *A National Report Card on Women in Firefighting*, International Association of Women in Fire and Emergency Services, April 2008a; Molly Dunigan, *Victory for Hire: Private Security Companies' Impact on Military Effectiveness*, Stanford University Press, 2011.

[4] Lynn M. Boorady, Jessica Barker, Shu-Hwa Lin, Young-A Lee, Eunjoo Cho, and Susan P. Ashdown, "Exploration of Firefighter Bunker Gear," *Journal of Textile and Apparel, Technology and Management*, Vol. 8, No. 2, Summer 2013, p. 1.

[5] U.S. Department of Justice, "Women in Law Enforcement," *Community Policing Dispatch*, COPS Office, July 2013.

police and fire departments and the Marine Corps infantry. The Marine Corps infantry is often the most extreme characterization of each category of the comparison rubric. Environmentally, the infantry is expected to operate in more austere and diverse environments for longer periods of time against more capable adversaries. Infantry Marines are expected to master a wider range of technical skills and equipment.[6] The Marine Corps infantry also has more formalized promotion and retention policies and procedures, and a much more complex organizational hierarchy. It is important to keep in mind that the Marine Corps infantry is more extreme than police or fire departments in every category of comparison.

There are two additional aspects to remember when interpreting integration lessons from police and fire departments. First, police and firefighters' unions were major stakeholders during the integration of those organizations. Unions strongly advocated against some integration policies (such as transitioning to task-based training and assessment), which departments had to address to the unions' satisfaction.[7] The closest equivalent stakeholders in terms of advocacy are veterans service organizations (e.g., American Legion, Veterans of Foreign Wars) and think tanks, but these are not nearly as influential and integral as the unions were to the integration efforts of police and fire departments.

Second, Marine Corps infantry integration will take place within an organization that is already significantly integrated. In some combat service support occupational specialties, de facto full integration occurred in 1977 with the disbanding of the office of the Director of Women Marines.[8] Other occupational specialties were opened in following years as legal and policy restrictions on female assignments were lifted, including several combat arms occupations in 2014.[9] This long process of integration means that many aspects of gender integration such as training, promotions, and equipment have already been addressed, or are being addressed.

---

[6] For a full listing of USMC infantry tasks, see U.S. Marine Corps, "NAVMC 3500.44A: Infantry Training and Readiness (T&R) Manual," 2012.

[7] For a more detailed narrative on the influence of unions in female integration of police and fire departments, see Kerry Segrave, *Policewomen: A History*, Jefferson, N.C.: McFarland & Co., 1995.

[8] Mary V. Stremlow, *A History of the Women Marines, 1946–1977*, Washington D.C.: History and Museums Division, Headquarters, United States Marine Corps, 1986.

[9] For a concise history of female military integration milestones, see David F. Burrelli, *Women in Combat: Issues for Congress*, Washington D.C.: Congressional Research Service, R42075, May 9, 2013. For the most recent lifting of female assignment restrictions, see U.S. Marine Corps, MARADMIN 493/14: *Announcement of Change to Assignment Policy for Primary MOS 0803, 0842, 0847, 2110, 2131, 2141, 2146, 2147, 2149, 7204, and 7212*, September 30, 2014.

Lessons Learned from Police and Fire Departments

We looked for gender-integration lessons for police and fire departments using three methods: literature review, a lawsuit analysis, and interviewing subject matter experts. We began by conducting a literature review of 78 books, newspaper and professional journal articles, and other reports and publications. We extracted the most relevant lessons learned by keeping the target context (the USMC infantry) and source context (police and fire departments) in mind. The fact that the USMC is partially integrated already was important for us to consider, since many of the gender-integration lessons learned by police and fire departments had to do with initial qualification and hiring, promotion, and assignment issues that are already being addressed by the Marine Corps.

Our literature review led us to conduct an in-depth analysis of lawsuits related to gender integration. The review indicated that fire departments represented a worst-case integration scenario that might be useful to consider. We chose to examine the eight lawsuits against the Fire Department of New York City (FDNY) related to gender, using the *New York Times* as a data source. Appendix B contains the full summary of the lawsuit analysis.

Ensure That Equipment and Uniforms Meet the Needs of Women

The literature on fire department gender integration indicated that proper equipment is an essential prerequisite for successful gender integration. Like infantry Marines, firefighters rely heavily on personal equipment to do their jobs. The first generation of female firefighters had to contend with ill-fitting clothing and personal protective equipment, such as breathing equipment. While gender-specific bunker gear[10] was available in 1997, most female firefighters currently wear bunker gear designed and sized for men.[11] In one survey of female firefighters conducted in 2004–2005, "79.7 percent of women survey respondents reported problems with ill-fitting equipment, four times the 20.9 percent reported by males. These problems involved gloves (for 57.8 percent of female respondents), boots (46.8 percent), turnout/bunker coats (38.9 percent), helmets (28.4 percent), and breathing masks (25.6 percent). In interviews, one particular complaint involved breathing apparatus hitting helmets, tipping them forward to impair vision."[12] Among departments responding to our survey that had women employees, 39.8 percent reported not having purchased size-adapted clothing

---

[10] Bunker gear is a coat-and-pant combination developed to better protect firefighters.

[11] Boorady et al., 2013, p. 1.

[12] Denise M. Hulett, Marc Bendick Jr., Sheila Y. Thomas, and Francine Moccio, "Enhancing Women's Inclusion in Firefighting in the USA," *The International Journal of Diversity in Organisations, Communities and Nations*, Vol. 8, No. 2, 2008b, p. 199.

and personal equipment.[13] This type of inaction has led to several lawsuits across the country related to ill-fitting equipment and clothing.

Our analysis of police departments found that some police departments provide personnel with great flexibility in choosing the type of weapon that both male and female police officers use. For instance, some departments allow personnel to buy their own weapons, whereas other departments supply smaller or shorter weapons for small-statured men and women.[14] Some police departments also indicated that the only pieces of equipment and clothing that are gender specific are the female bulletproof vest, which has darts by the bust area, and the female pant uniform (although most female police officers in this particular department have opted to wear the male pant instead of the female pant).[15] This department also indicated that while the male and female bulletproof vests are slightly different, there is no cost difference between the two vests.

Although female Marines in noninfantry occupational fields have deployed with the current selection of individual equipment throughout the last decade of operations, the Marine Corps should continue to closely monitor this issue. We spoke with several people with expertise on Marine Corps equipment issues; planned modifications are expected to improve the fit of equipment for both female and male Marines (see Chapter Seven).

Small-Unit Dynamics and Discipline Need to Be Closely Monitored

One of the most commonly cited integration challenges that fire and police departments have faced throughout the past 30 years is the continued problem of maintaining good order and discipline in small units undergoing integration. Female police officers and firefighters at various times had to contend with males harassing, overprotecting, marginalizing, and even (in the case of firefighting) refusing to assist women in life-threatening situations.

In some cases, males took a paternalistic or overprotective attitude toward women. Our literature review showed examples in which male police officers responded more quickly to female officers' requests for backup, tried to take the lead in interactions with suspects, and otherwise tried to shield their female colleagues from situations that they (males) felt were too dangerous for female officers.[16] However, overprotection was not observed in the fire department literature or lawsuit analysis.

In other cases, men marginalized the efforts of women. Our literature review showed that in some police departments, male supervisors relegated female officers to report writing, filing, and other support-type work incidental to patrol duties when

---

[13] Hulett et.al., 2008b, p. 199.

[14] Interview with staff from large U.S. metropolitan police department, October 10, 2014.

[15] Interview with staff from large U.S. metropolitan police department, October 10, 2014.

[16] Segrave, 1995.

female officers began patrolling in the 1970s.[17] Although these female officers were trained and qualified to take on regular patrol duties, there was a significant amount of sidelining of female officers during this period.[18] Male officers gave reasons for this ranging from the well meaning (female officers are better suited to those tasks) to the hostile (female officers are *only* suited for those tasks).[19]

In still other cases, male police officers and firefighters harassed their female colleagues. Our analysis of FDNY lawsuits showed that male firefighters subjected subordinate female firefighters to hazing, verbal and sexual harassment in the firehouse, and other abuses.[20] Our literature review showed that female police officers suffered similar harassment during the early days of integration.[21] However, it appears that there are fewer incidents in police departments today, while fire departments appear to continue to struggle with issues related to misconduct (e.g., sexual harassment).

The harassment problems of police and fire departments were compounded by the perception that department leaders did not take those issues seriously, ignored them, or even condoned the actions of male officers and firefighters.[22] Our lawsuit analysis showed that FDNY leaders were often criticized by outside groups for minimizing problems as internal matters or as isolated incidents.

While the number of harassment incidents that have come to light has lessened over the years for police and fire departments, this reduction appears to have been the result of changing norms, rather than as the result of deliberate action. It does not appear some fire or police departments managed to successfully curb harassment toward women through any deliberate intervention, such as training or disciplinary action. Rather, it appears that harassment decreased (but has not disappeared) only after female officers and firefighters proved to be competent in their tasks and part of the mainstream, and after older officers and firefighters retired.[23]

The challenges to good order and discipline that police and fire departments faced in integrating women into their ranks will likely have implications for Marine Corps leaders as they plan to integrate women into the infantry occupational field. Overpro-

---

[17] Patricia Weiser Remmington, "Women in the Police: Integration or Separation?" *Qualitative Sociology,* Vol. 6, No. 2, Summer 1983, p. 118.

[18] Remmington, 1983.

[19] Remmington, 1983.

[20] Our review of FDNY lawsuits showed that these incidents included male firefighters defacing female lockers, stealing badges, slashing boots or gluing them to the firehouse floor, dumping trash on females' bunks, and numerous incidents of degrading remarks about female firefighters' abilities, sexual orientation, and sexuality.

[21] Kimberly A. Lonsway, Rebecca Paynich, and Jennifer N. Hall, "Sexual Harassment in Law Enforcement: Incidence, Impact, and Perception," *Police Quarterly,* Vol. 16, No. 2, June 1, 2013.

[22] Allan T. Duffin, *History in Blue: 160 Years of Women Police, Sheriffs, Detectives, and State Troopers,* New York: Kaplan Publishing, 2010.

[23] Duffin, 2010.

tection, marginalization, and harassment will likely be issues that the leaders and multiple levels of command must monitor and mitigate when appropriate.

Integration Challenges Change and Mature over Time

Police and fire departments encountered new challenges as female police officers and firefighters were promoted and integrated further into each organization. Our lawsuit analysis indicates that initial integration challenges in establishing performance-based standards and hiring practices were eventually addressed. New challenges, such as professional development and promotion practices, took their place. As female police officers and firefighters were promoted and gained greater responsibility, they continued to push organizations to re-evaluate more of their practices, policies, and procedures.

However, our lawsuit analysis shows that harassment remained an integration challenge at all phases of integration. Lawsuits stemming from firefighter misconduct and harassment appeared to be a constant throughout the FDNY's process of integrating firefighters. The nature of the misconduct (e.g., tasteless pranks, sexual and verbal harassment) also appeared to remain constant.

These observations suggest that integration is a process that will require the continuous attention of leadership for many years after initial integration. As female infantry Marines advance in rank and positions of responsibility, the Marine Corps will need to continue to pay attention to the new challenges that those Marines will face. At the same time, there will be some integration issues, such as harassment, that will require constant attention.

Being Open to External Perspectives Can Better Facilitate the Integration Process

Many police and fire departments integrated while under immense public pressure. This pressure was intensified by the defensive tone that many department leaders took in response to the scrutiny. Department leaders were sometimes dismissive of legitimate criticism, indirectly belittled critics, and took other actions that may have resulted in even greater public scrutiny.[24] This was particularly prominent in our lawsuit analysis of the FDNY. Our review of FDNY-related articles showed that the tone and theme of the articles appeared to grow more suspicious of FDNY leaders over time, particularly during the initial integration phase.

While these observations do not identify causal factors, they do suggest that the Marine Corps leadership should continue to pay close attention to outside attitudes and perceptions during the integration of female Marines into previously closed MOSs. An external oversight council may also facilitate this and enable the Marine Corps leadership to pursue integration without having to contend with lawsuits, public hostility,

---

[24] Jihong "Solomon" Zhao, Ni He, and Nicholas P. Lovrich, "Pursuing Gender Diversity in Police Organizations in the 1990s: A Longitudinal Analysis of Factors Associated with the Hiring of Female Officers, " *Police Quarterly,* Vol. 9, No. 4, December 1, 2006.

and an environment generally suspicious of the Marine Corps' commitment to giving integration a fair chance at success.

Implications

The experiences of police and fire departments that integrated women into their ranks over the last 30 years offer limited but important lessons for the Marine Corps. The lessons that these organizations learned in properly equipping women, dealing with internal small-unit dynamics, and withstanding external scrutiny are applicable to the Marine Corps infantry and should be considered carefully within context. One of the most important insights from the experiences of these civilian organizations is that the issues and challenges that have arisen during the integration process have followed a process that corresponds to the career progression of women after integration. In the early stages of integration, issues and challenges focused on issues related to recruiting and hiring. Then, as women progressed in their careers, issues related to promotion and retention arose. These findings reinforce that the Marine Corps should be ready for integration issues and challenges to evolve over time, and that its implementation and monitoring plans should be flexible enough to adjust to those changes.

CHAPTER SEVEN

Integrating the Marine Corps Infantry: Representation and Costs

Introduction

In this chapter, we develop a simple model to approximate the costs of integrating the Marine Corps infantry occupational field. A key output of our model is the number of women serving in the infantry at any point in time; we also use this information to calculate the representation of women within the infantry over time and to estimate how representation is likely to differ based on the number and proportion of women and men who complete training, serve in the infantry, and remain in the Marine Corps beyond their first term.[1]

As a first step to estimating the monetary costs associated with opening the Marine Corps infantry to women, we divide costs into two categories: (1) one-time costs and (2) recurring costs. We define *one-time* costs as those costs that occur in a single time period (generally in preparation for or during the initial period of integration). Examples of one-time costs include any costs for short-term research and development, as well as costs associated with necessary changes to equipment or facilities. Costs of establishing gender training and communication plans, gender advisers, or other specific resources to assist women (such as hotlines) would also fall in this category.[2]

We define *recurring* costs as those costs that occur repeatedly over multiple years as a result of opening the infantry to women. A main driver of recurring costs will be differences in attrition or retention rates. To the extent that women complete training at a lower rate, or spend fewer months on average in the infantry, substituting women for men will result in fewer personnel serving in the infantry. Therefore, the Marine Corps will need to recruit or retain additional personnel to maintain the size of the infantry. Recurring costs could also include additional physical conditioning time as necessary, lost time necessary to recover from increased injury rates, as well as any other alterations to training or continued implementation of policy changes.

---

[1] Our model uses information from the largest infantry MOS, "Rifleman." However, many of our results are applicable across the occupational field.

[2] As discussed in Chapter Five, the experiences of foreign militaries suggest that communication plans, advisers, and other similar resources are linked to success in integration.

Thus, ongoing costs associated with gender training, gender advisers, or other specific resources would fall in this category.

To estimate costs, we began with a detailed literature review; our methodology also included interviews with key personnel in organizations that have integrated women into physically demanding occupations, as well as estimates from a straightforward model based on personnel data. Our model allows us to estimate the number of women in the infantry at each point in time over a 15-year framework; from this information, we derive an estimate of recurring costs. Because our estimates of recurring costs are based on personnel data, we are able to capture differences in attrition rates and overall length of service, but we are *not* able to capture or predict costs based on time lost due to differential injury rates.[3] In a similar manner, our personnel data allow us to determine who remains in the Marine Corps, but we cannot determine individual levels of fitness; we discuss the implications below.

When using personnel data, we focus most of our analyses on enlisted Marines. Because there are very few female Marine Corps officers, modeling changes in the proportion (or even the number) of women in the officer corps over time involves substantial uncertainty. However, most of the information presented in this chapter on one-time costs is general in nature and thus is equally relevant to enlisted personnel and officers. For example, gender integration plans as well as facilities changes will affect both enlisted personnel and officers. We also present some information on representation of women in several other military occupations in the final section of this chapter; in particular, we include some key occupations in the Marine Corps and in the Army.

In the next section of this chapter, we discuss our findings on one-time costs. Then, in the Recurring Costs section, we provide details on our model and focus on the key parameters (the number of women who enter the Marine Corps, the number of women who enter and complete infantry training, and the length of time women serve in the infantry). We present the proportion of women in the infantry based on the most likely circumstances, but we also discuss the sensitivity of the model to factors such as training completion rates. Next, we discuss our calculations of costs based on attrition and length of service. Finally, we compare our results to historical data on the growth of women in key military occupations that opened roughly 20 years ago. We conclude the chapter with a brief discussion of the implications of our findings.

---

[3]   Although we do not have access to data on injury rates, such information is collected by the Marine Corps and could be added to our model.

One-Time Costs

Data Sources and Findings

We attempted to obtain estimates of the cost of integrating physically demanding occupations from several different sources. First, we tried to find as much information as we could about the costs incurred by foreign militaries when they opened combat arms–like occupations to women. We discovered no publicly available information on costs of integration in foreign militaries. We also asked specific questions about costs in our in-depth interviews with points of contact in key foreign militaries. Both the Norwegian and the Canadian contacts indicated that they had no information or data on the costs of integration. In addition, we examined the Australian Defence Force (ADF)'s highly detailed integration plans for each of its services.[4] Each plan included at least 50 activities, but even in a plan of this detail, the only specific information about costs is contained in a single column, which indicates whether the specific activity is expected to have cost implications. The vast majority of activities were not expected to have cost implications, and we were unable to find additional information on the cost of integration in the ADF.

We also tried to find as much information as we could about the costs incurred by domestic civilian organizations when they integrated. For instance, we included questions about costs in our interview protocol. We also searched the available literature and other open-source documents on the experiences of relevant civilian organizations. Again, we discovered no information about the costs of integration from these sources. And our sources suggested that modifications made to open occupations to women were relatively modest.

We also searched for available information on the costs, or even on the general experiences, of opening key U.S. military occupations to women in the past. For example, many U.S. military occupations were opened to women in the mid-1990s when the "risk rule" was rescinded. While analysis of the extent of women's integration is available,[5] we discovered no documentation of the costs associated with integration.

Finally, we spoke with Marine Corps subject matter experts who are knowledgeable about costs and budgeting for the Marine Corps as an organization, or about specific aspects of facilities or equipment. This line of inquiry also did not reveal any available estimates of the likely costs of integration. Interviewees indicated that many of the changes to facilities currently in the planning or execution stages will serve to improve the overall condition of facilities, which will benefit all Marines. These same changes will also assist with the integration of women, should the Marine Corps decide to open the infantry to women. These changes were undertaken to improve facilities,

---

[4]   Australian Government, Department of Defence, 2013a.

[5]   Laura L. Miller, Jennifer Kavanagh, Maria C. Lytell, Keith Jenning, and Craig Martin, *The Extent of Restrictions on the Service of Active-Component Military Women*, Santa Monica, Calif.: RAND Corporation, MG-1175-OSD, 2012.

not to ready facilities for women, but personnel indicated that only minor additional changes would be necessary to accommodate women. Our conversations indicated that cost analysts who work for the Marine Corps are well aware of the potential for increased costs in the wake of integrating the infantry. However, their greatest source of concern over costs of integration is linked not to the areas they oversee, such as short-term personnel or facilities costs, but to those costs likely to emerge in the future. In particular, Marine Corps personnel mentioned long-term medical costs as a source of concern and uncertainty.[6]

Marine Corps subject matter experts who work with equipment told a similar story. In one case, we discovered that current modifications to body armor will serve to improve the fit and functionality for most women, but also for some men. All Marines, not only those in the infantry, are issued body armor. Because approximately 92 percent of Marines are male, modifications that help a relatively large percentage of female Marines and a relatively small percentage of male Marines will actually impact more men than women. For example, an alteration to a vest that improves fit for·75 percent of female Marines and for only 25 percent of male Marines will improve fit for roughly four times as many males as females.[7] Consistent with this example, our conversations suggested that many more males than females would benefit from several proposed changes.

Key Themes

A couple of key themes emerged from our research and conversations concerning one-time costs. In particular, there is no cost information available from past gender-integration efforts; also, there is no clear precedent or accepted method for estimating costs of integration. One explanation for the scarcity of information is that costs are not tabulated in a gender-specific manner. While certain key adaptations (such as the establishment of "gender advisers" or similar) can be clearly linked to the opening of occupations to women, most costs are not classified in such a manner and, given the ever-changing and uncertain aspect of costs, it would be difficult even in retrospect to link opening occupations to specific one-time costs. We turn next to recurring costs—those costs that are expected to occur on a regular basis.

---

[6]   Estimates of differences in medical costs between male and·female Marines are not readily available, and estimates of overall differences from the civilian population or even other services may not be accurate for the Marine Corps given the age and fitness distributions of Marines. However, it is worth noting that first-term female Marines are far less likely than first-term male Marines to be married to civilians; this suggests that although female Marines' individual medical costs are likely to be higher than those of male Marines, the overall impact of opening the infantry to women on the total Marine Corps health costs is unclear. Per capita health care costs from the Office of the Assistant Secretary of Defense (Health Affairs), "Per-capita DoD Costs for TRICARE Programs in FY2012," unpublished spreadsheet provided to RAND. For marriage rates, see Defense Manpower Data Center, "Active Duty Marital Status," spreadsheet, April 2010.

[7]   This calculation is accurate when we use data on only enlisted personnel in the Marine Corps, and when we use data that combines enlisted personnel and Marine officers.

Recurring Costs

As was the case with one-time costs, we discovered no estimates of the recurring costs of opening physically demanding occupations to women in the existing literature. Specifically, publicly available information on foreign militaries included no estimates of recurring costs; our points of contact in key foreign militaries and civilian organizations also could not provide estimates of ongoing costs. Finally, there are no estimates of recurring costs of integration for civilian or military occupations that opened to women in the past. Indeed, there is no established or accepted methodology for estimating or calculating these costs.

Therefore, we estimate recurring costs based on personnel data. To be specific, we estimate our costs based on the number of personnel serving in key occupations at any point in time. This is appropriate because personnel costs (including basic pay, housing allowances, subsistence allowances, retirement set-asides, and funds for recruiting and training personnel) constitute the majority of the Marine Corps budget.[8] Moreover, the total cost of any given policy change is closely linked to the rank and years of service distributions of the personnel involved. Personnel data allow us to estimate such costs.[9]

These data indicate the date at which personnel enter the Marine Corps and the start and end dates for each MOS held by each Marine. Thus, it is possible to calculate the overall attrition rate, the boot camp attrition rate, and the amount of time each Marine serves in the Marine Corps or in any individual MOS. As noted above, these data do not indicate any gradations in performance. For example, they do not indicate which personnel have minor injuries that result in light-duty status or which personnel perform at a higher level than their peers; data indicating such outcomes are not readily accessible. While the level of performance certainly has an effect on overall personnel costs, the number of personnel at each point in time drives the overall costs. Thus, we estimate costs by using personnel data to determine the likely growth of women within key occupations and to determine whether additional recruiting or retention resources may be necessary to prevent the size of a key MOS from shrinking after the MOS is opened to women.

The Marine Corps has control over many decisions that will affect costs should the infantry be opened to women. In particular, the Marine Corps often has chosen to retain a relatively small proportion of personnel at the end of the first term. In contrast, first-term retention rates have been higher than the historical average in recent years. This decision has implications, both in terms of the months Marines serve in the infantry and in terms of personnel costs; we discuss these issues later in the chapter.

---

[8]   See, e.g., the Department of the Navy's Financial Management and Comptroller website, which provides details on the Department of the Navy's FY15 budget.

[9]   Again, our personnel data do not allow us to estimate costs based on differences in injury or deployment rates.

As a first step, we describe the typical Marine Corps infantry career and discuss relevant aspects of our personnel data. Because we identify infantry personnel based on their MOS, the manner in which MOSs are assigned in the Marine Corps is relevant to our analyses. Newly enlisted personnel (those in boot camp) hold a general training MOS.[10] At this point in a Marine's career, our personnel data include no indication of the intended occupation; therefore, we cannot determine how the boot camp attrition rate of enlisted personnel who intend to serve in the infantry differs from the boot camp attrition rate of those who intend to serve in other occupations (this information is available to the Marine Corps based on contract data). After completing boot camp, Marines who will serve in the infantry next complete infantry training; this training takes approximately two months. Marines who are completing infantry training initially hold an MOS of 0300. Finally, upon completing infantry training, Marines receive an infantry-specific MOS. The most common infantry-specific MOS is 0311 (Rifleman). However, several other MOSs are part of the infantry.[11]

For clarity, we focus our cost model on the largest Infantry MOS (0311, Rifleman). We do this for several reasons. First, focusing on this MOS allows us to capture the majority of the infantry. Rifleman is the most common Infantry MOS; our data indicate that roughly one in eight enlisted Marines holds this MOS at some point during his career. Also, while training for all Infantry MOSs is very similar, there are small differences in the training pipeline. Focusing on 0311s allows us to examine a group with consistent training. Finally, in the past, the services have opened occupational fields by MOS (for example, women may serve in some enlisted Engineering MOSs in the Army but not in others).

While we focus on a single MOS, we also note that our cost model and our cost estimates are based on the *total* number of women who enter the infantry; therefore, all of our total cost results are completely applicable, even should the Marine Corps choose to open additional MOSs. When we calculate the percentage female in the infantry later in this chapter, that percentage is based on opening only MOS 0311; therefore, should additional MOSs be opened as well, the percentage of women would be different (lower) than we calculate, but the total cost estimates would be exactly the

---

[10] The vast majority of the Marines in our sample hold an initial training MOS of 8100, 9900, or 9971. This is also the case among those who eventually serve in the infantry. During initial training, there is no indication in our personnel files of the intended occupation; therefore, we cannot determine how the boot camp attrition rate of enlisted personnel who intend to serve in the infantry differs from the boot camp attrition rates of personnel who intend to serve in other occupations. The services assign occupational codes in different ways; in the Army, for example, personnel may change MOSs over time, but even personnel in boot camp are assigned an MOS indicating their planned occupation. This has implications for comparing the representation of women across services; we discuss this when we compare the growth of women in USMC versus Army occupations.

[11] Specific examples of other infantry MOSs include 0313 (LAV Crewman), 0331 (Machine Gunner), 0341 (Mortarman), 0351 (Infantry Assaultman), and 0352 (Antitank Missleman). Additionally, the MOS 0369 (Infantry Unit Leader) is held only by Marines who have achieved at least the rank of staff sergeant; Marines who hold this MOS generally held a different infantry MOS prior to receiving 0369 (most often 0311).

same. Therefore, throughout this chapter, our use of the word *infantry* refers specifically to MOS 0311.[12]

Infantry training consists of several distinct phases:

- Boot camp, approximately 90 days
- Infantry training, 59 days
- Predeployment training (PTP) at first duty station, approximately six months.

Boot camp and infantry training constitute formal training. Together, they take approximately six months (there is generally a short break between boot camp and infantry training). After completing this formal training, personnel are considered part of the infantry. However, training continues, albeit in a less formal manner, at their first duty station (this is PTP, or predeployment training). We estimate that infantry personnel are fully trained and become productive after about six months at their first duty station (i.e., after being in the Marine Corps for approximately one year and holding an infantry MOS for about six months). After completing all training, Marines serve in the infantry for the rest of their careers. On average, Marines in the infantry spend about 45 months in the infantry; therefore, we estimate that they spend about 39 months as fully trained infantry personnel. Next, we model the number of Marines at each stage of this process.

Recurring Costs: Personnel Model

Our model uses several assumptions to determine the number of Marines at key career points. We use the historical personnel data to obtain retention rates at key points, and then we apply these rates to all personnel in our model. In this manner, we can estimate the number of female and male Marines who complete boot camp, enter infantry training, complete infantry training, and enter the infantry, as well as the overall size of the infantry and the proportion of infantry Marines who are female.[13] We explicitly acknowledge that the time period covered by our data may not accurately reflect

---

[12] In our calculations of the size of the infantry, we also include Marines who first held the MOS of 0311 and then obtained the MOS of 0369 (Infantry Unit Leader) as 0311s. These staff sergeants make up a small proportion of our data; excluding them does not qualitatively change our results, although the proportion of the infantry that is female increases somewhat when we exclude 0369s.

[13] Our data sets are based on two separate Defense Manpower Data Center (DMDC) files: the Work Experience file and the Defense Enrollment Eligibility Reporting System file. In each case, we select information on Marines who served from January 1996 through December 2012. Our files do not include the exact dates that Marines complete boot camp. Therefore, we use three-month attrition rates to approximate boot camp attrition, but we recognize that true boot camp attrition rates are slightly higher because some Marines repeat portions of boot camp (see Aline O. Quester, "Marine Corps Recruits: A Historical Look at Accessions and Bootcamp Performance," Center for Naval Analyses, annotated briefing, D0023537.A1, 2010).

the future of the Marine Corps, especially in terms of deployment schedules, recruiting resources, and the propensity to enlist. And of course, we have no information on women serving in the Marine Corps infantry because the infantry is currently closed to women. Therefore, we test the sensitivity of our model to our assumptions by allowing key attrition and continuation rates to vary, and then determining how much our results change in response to these variations. Also, we model enlisted behavior only because the enlisted force is much larger than the officer corps; in particular, there are very few female officers, which makes any estimates inherently uncertain.

In general, we set up the model so that the size of the infantry would remain approximately constant over time, if no women enter the infantry. Of course, the size of the infantry could increase or decrease based on the needs of the Marine Corps, but holding the infantry to a constant size allows us to demonstrate the impacts of changes in retention and the number of women entering the infantry.

Retention Model: Inputs
Number of Women and Men

For the purposes of this analysis, our model assumes that 3,000 recruits enter boot camp each year with the intention to serve as riflemen in the infantry, and we initially assume that the total number of recruits will stay the same if the infantry opens to women. Thus, a key parameter is the number of women (and men) among recruits who intend to serve in the infantry. We bound this parameter by first modeling the total number of female Marine recruits.

In the Marine Corps, both the total number of recruits and the number of female recruits have varied over the years since the advent of the AVF, although changes to Marine Corps recruiting have been less dramatic than those experienced by the other services. During the early to mid-1970s, before the advent of the AVF, Marine Corps Non-Prior Service (NPS) accessions were over 45,000 per year; for the rest of the Cold War period, accessions averaged about 35,000 per year.[14] During the 1990s, missions were smaller, and accessions averaged slightly less than 30,000 per year. In the years soon after September 11, 2001, Marine Corps accessions increased somewhat to over 31,000 per year; accessions increased further in FY 2007. At the same time, the proportion of accessions (and of Marines) who are female has increased very slowly, but fairly steadily, over the period from 1973 to today. This trend—growth in the percentage of female service members—holds across the services for officers and enlisted personnel. The other services have a higher proportion of women than the Marine Corps at each point in time, perhaps because of the very central and large role that combat arms–like MOSs and the 0311 MOS in particular play in the Marine Corps.

---

[14] Except where noted, all service-level accession information in this section comes from the Population Representation Reports; see, especially, the 2011 report, Appendix C. The information is quite consistent with our personnel files (the Reports use DMDC data) but includes accession information from a longer time frame.

In the last two to three years the number of women enlisting in the Marine Corps has trended upwards. For instance, in FY 2013, NPS female accessions exceeded 2,800 (this is the largest number of women ever to enter the Marine Corps in a single year), and women made up over 9 percent of all accessions.[15] But even including the most recent years, the number of female accessions has increased by only about 75 women per year in the post-9/11 period. Thus, assuming the number of women will continue to increase at a rate of 75 per year over the next few years is the most straightforward way to estimate the number of women likely to enter the Marine Corps in future years. But such a simplistic assumption is not sustainable in the long term and does not utilize all available information on current trends. In particular, a steady increase of 75 women per year does not constitute an equilibrium; at some point, we would expect the number of women (and men) entering the Marine Corps to stabilize.

For these reasons and because the number of women has trended upwards in recent years, we also predict the number of women likely to enter the Marine Corps in the future using a more sophisticated technique. We form a data set including the number of female accessions, as well as the total number of accessions into the Marine Corps each year and use regression analysis to determine the relationships between the number of female accessions, the total number of accessions, and a time trend. We then use this information to predict the number of women who will enter the Marine Corps each year in the near future.[16] Our models consistently predict that the number of women entering the Marine Corps will increase by approximately 100 per year. Of course, these are out-of-sample predictions (assuming that current trends will continue into the coming years).[17] Major changes in the recruiting missions, or in the use of recruiting resources, could certainly result in markedly different numbers of female accessions. Indeed, opening the infantry to women could have a positive effect on recruiting.

Our actual goal is to predict the number of women who will enter the Marine Corps with the intention of serving in the infantry each year. Should the infantry be opened to women, it is not clear exactly how many female recruits will enlist with the intention to serve in the infantry. Having an idea of the total number of women entering the Marine Corps will help us to bound our estimates and determine how opening

---

[15] Most recent years of accession information supplied by Operations Analysis Division, Marine Corps Combat Development Command, and therefore may not be exactly comparable to numbers from earlier years. FY 2014 numbers were not available during the analysis phase of this project.

[16] This estimate is quite insensitive to changes in the years of data used; variations on this model consistently suggest that the number of female accessions is likely to increase by 75–100 per year. See Appendix C for regression results and more information about the data.

[17] An "out-of-sample" prediction or forecast uses current and past measures to predict likely future outcomes. Forecasts are "out of sample" by definition; thus, all forecasts involve making assessments of the extent to which current trends will continue in the future.

the infantry to women is likely to affect costs, but this result does not tell us how many women are likely to enter the infantry.

Therefore, we consider a series of scenarios in which the total number of women intending to enter the infantry varies between zero and 400 per year. Thus, the number of men entering the Marine Corps with the intention to serve in the infantry varies between 2,600 and 3,000. The extent to which the number of women entering the infantry represents additional recruits, versus a reorganization of the women in the Marine Corps, has implications for the overall cost of opening the infantry to women. For example, if an additional 100 women enter the Marine Corps in the near future, but 400 women enter infantry training, then there will be fewer female Marines serving in noninfantry MOSs. We discuss this in more detail in the last section of the chapter.

Boot Camp

Our model begins with new recruits who enter boot camp. As discussed above, we lack the information necessary to identify the recruits who intend to enter the infantry. Thus, we identify a set number of recruits as infantry-bound and then apply the boot camp and training attrition rates to the numbers. Here, we assume boot camp attrition is the same among potential infantry personnel and among others.[18] To produce an infantry of approximately 16,500 personnel, we "assign" 3,000 entry-level recruits to the infantry each year (this also produces a realistic number of infantry trainees at each point in time).

We use boot camp completion rates of 92 percent for men and 88 percent for women. These rates reflect the three-month attrition rates in our personnel data over the last five years. We note that these rates are somewhat lower than rates in earlier years.[19] While boot camp attrition certainly affects costs, the impact on our results from small changes in boot camp attrition is minimal. (Assuming attrition increases proportionally for men and women, an increase in boot camp attrition will mean that the Marine Corps will need to use additional recruiting resources to attain the same size force, but such attrition increases will affect our model primarily by decreasing the average amount of time recruits would be expected to serve in the infantry.)

---

[18] Many Marines serve in the infantry, so the male boot camp attrition rate is likely to be similar or lower among those who enter the infantry versus those who do not. Indeed, if recruits who intend to serve in the infantry enter the Marine Corps more physically fit than other recruits, those headed for the infantry may in fact have lower boot camp attrition rates than other Marines; this would cause our estimated costs to be slightly higher than the true costs of infantry training.

[19] For a complete discussion of early-term attrition rates in the Marine Corps over the last 35 years, see Quester, 2010. This document also points out that boot camp attrition rates tend to be slightly higher than three-month attrition rates (our files allow us to calculate only the three-month rates), and that boot camp attrition rates have been as high as 15 percent for men and 25 percent for women in past decades.

Infantry Training

Next, those who complete boot camp enter infantry training. The number of women in the infantry depends heavily upon the number of women who enter infantry training, *and* on the number of women who successfully complete infantry training.[20] Infantry training is challenging, but the completion rate of *men* who enter this training is quite high. Our personnel data indicate that about 95 percent of men who enter infantry training complete the training and go on to serve in the infantry. Those who successfully complete infantry training go on to attain an infantry MOS; at that point they become a part of the infantry.

Of course, we do not know what the completion rate will be for women who enter infantry training (women who have entered infantry training to date have had a relatively high attrition rate, but these women entered the infantry without passing the gender-neutral physical screening being developed). Based on other attrition data, we would expect the completion rate of women to be lower than that of men, but this rate depends on a number of factors, including how accurately the physical standards required for entry into infantry training predict women's performance in training. While we do not know how many men would successfully complete training if the standards were set at a different level, the standards seem highly predictive for men—most men who meet them and enter training go on to successfully complete the training. If the standards accurately predict women's success, the likely result is that relatively few women will enter infantry training, but those who do enter will complete the training at a high rate. If, in contrast, the standards do not accurately predict women's success, then we may see many more women entering training, but the completion rate may be much lower. In our model, we initially produce estimates based on an 85-percent completion rate, but we also produce estimates based on a much lower 45-percent completion rate.

If physical standards do *not* predict women's success in infantry training, then finding an alternate career path for the women who do not complete the training will be key for several reasons. A main reason is related to costs—if the Marine Corps pays to recruit and train women who do not complete infantry training and these women then leave the Marine Corps, this represents a lost investment. Of course, the vast majority of Marines in the infantry are men, so working to retain *male* Marines who do not complete training also represents an opportunity to conserve resources.[21] Retaining personnel who do not successfully complete infantry training and moving those personnel into an alternate MOS represents a way to minimize costs associated

---

[20] We assume that Marines who complete infantry training will go on to serve in the infantry.

[21] We emphasize that retaining the men who do not complete infantry training is likely to represent at least as large a savings as retaining the women who do not complete infantry training. For example, if 200 women enter infantry training each year and 2,800 men enter, and men wash out at a 5 percent rate and women wash out at a 55 percent rate, those who fail to complete training will include 140 men and 110 women. (Our models suggest the number of women entering infantry training each year is likely to be lower than 200.)

with opening the infantry to women. While time spent attempting infantry training will still have a cost, any level of infantry training is also likely to have benefits for Marines who go on to serve in other MOSs. We note that well-designed physical standards will, by definition, display no gender bias and thus will predict equally well for men and women. Thus, if physical standards do not predict success, we would expect standards to be adjusted. This suggests that retaining personnel who do not complete infantry training may be necessary in the short run but may become less important over time.

Results: Retention Model

The primary outcome from our model is the number of Marines in the infantry at each point in time, by gender. We also calculate the number of infantry trainees at each point in time, by gender.[22, 23] We begin by presenting results from our basic model; next, we allow training completion rates to vary. Then, we explore the effects of post-training continuation rates and present some results from an alternate version of the model that allows continuation rates to vary over time. Finally, we calculate years of service and present cost estimates. Table 7.1 indicates the key retention rates in our model, the extent to which we allow these rates to vary, and other key inputs.

Results: Basic Model

Figure 7.1 presents the basic results from our model. In this figure, we calculate the proportion of infantry personnel who are female as a function of the number of women who enter boot camp intending to serve in the infantry each year. In each case, we apply the retention rates listed in Table 7.1. We assume that, among those who complete boot camp and enter infantry training, 85 percent of women complete infantry training; we set women's continuation rates after the first year at 75 percent (consistent with personnel data).

Figure 7.1 demonstrates that the growth of women in the infantry is likely to be fairly slow, taking at least seven to ten years to level off. For example, if 100 women enter the Marine Corps each year with the intention to serve in the infantry, our model predicts that women will eventually make up about 2 percent of the infantry. In contrast, to exceed 8 percent representation would require about 400 women per year entering the Marines with the intention to enter the infantry, and about 300 per

---

[22] As discussed above, infantry trainees hold a training MOS and are not yet considered to be a part of the infantry.

[23] In our model, we assume that if the Marine Corps opens the 0311 MOS to women, women will initially enter training during FY 2016. Therefore, at the beginning of FY 2016 there are no women in the infantry, but by the end of FY 2016 a group of women have completed training and become part of the infantry. (Our year-specific results should be interpreted as indicating the number of women and men in the infantry at the end of each fiscal year.) Of course, should the Marine Corps choose to open the infantry to women during an alternate year, our results would still be consistent, but women would begin to enter the infantry during the alternate year rather than FY 2016.

Table 7.1
Retention Model: Key Assumptions, Infantry Training

Career Milestone	Retention Rate, Men (%)	Retention Rate, Women (%)
Boot camp	92	88
Infantry training	95	85 (45–90)
Infantry continuation rate	83	75 (70–80)

Other Key Inputs

Number of infantry personnel (0311s): ~16,500

Trainees per year: 3,000

Female trainees per year: 0–400

NOTE: Rates and inputs are estimates based on RAND analysis of Defense Manpower Data Center Personnel Files.

year actually entering the infantry after boot camp and training attrition for most of the next 15 years. Recall that 400 women per year entering the infantry is quite optimistic based on our estimates of the total number of women entering the Marine Corps. However, also note that our model allows a steady number of women to enter the infantry each year, and that we assume a relatively high proportion of women complete infantry training. Therefore, scenarios in which fewer women enter the infantry

Figure 7.1
Predicted Representation of Women Among USMC Infantry Enlisted Personnel Based on Initial Assumptions of Accession and Training Completion Rates

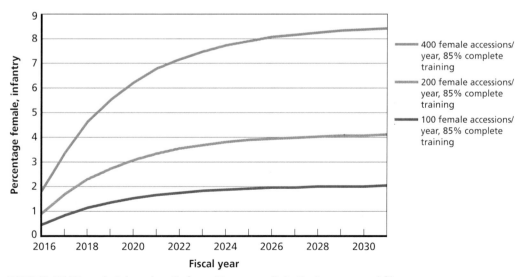

SOURCE: RAND analysis based on Defense Manpower Data Center personnel files.
RAND RR1103-7.1

are more likely, especially in the near term. If, in fact, the number of women entering the infantry and completing training *increases* over time, we might expect that the percentage female will be in the area of the blue line in the near future but will eventually approach the orange line. However, achieving a situation in which more than 5 percent of infantry personnel are female would require substantial numbers of women completing training for a number of years. This accords with the results from our review of the literature of foreign militaries and their experiences with integrating combat arms–like occupations; when information was available, it suggested that the proportion of women in these occupations remained very low, even when the occupations had been opened to women for relatively long periods.

Results When Training Completion Rates Vary

Next, we allow some of our key assumptions to vary. First, we consider the implications of women completing infantry training at rates well below 85 percent. In this case, their representation in the infantry will grow much more slowly. Figure 7.2 demonstrates the effect of training completion. In this figure we present the same information shown in Figure 7.1, but we also add dashed lines to indicate how much future representation would change if the training completion rate were 45 percent rather than 85 percent. Figure 7.2 indicates that cutting the training completion rate by nearly 50 percent also causes representation to be nearly 50 percent lower in each scenario.

Figure 7.2
Predicted Representation of Women Among USMC Infantry Enlisted Personnel Depends on Training Completion Rate

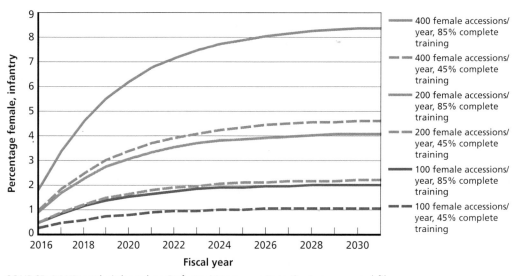

SOURCE: RAND analysis based on Defense Manpower Data Center personnel files.
RAND RR1103-7.2

Results When Continuation Rates Vary

Even if women complete infantry training at a relatively high rate, longer-term continuation rates also have the potential to impact representation. Figure 7.3 presents the same information as in Figure 7.1 but adds dotted lines to indicate the effect of lower continuation rates *after* training. In each figure, men in the infantry have a yearly continuation rate of 83 percent after training (roughly the rate reflected in the personnel data). If women in the infantry have a yearly continuation rate of 75 percent after initial training, the solid lines indicate their representation. But if women have a yearly continuation rate of 70 percent after initial training, the dotted lines in Figure 7.3 indicate their representation. Here, the pattern is similar to Figure 7.1 in the first years, but over time the difference in continuation begins to influence representation. Indeed, the effect of this relatively small change in continuation rates is substantial, decreasing the representation of women by about 15 percent. This suggests that longer-term continuation rates will affect the representation of women in the infantry. In other words, retention is also likely to be a key metric. Therefore, we next explore the implications of continuation/retention in our model in more detail.

Assuming a constant continuation rate simplifies our model while still allowing us to represent the size of the infantry in an accurate manner. In reality, of course, Marines do not have a constant continuation rate after initial training. The Marine Corps is a young force, and the first-term retention rate tends to be lower than the rate found in the other services. In our data, at any point in time, 18–25 percent of

Figure 7.3
Representation of Women Among USMC Enlisted Infantry Personnel Depends on Continuation Rates

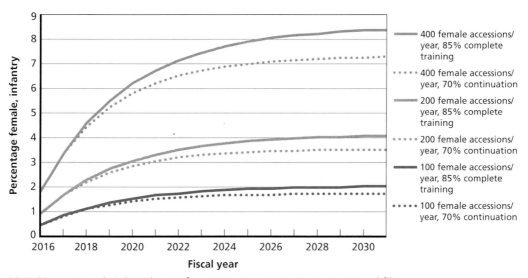

SOURCE: RAND analysis based on Defense Manpower Data Center personnel files.
RAND *RR1103-7.3*

those holding the MOS of 0311 have between 12 and 23 months of service experience. Across all occupations, there have been 14,000–16,000 enlisted Marines with four years of service in recent years, but only about 7,000–9,000 enlisted Marines with six years of service. During most years between 1980 and 2006, the first-term reenlistment rate hovered around 30 percent.[24] Thus, the number of Marines in each cohort drops sharply after the end of the first term, and a "typical" Marine would complete four years and then leave the Marine Corps.

To test the implications of these continuation patterns, we constructed an alternate model that allows continuation rates to vary over time. In this model, we set the male continuation rates to 97 percent per year between initial training and the end of the first term, while female continuation rates were set to 95 percent per year in this period. Then, we set the continuation (reenlistment) rate at the end of the first term at either 30 or 45 percent.[25] Figure 7.4 demonstrates the results of this model.

In this model, we allow 200 women and 2,800 men to enter the Marine Corps with the intention to serve in the infantry. Our model with a constant continuation rate predicted that about 4.1 percent of infantry personnel would be women, while this model predicts about 4.2 percent if men have a reenlistment rate of 45 percent and women have a reenlistment rate of 30 percent.[26] Figure 7.4 also demonstrates that lower continuation rates among men *and* women will tend to produce faster growth in representation (because the infantry is "turning over" faster). Similar to Figure 7.3, Figure 7.4 suggests that continuation rates are likely to have a large influence on the representation of women in the infantry. This suggests that first-term reenlistment rates are another important indicator to track. The overall implications of the two models are very similar.

Results: Years of Productive Service

Next, we discuss the amount of time personnel are likely to serve in the infantry and the cost implications of potential gender-based differences in productive time in the

---

[24] During the past decade, the Marine Corps expanded the reenlistment bonuses available and purposefully increased first-term reenlistment rates. For example, all Marines who reenlisted between October 1, 2006, and February 26, 2007, received a $10,000 bonus; during this period, all eligible Marines were allowed to reenlist, producing reenlistment rates of roughly 40 percent (see Diana S. Lien, Aline O. Quester, and Robert W. Shuford, "Marine Corps Deployment Tempo and Retention from FY04 Through FY07," Center for Naval Analyses Research Memorandum D0018757.A2, 2008). This strategy served to increase the size of the Corps quickly, but we do not expect this to be the norm in future years. During earlier years, the first-term reenlistment rate was roughly 30 percent; see Aline O. Quester, Anita Hattiangadi, Gary Lee, Cathy Hiatt, and Robert Shuford, "Black and Hispanic Marines: Their Accession, Representation, Success, and Retention in the Corps," Center for Naval Analyses Research Memorandum D0016910.A1, September 2007. In contrast, the Army's first-term retention rate has often been above 45 percent; see, for example, Richard J. Buddin, *Success of First-Term Soldiers: The Effects of Recruiting Practices and Recruit Characteristics*, Santa Monica, Calif.: RAND Corporation, MG-262-A, 2005.

[25] Thirty percent approximates the historic rate, while 45 percent represents a slightly higher rate than that observed during the recent buildup.

[26] These figures roughly approximate the constant reenlistment rates used in our basic model above.

Figure 7.4
Representation of Women Among USMC Enlisted Infantry Personnel with Varying Continuation Rates

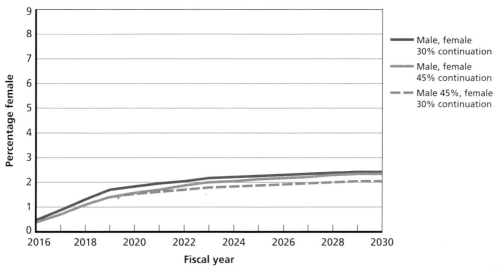

SOURCE: RAND analysis based on Defense Manpower Data Center personnel files.
RAND RR1103-7.4

infantry. After infantry training, Marines are assigned to a unit and at this point are considered part of the infantry. Next, Marines prepare to deploy. During the first months in their unit, although training is less formal, Marines are still learning how to be members of the infantry. At the end of approximately six months in the unit (and approximately 12 months in the Marine Corps), we consider the trained Marines to be productive members of the infantry. This is the period in which the Marine Corps can recoup the investments (e.g., costs related to recruiting and training).

Therefore, the final key assumption in our model is the number of months that each Marine is expected to serve in the infantry. Again, we base this on our personnel data. The data indicate that Marines who complete infantry training and enter the infantry are expected to spend about 52 months in the Marine Corps on average (this number includes all first-term attrition). This consists of six months of formal training, followed by 46 months in the infantry, the first six months of which is spent in informal training.[27] This suggests that men in the infantry spend about 40 "productive" months serving in the infantry after completing boot camp, infantry training, and informal training. Of course, we do not know how many months women will spend

---

[27] We calculate this figure by examining all Marines who hold the MOS of 0311 and had left the Marine Corps by the end of 2012 (to avoid right-censoring). As noted above, infantry MOSs such as 0369 "Infantry Unit Leader" are held by Marines with previous experience in 0311; we include this time in our calculations to count all productive infantry time.

in the infantry, but continuation rates suggest that women tend to spend about six months less than men in the Marine Corps. Therefore, women·are assumed to spend about 46 months in the Marine Corps; this consists of six months of boot camp and infantry training followed by six months of informal training and about 34 "productive" months in the infantry. These numbers are consistent with the predictions from our basic model. We note that the number of productive months in the infantry is affected by many factors. In particular, if the Marine Corps chooses to increase the first-term retention rate, the average number of productive months served will increase.

We next calculate the total number of years of productive service of all personnel in the infantry (we refer to these as *infantry-years*). This calculation is simply the product of the number of personnel entering the infantry and the expected amount of time each will serve; the disparity is due to the six-month difference between men's and women's expected service. Based on the attrition rates above (see Table 7.1), for every 100 women who enter boot camp with the intention to join the infantry, about 75 women will complete infantry training; for every 100 men who enter the infantry; about 87 will complete infantry training. This difference, and the six-month difference in expected months of service, imply that, as the number of women entering the infantry increases, the total years of infantry service falls.

We repeat this calculation with different numbers of men and women and compare the outcomes. Table 7.2 shows the numbers of infantry-years as a function of the number of women and men entering the infantry each year. These figures represent the service expected from infantry personnel. The table indicates that, for every 100 women who enter boot camp with the intention to serve in the infantry, the total number of infantry-years falls by about 75. This is because women have lower completion rates through boot camp and infantry training, and then are expected to serve fewer months on average in the infantry. Thus, our model predicts that there will be fewer people in the infantry than had the infantry remained closed to women. Therefore, keeping the infantry at the same size (in terms of productive time) will require additional Marines. Based on the average amount of time served in the infantry, the shortfall in infantry-years will require enough additional personnel to serve about 75 additional years in the

Table 7.2
Infantry-Years of Service

Number of Women/Men Entering Boot Camp	Number of Women/Men Entering the Infantry	Total Infantry-Years
0 women/3,000 men	0/2,622	8,740
100 women/2,900 men	75/2,535	8,663
200 women/ 2,800 men	150/2,447	8,582
400 women/ 2,600 men	300/2,272	8,423

infantry. This implies an additional 23 or so Marines would need to enter the infantry if each served 40 productive months.

To make up for this shortfall, there are two main ways to achieve additional service: recruit additional personnel, or retain additional personnel at the end of the first term. To achieve the same amount of infantry service, the Marine Corps would need to retain about 23 additional male Marines at the first enlistment point or to recruit about 27 additional male Marines for each 100 women who enter boot camp with the intention to serve in the infantry. Of course, the Marine Corps could also retain or recruit additional women, or a combination of men and women.

Should the Marine Corps decide to recruit additional personnel, it is possible to estimate this cost with reasonable precision. The overall recruiting budget is about $600 million.[28] This suggests that the average cost per recruit is roughly $20,000, but additional high-quality recruits are thought to cost more, perhaps $25,000 per recruit.[29] Thus, for every 100 women who enter the Marine Corps with the intention of serving in the infantry, additional recruiting resources representing about 0.1 percent of the total recruiting budget are likely to be necessary to keep the total number of infantry-years constant.

Should the Marine Corps decide instead to retain additional experienced Marines, research suggests that the cost of an additional *year* of service is roughly $20,000–$25,000.[30] This, coupled with the number of months Marines typically serve in the infantry, suggests that retaining 75 additional infantry-years of service is likely to cost 2–3 percent of the current selective reenlistment bonus (SRB) budget. (The Marine Corps SRB budget was about $60 million in FY 2014 and was projected to be roughly $55 million in FY 2015).[31] However, this is likely an overestimate for a couple of reasons. First, although it is difficult to quantify, experience is valuable. Therefore, retaining experienced Marines (rather than recruiting inexperienced Marines) may be preferable from a productivity standpoint. Indeed, it may be possible to retain fewer Marines

---

[28] See the Department of the Navy website, which provides details on the Navy's FY15 budget as well as some information about historical spending (U.S. Department of the Navy, "Department of the Navy Releases Fiscal Year 2015 Budget Proposal," *Navy News Service*, March 4, 2014).

[29] While there are no recent estimates for the marginal cost of an additional "high-quality" Marine Corps recruit, this figure is consistent with estimates found in Beth J. Asch, Paul Heaton, James R. Hosek, Francisco Martorell, Curtis Simon, and John T. Warner, *Cash Incentives and Military Enlistment, Attrition, and Reenlistment*, Santa Monica, Calif.: RAND Corporation, MG-950-OSD, 2010; Edward J. Schmitz, Michael J. Moskowitz, David Gregory, and David Reese, "Recruiting Budgets, Recruit Quality, and Enlisted Performance," Center for Naval Analyses Research Memorandum D0017035.A2, 2008. In manpower research, "high-quality" generally implies that the recruit possesses a high school diploma or the equivalent and scored at least 50 on the Armed Forces Qualifying Test (AFQT).

[30] See Asch et al., 2010, which estimates the cost of an additional year at the first reenlistment point to be between $14,000 and $17,000 in FY07.

[31] See the Department of the Navy's website for details on the Navy's FY15 budget (U.S. Department of the Navy, 2014).

without sacrificing productivity or readiness. Also, retaining additional Marines may not require this many resources. In many years, the Marine Corps holds first-term reenlistment to a low rate; allowing a higher level of reenlistment could result in additional infantry-years for fewer resources than we calculate here.

Of course, retaining additional Marines (rather than recruiting additional Marines) has different implications for the years of service (YOS) profile. Combining additional recruiting with additional retention would allow the YOS profile to remain unchanged. In either case, the resource costs are likely to be quite manageable, representing a small percentage of overall personnel costs. This result is driven by the small numbers of women expected to enter the infantry and by the relatively modest differences in months of service between men and women.

Representation of Women in Previously Opened Occupations

While there are no women in the infantry today, there are women in other previously closed occupations in the Marine Corps. In particular, the services opened a significant number of positions to women in the mid-1990s after the "risk rule," barring women from units or missions where the risk of exposure to direct combat, enemy fire, or capture equaled or exceeded the risk in the units the women supported, was rescinded. As points of comparison, we track the proportion of women serving in several previously closed occupations in the Marine Corps and in the Army. Specifically, we look at the proportion of engineers who were women over time (among the enlisted force) and the proportion of pilots who were women (among the officers). We chose these occupations because they represent relatively large occupations that have some comparability across the Army and the Marine Corps.[32] We also look at the number of women who entered the surveying and aviation mechanics occupations in the Marine Corps (these occupations also opened to women in the mid-1990s). To determine the proportion of women in these occupations, we use the same DMDC personnel files as discussed above. While the Marine Corps infantry differs in important ways from other occupations, tracing the representation of women in previously closed occupations may provide information about the likely representation of women in the infantry over time.

In each case (engineers and pilots in the Marine Corps and the Army), we tabulate the number of personnel who held that MOS at some point during each year and then determine the male-female breakdown within the MOS.[33] In the Marine Corps,

---

[32] See Harrell and Miller, 1997, for more details on the occupations that opened during this period. Note that aviation occupations differ between the Army and the Marine Corps in terms of training pipelines and day-to-day activities. However, in each service, the aviation occupations require relatively long and expensive training, and these occupations were opened to women at roughly the same time.

[33] We use the term Military Occupational Specialty, or MOS, to refer to occupations throughout this report; technically, the occupations of commissioned officers in the Army are referred to as Areas of Concentration.

the proportion of women in engineering and aviation grew slowly but steadily over the time period—about 3 percent of the Marines in each occupation today are women (see Figure 7.5).

Among Army personnel, the proportion of women in the engineering MOS grew rapidly in the years soon after the occupation was opened; female representation leveled off and then decreased over the last ten years (see Figure 7.6). Among pilots, the pattern is somewhat different. Quite a few women entered the occupation during the mid-1990s, and their representation grew fairly quickly before leveling off. But women have never represented even 10 percent of pilots (see Figure 7.6). This pattern is somewhat similar to the growth of women among pilots in the Marine Corps in that the proportion of women in the MOS is fairly stable and is smaller than the proportion of women across the service. Differences in the initial growth may be due to service-specific differences in the training pipelines.

We also explored several other occupational fields, though these fields may be less comparable across the services. For instance, we examined the growth of women among Marine Corps officers serving as engineers and among Army officers serving as engineers. In the case of the Marine engineering officers, the proportion of women in the occupation expanded more rapidly than in the case of the pilots, but not as rapidly as in the case of Army enlisted personnel. Unfortunately, in the case of Army officers serving as engineers, changes in the coding of the MOS over time made our sample

Figure 7.5
Percentage Female, Engineers and Pilots, USMC, 1997–2013

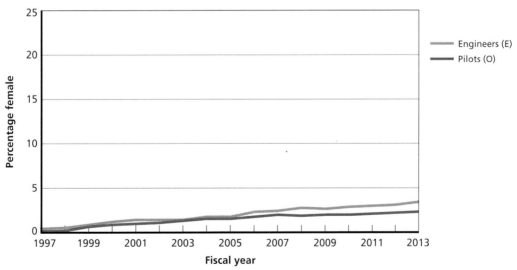

SOURCE: RAND analysis based on Defense Manpower Data Center personnel files.
RAND RR1103-7.5

Figure 7.6
Percentage Female, Engineers and Pilots, Army, 1997–2013

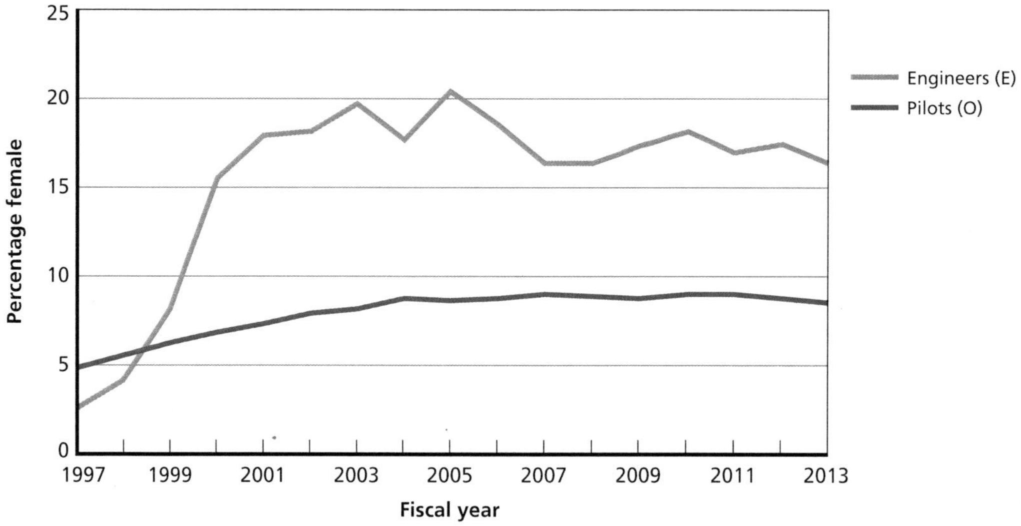

SOURCE: RAND analysis based on Defense Manpower Data Center personnel files.
RAND *RR1103-7.6*

nonrepresentative.[34] We also looked at enlisted surveyors in the Army. Women made up a smaller proportion of surveyors than of engineers at each point in time, but the patterns of growth in representation over time were quite similar. Finally, we examined a group of enlisted Marine Corps occupations that includes various types of aviation mechanics. The pattern of growth of women in these occupations was similar to that shown in Figure 7.5 for female engineers.

To summarize the trends across some of the occupations that opened to women in the mid-1990s:

- In the Army, the proportion of women among enlisted engineers grew quickly and then stabilized; women are represented among engineers at a rate that is similar to their overall representation in the enlisted Army. The pattern is generally similar among surveyors (not shown), although representation of women is somewhat lower.
- In the Marine Corps, the proportion of women among enlisted engineers grew more slowly; today, women make up 2 to 3 percent of enlisted engineers. Women

---

[34] Over the years included in our sample, the MOS indicating that Army officers served as engineers changed multiple times. It appears that our data did not capture all of the changes in an accurate fashion; our data suggest that the number of Army officers serving as engineers fell by more than 80 percent between 2003 and 2004 and increased after 2004, but never attained the original total. This suggests that in the early years, some personnel serving in other occupations are classified as engineers, while the opposite is likely to be true in some of the later years.

make up a higher proportion of engineering officers in the Marine Corps (not shown), but again the entry of women into this field was fairly slow.

- Among Army pilots, the proportion of women remains lower overall in the occupation than in the rest of the Army, but the initial increase was fairly rapid.
- In the Marine Corps, in contrast, the growth of women in aviation has been slower; today 2 to 3 percent of pilots in the Marine Corps are women.
- The growth and representation of women among aviation mechanics (not shown) is similar to that shown for enlisted engineers and for pilots in the Marine Corps.

A number of factors could influence these differences. A detailed examination of this topic would require tracing the number of trainees and determining the extent to which women in each occupation were eligible to reenlist, chose to reenlist, and were eligible for promotion, and such analysis is clearly beyond the scope of this effort. However, we do note that the timing of assigning MOSs differs in the Army versus the Marine Corps, and this alone makes a direct comparison between the services potentially misleading. In general, Army personnel are assigned a final MOS during the training period, while Marine Corps personnel instead hold a training MOS during this period. For this reason, even if the proportions of women in training and in the occupation were equal across the services, the proportion of women would appear to increase more quickly in the Army than in the Marine Corps, and the overall proportion in the Army would appear to be somewhat higher at each point in time due to the treatment of trainees. Additionally, other differences in the training pipelines are likely to influence the proportion of personnel in a given occupation who are women. But the information in this section indicates that the representation of women in newly opened occupations within the Marine Corps is likely to grow quite slowly. This is the case across enlisted personnel and officers and across multiple MOSs. Based on this, we would expect the growth of women in the Marine Corps infantry to be quite slow. This would also be consistent with the results from our cost model, presented above, and with the experiences of various foreign military organizations discussed in Chapter Five.

Implications

In this chapter, we trace out the implications and potential costs of opening the infantry to women. Despite a thorough review of the available literature and interviews with a number of subject matter experts, we were not able to discover any estimates of the likely one-time or recurring costs of opening the infantry to women. However, the information that we gathered suggests that many of the one-time costs may be manageable because periodic updates to facilities and equipment can serve to ready the infantry for women while improving facilities and services for all Marines. In terms of recurring costs, we focus on those costs that can be estimated with personnel data. We form our estimates based on personnel costs because personnel costs make up the majority of the Marine Corps' costs and are driven by the number of personnel as well as the rank and years of service distributions. We note again that other aspects of service will influence costs. We do not have access to information on the rates of injury or deployability/deployment of male and female Marines, but we recognize that this information has cost implications, and we recommend that the Marine Corps carefully track such information (see Appendix D for recommendations for monitoring costs).

The recurring costs in our model are driven by differences in attrition and retention, as well as by the total number of women who enter the infantry. Based on our exploration of costs and our model of recurring costs, there are a number of implications and takeaways that will be relevant as the Marine Corps considers opening the infantry to women. Here, we provide a brief list, followed by a discussion of key points:

- There are no existing estimates of the likely (one-time or recurring) costs of integrating physically demanding occupations; one reason for the lack of existing estimates is that costs generally are not itemized in a manner that allows assignment by gender.
- Many of the current improvements to facilities and equipment that are ongoing would be necessary should the Marine Corps decide to integrate the infantry; in any case, these changes are likely to have positive effects on many Marines (male and female).
- Our estimates, as well as experiences when the Marine Corps opened previously closed occupations to women in the past and experiences of foreign militaries, suggest that the number of women entering the infantry will be modest, and the increase in representation will be slow.
- Likewise, we expect the total number of women entering the Marine Corps to continue to grow in the near future, but at a modest rate.
- Our model suggests that opening the infantry to women will have costs because we expect women to have higher levels of attrition during training and fewer months of service in the infantry than men.
- The rate at which women successfully complete infantry training will be linked to costs; if women who do not successfully complete the training are retained in other MOSs, this offers a mechanism for cost saving. Retaining men who do not complete the training could have even larger cost implications.
- Policies that encourage reenlistment at the first retention point have the potential to decrease the costs of integration.
- The Marine Corps should be able to make up any shortfall in the infantry effectively through increased recruitment, increased retention, or both.
- We expect overall personnel costs associated with the shortfall to be modest (when compared to total recruiting or retention budgets).

Next, we discuss a few of these key points in more detail.

Of course, we have no specific information on the number of women likely to enter the infantry, but we do know how many women chose to enter the Marine Corps in past years, and we use these data to predict the likely rate of female accessions in the near future. Under most assumptions, our models predict modest growth in the number of women entering the Marine Corps each year in the near future—perhaps an additional 100 women per year. It is certainly possible that the Marine Corps could use recruiting resources and could achieve significantly higher growth rates among women. However, based on past data as well as the experiences of foreign militaries, we would expect modest growth in the number of women entering the Marine Corps in the near future.

This data point will impact the overall cost of opening the infantry to women. Assuming modest growth of women in the Marine Corps, the number of women entering the infantry is also likely to be small. For example, if accession increases by 100 women *each year* and *every* additional woman intends to enter the infantry, no more than 75 women will complete infantry training in the first year, and it will take four years for the number of women entering the infantry to grow to 300. Even in this case, growth will still be relatively slow, although the number of women in the infantry will eventually begin to grow substantially. In a more extreme case, if the growth of women in the infantry actually exceeds the overall growth of women in the Marine Corps, then there may actually be *fewer* female Marines in other occupations due to opening the infantry to women. This, too, will affect overall costs; because female Marines generally serve fewer months than male Marines in all occupations, "shifting" Marines between occupations will have fewer costs than increasing the overall number of female Marines. However, based on our analysis and the experiences of other organizations, we would expect that relatively small numbers of women will enter the infantry each year and that the proportion of women will grow quite slowly, similar to the pattern seen among Marine Corps pilots and engineers over the 20 years after those occupations opened to women.

Another significant unknown is the rate at which women will complete infantry training. This rate will substantially impact the growth of women in the infantry (see Figure 7.2). In particular, if many women do not complete infantry training, planning to move these Marines into alternate occupations offers a way to contain costs. (We note that moving male Marines who do not complete infantry training into alternate occupations offers another, potentially larger, opportunity for cost savings.) If physical standards predict women's capacity to complete training, then most women who enter training will be likely to complete it; in this case, moving women into alternate occupations will be less important. Finally, continuation rates (especially first-term reenlistment rates) will have a large impact on the long-term growth of female representation in the infantry. The Marine Corps generally maintains a structure that allows relatively few experienced Marines to reenlist. Because Marines often compete to reenlist at the end of the first term, the extent to which women have the opportunity to reenlist may be another cost driver, as well as a data point that helps to predict the success of opening the infantry to women.

CHAPTER EIGHT

Developing a Monitoring Framework

Introduction

Developing and following a comprehensive and clear monitoring framework is a challenging yet crucial aspect of planning for successful USMC gender integration in the years to come. This chapter proposes a monitoring framework comprising two phases: (1) the planning phase (before integration) and (2) the first phase of implementation (e.g., annual requirements up to five years after integration). At the five-year point after integration, we recommend that the USMC carry out a comprehensive evaluation of the integration process and reevaluate monitoring priorities, and that the USMC continue to sustain the monitoring effort in the long term. This chapter also discusses broader, strategic monitoring considerations.

We begin by presenting our approach in developing the monitoring framework. Our approach included drawing on sources from the USMC; international organizations; and lessons from foreign militaries, domestic civilian organizations, and other U.S. military services. To develop a comprehensive and well-informed framework, it was a very useful exercise to review lessons from previous similar efforts and understand how those lessons might inform the Marine Corps' infantry gender-integration monitoring framework. Next, this chapter presents the gender-integration monitoring framework we have developed for the USMC. This monitoring framework focuses on using existing data and developing new data systems to measure specific aspects of gender integration that are important during the first few years of transition. We also identify potential ways to measure progress in each monitoring category and methods for collecting relevant data. Finally, we discuss broader, strategic monitoring considerations. These considerations include

- the importance of internal and external oversight
- the significance of gender advisers
- cultural change and understanding of gender issues
- the importance of consistent monitoring.

This framework is not intended to be a finalized and complete monitoring plan, but rather to present a suggested approach and discussion of the important elements to include in the final monitoring plan that the USMC ultimately develops.

Developing a Monitoring Framework

We developed a short- to medium-term monitoring framework to provide an example of common practices used by other organizations that have implemented gender integration. This plan is broken into two phases: the Planning Phase (before the decision whether or not to integrate has been made) and Phase One (up to five years after integration). At the five-year point, we recommend that the USMC conduct a comprehensive evaluation of the integration process to reevaluate monitoring priorities. Regardless of the outcome of this evaluation, we also emphasize the need for long-term, sustained monitoring to identify potential problems quickly as they evolve over time. See Appendix D for the complete spreadsheet of the monitoring framework.

Monitoring Framework Definitions

We organize our monitoring framework by levels (individual, collective, and institutional), categories, and subcategories. For the categories, we followed the Doctrine, Organization, Training, Materiel, Leadership and Education, Personnel, Facilities, and Policy (DOTMLPF-P) structure but added a category termed *Attitudinal*, which includes well-being, welfare, morale, and misconduct. The subcategories are defined in Table 8.1.

Monitoring Framework Structure

In this monitoring framework, we included types of issues ("what are you measuring?"), metrics ("how are you measuring progress, and what information do you need?"), and methods ("how are you collecting the information that you need to measure progress?"). The USMC is in the best position to identify existing data systems that could be leveraged for monitoring the gender-integration process; therefore, the goal of this monitoring framework is to identify broad types of data systems and data collection methods that could be used to help monitor various integration issues. In the Planning Phase, the metrics are designed to track progress in program and policy development over time. In general, the metrics are designed to offer suggestions for ways to track and evaluate those measures; however, there are several different ways to measure progress on integration issues. We also present several different methods for collecting data as well and discuss the value of considering a variety of methods to measure different types of integration issues. These suggested methods of data collection include administrative data, surveys, focus groups, and interviews.

- *Administrative data*: Administrative data are data gathered by different USMC organizations. The data may be gathered for a variety of different reasons. Leveraging existing data collection efforts can be a valuable means of monitoring the gender-integration process.
- *Surveys*: Surveys generate generalizable data and results based on a substantial sample size. Surveys can be used as a means to understand a population's sentiment and perception.

Although administrative data and surveys are useful data collection methods for some metrics, smaller-scale data collection methods are also crucial to identifying concerns quickly and to providing detailed information on trends or on concerns. Focus groups and interviews are important for identifying issues to pursue through administrative or survey data, interpreting findings from survey or administrative data, and exploring complex issues difficult to measure with other types of data. Some issues that may emerge in focus groups or interviews may be good candidates for follow-up in a survey, which can provide information for a representative sample of the population of interest.

- *Focus groups*: Focus groups gather information on collective views and generate an understanding of participants' beliefs and experiences.
- *Interviews*: Interviews gather information on individual views, experiences, and beliefs. Since interviews can be conducted one on one, they are usually more appropriate for more sensitive topics that may not be openly discussed in a group setting.

Strategic Monitoring Considerations

There are several broader strategic monitoring considerations that should also be taken into consideration. These include

- importance of internal and external oversight
- significance of gender advisers
- cultural change and understanding of gender issues
- importance of consistent monitoring.

In this section, we discuss these issues and their significance.

Importance of Internal and External Oversight

Gender-integration oversight boards will be a crucial piece in not only conducting the monitoring, but also in setting and defining requirements for longer-term prog-

Table 8.1
Monitoring Framework Definitions

Category	Subcategory
Organization	**Unit and individual readiness:** Includes all unit and individual readiness aspects regarding the integration of women into previously closed MOSs. Excludes unit training issues.
Training	**Initial entry training:** Issues concerning performance of female Marines in initial entry training (e.g., recruit training/Officer Candidate School, Infantry Training Battalion, The Basic School (TBS), Infantry Officer Course (IOC)).
Training	**Unit training:** Issues concerning the impact of the presence of female infantry Marines on a unit's ability to successfully complete its predeployment training plan (PTP).
Materiel	**Individual clothing and equipment:** Issues concerning the fit, comfort, and functionality of individually issued items, such as uniforms, footwear, Personal Protective Equipment, and load-bearing equipment.
Materiel	**Individual weapons and optics:** Issues concerning the fit and functionality of individual and crew-served weapons, optics, image enhancement equipment, and other serialized items.
Leadership and education	**PME:** Issues concerning female infantry Marines' access to professional military education (PME) opportunities. Includes MOS-specific professional military education opportunities and required PME.
Leadership and education	**Mentorship and support:** Availability and quality of informal mentoring, counseling, and advice to female infantry Marines from their unit's chain of command.
Leadership and education	**Career development:** Issues concerning assignment within Monitored Command Codes (e.g., to key leadership billets) that can affect the promotion and retention opportunities of female infantry Marines.
Personnel	**Recruitment:** Issues concerning the sufficient accession of female recruits and officer candidates to ensure a viable pool of qualified individuals for infantry MOS training.
Personnel	**Assignment:** Issues concerning the assignment of trained female infantry Marines to units in the Operating Forces and the Supporting Establishment.
Personnel	**Promotion:** Issues concerning policies that give the most equal opportunity for promotion possible to qualified male and female infantry Marines.
Personnel	**Retention:** Issues concerning the retention of qualified female infantry Marines.
Personnel	**Attrition:** Issues concerning the reasons female infantry Marines (who have completed MOS training) leave the Marine Corps.

Table 8.1—Continued

Category	Subcategory
Facilities	**Infrastructure:** Issues concerning changes to Marine Corps facilities to accommodate female infantry Marines. Facilities that may require changes include barracks, office buildings, and training facilities.
Policy	**Oversight:** Issues concerning the formation, resourcing, and support to the external oversight group monitoring the integration process.
Policy	**Integration execution:** Issues concerning the temporary policies, organizations, and resources required to support the transition period.
Policy	**Integration cost:** Issues concerning the planning, programming, budgeting, and execution of one-time integration costs.
Attitudinal	**Misconduct:** Issues concerning the impact of female integration on infantry unit misconduct rates, incidents, and punishments.*
Attitudinal	**Cohesion and morale:** Issues concerning the impact of female integration on the unit's cohesion and morale.
Attitudinal	**Welfare:** Issues concerning female infantry Marines' sense of satisfaction, usefulness, and morale separate from the cohesion and morale category.

* This includes sexual harassment and sexual assault.

ress. The NZDF established a Women's Development Steering Group to ensure that integration policies are followed and women are afforded the requisite opportunities to enable integration.[1] In addition, the International Association of Chiefs of Police created an Ad Hoc Committee on Women in police to promote progress of women in policing.[2] An oversight board should have broad authority to task any USMC organization and should have full support from top USMC leadership. It will be a key aspect of consistency to execute and enforce the monitoring plan over the long term. Although our initial monitoring plan is recommended for up to five years, conducting a full-scale reassessment at the five-year mark would be beneficial to determine progress and identify areas of continued development.

External oversight is also important, as external organizations can provide an objective assessment of integration progress (or lack thereof) and could play an important independent role in making recommendations. For example, the 1998 Canadian Forces audit report recommended more effective use of an external advisory panel for transparency during the process of gender integration.[3]

Insights from Foreign Militaries

In the foreign militaries we reviewed for our report, oversight and monitoring of the integration of women into combat positions combines monitoring conducted internally (by military leaders and military organizations themselves) and externally (by civilian organizations, courts, and experts). While internal monitoring helps ensure consistent attention and leadership commitment, external monitoring provides objectivity, transparency, and accountability. Monitoring to support public reporting for purposes of transparency and accountability is also very different from internal monitoring to inform leaders with responsibility at different levels for outcomes.

Organizational structure of internal oversight and monitoring mechanisms—Internal monitoring appears to come from two primary sources. First, much oversight is concentrated at the leadership level. This oversight primarily involves audits and reviews of the integration progress mandated by senior leaders and carried out by sources within the military itself. In Canada, for example, military leaders commissioned a review of integration in 1996 to assess the military's progress in incorporating women into the armed forces. They then used this report to direct the individual services to develop new integration plans and strategies. Now, Canadian military leaders continue to assess the progress of integration of various subgroups each year in the annual equity report, which reports statistics, such as the number of female recruits by occupation, attrition

[1]   "Defence Force Launches Women's Development Steering Group," 2013.

[2]   International Association of Chiefs of Police, *The Future of Women in Policing: Mandates for Action*, Fairfax, Va.: International Association of Chiefs of Police, November 1998.

[3]   Chief Review Services, 1998.

rates, and promotion rates.[4] In Sweden and Norway, integration is monitored on a more constant and direct basis by gender coaches and advisers who work directly with military commanders and personnel to promote and monitor gender equity in training, everyday missions, and deployments.[5] These many sources of oversight are periodically integrated into annual reports on gender equity given at North Atlantic Treaty Organization (NATO) conferences and reviewed by military leadership. Finally, in Australia, monitoring and evaluation is built into each stage of the implementation plan. Each of the services has its own plan and infrastructure for monitoring. In the army, for instance, monitoring and review of integration is conducted at the headquarters level, within the personnel division, and is described as an ongoing task.[6]

In addition to oversight that occurs from the top down, some internal monitoring occurs through women's advocacy groups (made up of military personnel and civilians), who monitor the integration of women, identify new opportunities for their development, and vocalize their concerns and complaints. As an example, the NZDF Women's Development Steering Group (made up of military personnel) works to identify development opportunities for women and to identify continuing challenges to integration.[7] Similarly, in Canada, the Defence Women's Advisory Organization (chaired by an elected civilian representative and a military member) works with military leaders to discuss and address issues such as harassment, family policy, work-life balance, and the development of gender-free physical standards.[8] There is also a Women's Affairs Division in the Israeli Defense Forces whose job it is to address challenging issues faced by women, including sexual harassment, discrimination, and other obstacles.[9]

Overall, our review of internal monitoring in foreign militaries suggests that internal oversight can help ensure that various oversight initiatives are integrated and coherent and that leadership commitment to integration is apparent. At the same time, monitoring efforts should "trickle down," meaning that they should incorporate mid-level commanders and leaders as well, to ensure that the oversight of integration becomes consistent. While periodic reviews are valuable, monitoring of integration on a constant basis is important because it keeps integration as a priority, demonstrates leadership commitment, and helps keep the integration process constantly moving forward.

Organizational structure of external oversight and monitoring mechanisms—Externally appointed panels of experts intended to provide an independent review of the

---

[4] Canadian Ministry of Defence, 2012–2013.

[5] Norwegian Report to Committee on Women in NATO Forces, 2002.

[6] Australian Government, Department of Defence, 2013a.

[7] New Zealand Defence Force, "Defence Force Launches Women's Development Steering Group," press release, March 8, 2013.

[8] Canadian Ministry of Defence, 2012–2013.

[9] Sasson-Levy and Amram-Katz, 2007.

integration process often conduct monitoring and reviews. In New Zealand, both the 1998 and 2005 diversity audits were carried out by independent organizations, outside of the military hierarchy, in order to provide additional objectivity and, ideally, a more thorough and realistic review as a result.[10] In Israel, much of the monitoring of the integration of women into combat units focuses on physical fitness, training, and injury rates. External experts, scientists who collect data and study issues related to physical performance among women, also monitor these issues.[11] In other cases, external monitoring is carried out by a preexisting organization (such as a court, tribunal, or research organization) tasked with the responsibility of monitoring the integration process and the treatment of women in the military. As an example, following its 1989 ruling, the Canadian Human Rights Tribunal conducted periodic reviews of the military's progress on integrating women into the armed forces and into combat positions.

Our review suggests that external monitoring of integration can be extremely valuable and can serve as a powerful catalyst for progress on integration. External reviews conducted by experts, former military personnel, and civilians provide objectivity and accountability that internal reviews sometimes lack. As a result, they can often be more powerful in diagnosing problems with the integration process and promoting change where obstacles exist.

Oversight and monitoring timelines—Monitoring and oversight, whether external or internal, typically occurs on three primary timelines. First, there is routine ongoing monitoring and oversight. Several examples of this everyday monitoring were mentioned previously, including the approach outlined in Australia's monitoring plan and the gender coaches and advisers used in Sweden and Norway. This type of monitoring, while the most informal, is also some of the most important, as it is the most immediate and often the first place a problem or challenge is identified. Second, there are periodic reviews and monitoring that occur on a set schedule, such as annual reports on equity, diversity audits, and five-year progress reports. Reports to the NATO Committee on Women and the Canadian Equity Report are two examples of this type of monitoring. Finally, there are reviews mandated in response to specific events, such as a major complaint or harassment case. For example, in New Zealand, reports of harassment at the New Zealand Defence College led to several follow-up reports that assessed the problem and later progress in resolving it.[12]

Insights from Domestic Police Departments

Police oversight organizations have long been accepted as a part of the practice of policing. Although the origins and goals of these oversight organizations are somewhat different from the goals of gender-integration oversight, the relatively long history

---

[10] Bastick, 2011.

[11] Randazzo-Matsel, Schulte, and Yopp, 2012; Sasson-Levy and Amram-Katz, 2007.

[12] Selenich, 2012.

of police oversight organizations does provide useful insights into how to potentially monitor the gender-integration process beyond the supervision provided by unit chains of command. The experiences of police and fire departments also highlight the need for access to data while monitoring the integration process.

Police oversight has long been a concern of elected officials and the general public. In particular, the widespread perception of police corruption and abuse of power following the social upheavals of the 1960s drove many municipal governments to seriously consider the need for an independent oversight organization to hold police departments and officers accountable for their actions. [13] High-profile incidents of police abuse through the 1980s and 1990s (including the Rodney King beating) sustained this interest.

Although only an estimated 18 percent of police departments in the United States today have oversight organizations, independent oversight is an accepted part of American policing. In many cases, oversight organizations were set up in response to an incident of police abuse of authority that resonated with the public.[14] In fact, a review of 30 police oversight organizations by the Police Assessment Resource Center shows that over two-thirds of those organizations were organized after an incident of police abuse, often at the recommendation of an independent investigation.

Many of these organizations act as a means of ensuring that police departments handle incidents of possible abuse fairly and impartially. Some organizations, such as the Review Commission of the St. Paul (Minn.) Police Department have the authority to review only abuse cases that are internally investigated to ensure procedural fairness and accuracy.[15] These *review and appellate* organizations are useful only when civil or police authorities take their reviews and assessments seriously.

Other organizations, such as the San Francisco Police Department's Office of Citizen Complaints, have the authority to assist internal investigators or investigate incidents independently.[16] These *investigative and quality assurance* organizations have more authority but still focus only on individual cases, rather than on the systemic issues and trends that enable police abuse.

A third type of oversight organization assesses and advises police leadership on broad trends related to police abuse. These *evaluative and performance-based* organizations tend to concentrate on strategic issues within the organization, such as policies and organizational climate. They usually do not investigate individual cases and are

---

[13] Eduardo L. Calderon and Maria Hernandez-Figueroa, "Citizen Oversight Committees in Law Enforcement," California State University Fullerton, Center for Public Policy, 2013.

[14] Police Assessment Resource Center, "Review of National Police Oversight Models for the Eugene Police Commission," Police Assessment Resource Center, February 2005.

[15] Police Assessment Resource Center, 2005.

[16] Police Assessment Resource Center, 2005.

focused on proactively minimizing the risk of police misconduct by identifying patterns and practices that lead to police misconduct.

All three types of organizations may comprise sworn officers, unaffiliated professionals, or some combination of both. The first police departments to experiment with oversight organizations staffed them with sworn officers. The officers had the expertise to credibly evaluate other officers' actions, but they were perceived to be less responsive to citizen concerns.[17]

In response, some departments staffed their organizations with unaffiliated professionals, often volunteer lawyers or former elected officials. While these groups were perceived by citizens to be more responsive, they often lacked the expertise and access to properly do their jobs.

Eventually, police departments started to experiment with hybrid models staffed by a combination of sworn officers and unaffiliated professionals. These hybrid organizations have the access and expertise necessary to conduct rigorous investigations but still retain the support of citizens and elected officials. By the early 2000s, these organizations became the norm in police departments with oversight organizations.

Organizational structure of oversight and monitoring mechanisms—These oversight organizations highlight the need for a mix of internal and external members on the oversight committee in order to balance the expertise of insiders with the wider points of view of nonpolice members. In the context of police oversight organizations, this has included sworn officers, nonpolice legal professionals, and executive-level individuals (e.g., CEOs and former elected officials). For the Marine Corps, this might mean an oversight committee that includes a wide range of individuals: infantry and noninfantry, male and female, officer and enlisted, for instance.

The experience of performance-based oversight organizations also highlights the need for a high level of authority and autonomy. The wide-ranging charter of performance-based oversight organizations required these organizations to have unmistakable support from the police department leadership and unfettered access to any information or individuals that the organizations needed to carry out their evaluative tasks. In the context of police oversight, this meant that the best organizations had the ability to access any and all records, documentation, or files in the department, as well as the authority to subpoena individuals for oversight hearings. Within the Marine Corps, such an oversight organization will likely require high-level support from Marine Corps leadership (e.g., Commandant of the Marine Corps and Sergeant Major of the Marine Corps), access to all data (including records held at the unit level), and the ability to speak to any individuals that the committee needs to speak to. This may be similar to the authority that an investigating officer might have, but at an organizational level.

---

[17]   Calderon and Hernandez-Figueroa, 2013.

Significance of Gender Advisers

Gender advisers are positions specifically designated to advise leadership on issues related to gender integration. These should be thought of as separate and distinct from a gender-integration oversight board, as the gender adviser positions are full-time advisers, whose roles are to advise leadership on the day-to-day aspects of gender integration. Although gender advisers may be involved in periodic assessments conducted by the oversight board, they will be a distinct function. Gender advisers can operate at all levels and have been used in Norway, Sweden, Bulgaria, and South Africa, among others. For example, Sweden relied on gender coaches and field advisers at various levels—from senior leadership down through individual unit commanders.[18] The Marine Corps should consider the creation of a gender adviser billet to facilitate the integration process.

Cultural Change and Understanding of Gender Issues

The Gender Self-Assessment Guide referenced earlier in this chapter discusses the importance of institutional culture and understanding of gender issues. It defines institutional culture as the "collection of values, history and ways of doing things that form the unstated 'rules of the game' in an institution . . . can be a powerful ally in making work on gender equality a valued part of the institution's work, or can block progress on gender issues."[19] The Army reported that one of the major successes of the 2012 Exception to Policy implementation was that the Equal Opportunity and Sexual Harassment/Assault Response and Prevention training conducted by unit commanders aided the integration of women into maneuver battalion headquarters in Brigade Combat Teams.[20] Some recommendations to measure cultural change in understanding gender issues include conducting surveys, focus groups, and interviews to determine understanding of the importance of addressing gender issues, extent of dissemination of gender-related policies, perception of gender equality and issues, prevalence of gender stereotyping and discrimination, and prevalence of sexual harassment.

Importance of Consistent Monitoring

One common theme throughout all the monitoring plans and gender audits that we reviewed was the lack of consistent monitoring. Canadian Forces had several intermittent studies conducted on various aspects of gender integration but conducted a formal assessment of progress only in 1999—at the defined deadline, ten years after the gender integration was mandated. By not conducting intermediate studies, the CF lacked a comprehensive understanding of progress (or lack thereof) during that

---

[18] Egnell, Hojem, and Berts, 2012.

[19] Bastick, 2011, p. 36.

[20] Office of the Under Secretary of Defense (Personnel and Readiness), *Report to Congress on the Review of Laws, Policies and Regulations Restricting the Service of Female Members in the U.S. Armed Forces*, February 2012.

ten-year period, so it was not able to adjust and adapt its overall policies. The NZDF conducted organizational audits in 1998, 2005, and 2014, which were valuable—but without a set timeline or defined goals for assessment, progress is difficult to assess. As mentioned previously, the most consistent monitoring was conducted by the National Center for Women and Policing, which conducted five annual studies looking at women's representation in policing.[21] Clearly defining the monitoring terms, requirements, and timeline over the long term is an important aspect of a sound monitoring plan. In addition, monitoring consistently and enforcing results and recommendations are also important aspects of monitoring gender integration.

Conclusion

As indicated by the experiences of foreign militaries and domestic civilian organizations, gender integration will not happen overnight, but rather it will be a long process that will not be without its challenges and obstacles. Monitoring something as sensitive and significant as gender integration in combat roles in the USMC requires constant vigilance from leadership and the institution itself. It is not enough to conduct yearly reviews on personnel policies or collect data or statistics. A monitoring plan must consist of long-term and deliberate methods of measuring progress and must include strategies to measure institutional and cultural change over time. Based on our research and analysis of other monitoring efforts, this chapter was intended to present and discuss ideas and suggestions for what might be included in such a monitoring plan. For our completed monitoring framework, see Appendix D of this report.

---

[21] National Center for Women and Policing, 2002.

CHAPTER NINE

Cross-Cutting Implications and Recommendations for Implementation

As the Marine Corps moves closer to the January 2016 deadline, the findings in this report offer critical insights into the integration implementation planning process. The implementation planning phase presents the Marine Corps with a critical window of opportunity to develop integration strategies, plans, and policies, as well as to put the necessary data systems in place to monitor integration progress over time. When looking across all of our study findings, we find the following areas are particularly relevant to informing the Marine Corps' implementation planning process: (1) leadership is key to integration success on many fronts; (2) develop a detailed implementation plan and assign accountability; (3) establish oversight mechanisms; (4) monitor standards and training, which are critical; (5) consider long-term career progression issues; (6) develop customized integration strategies through experimentation; (7) monitor integration progress over time; and (8) manage expectations. We discuss each of these issues below.

Leadership Is Key to Integration Success on Many Fronts

Across the findings from our study, it is striking how much agreement there is on the importance of leadership during the integration process. For instance, in our analysis of foreign militaries, institutional commitment and strong leadership were key variables that seem to be associated with integration success. Without this commitment from key stakeholders and without visible involvement by senior leaders, progress on integration is difficult or impossible to achieve. Integration needs to be supported by legal and policy changes, and senior leaders are uniquely positioned to implement and enforce these types of changes.

Leadership (at all levels of the chain of command) is also key to setting the tone for the integration process and ensuring that cohesion is not negatively affected by integration. Our findings from the cohesion literature indicate that integration can rarely succeed without the support of leadership. Leaders can set the command climate and enforce good order and discipline to prevent issues of misconduct (e.g., sexual harassment) that can have negative impacts on cohesion. This finding was reinforced by our analysis of civilian organizations. We found that when leadership in civilian organizations ignored integration challenges, this resulted in lower morale and ultimately led to litigation.

In addition to setting the tone for the integration process, leadership also plays a critical role in disseminating a consistent message about integration to both internal and external audiences. As the Marine Corps moves forward into its implementation planning stage, it would be prudent to develop both internal and external communications strategies. These communications strategies will be especially critical when a decision regarding implementation is made. Regardless of the decision, there will likely be both external and internal proponents and opponents to the decision. Our findings suggest that a clear communications strategy can help facilitate the integration process as a whole by clarifying integration goals. We found that it is especially critical for leadership to provide a clear, consistent explanation of the reasons integration is beneficial to the organization's mission effectiveness. This is particularly important for internal constituencies, because without a firm understanding of what additional capabilities women bring to the Marine Corps infantry's mission, resistance to integration may develop or continue.

Develop a Detailed Implementation Plan and Assign Accountability

Our analyses of the integration experiences of foreign militaries and of civilian organizations indicate that the development of a detailed implementation plan is another key element of successful integration efforts. Although some countries have opened combat occupations without an implementation plan, having an implementation plan facilitates a smoother transition and ensures that integration occurs alongside the necessary training, mentorship, monitoring, and institutional support. Well-designed implementation plans that assign responsibility, identify risks, and outline mitigation strategies are particularly effective in streamlining the integration process. These types of implementation plans clarify the goals of integration and identify the risks associated with integration, as well as the actions that the organization will need to take to mitigate those risks. We also found that it is critical that the implementation plan assign responsibility and accountability for the various elements of integration. Without such accountability, the integration process can stagnate or atrophy all together.

As the Marine Corps continues to think about implementation planning, the development of a detailed implementation plan will ensure that the entire organization will be using the same guidance once a decision about integration is made. Therefore, during the implementation planning phase, it is important to begin to think about the entities that will be responsible for and accountable for the various elements of the implementation plan. If these decisions are made during the implementation planning phase, the various responsible entities can begin to gear up for their assigned implementation responsibilities and begin to carry them out as soon as a decision on integration is made.

The implementation plan's success also hinges on the plan being effectively communicated to all parts of the organization. As mentioned in the previous section on leadership, leaders will play a vital role in communicating the Marine Corps' integration goals, strategies, plans, and policies. Once an implementation plan is ready to be rolled out to the broader Marine Corps, leaders at all points along the chain of command will need to reinforce the plan and the overall goals that it strives to achieve.

Establish Oversight Mechanisms

Our findings also indicate that gender integration oversight boards have been used elsewhere to conduct oversight and monitoring, but also in setting and defining requirements for longer- term progress. Oversight typically occurs on three primary timelines. First, there is the "everyday" monitoring and oversight that occurs on a normal basis and covers routine ongoing progress on integration. Second, there are periodic reviews and monitoring that occur on a set schedule, such as annual reports on equity, diversity audits, and five-year progress reports. Finally, there are reviews mandated in response to specific events, such as a major complaint or harassment case. However, it is critical to keep in mind that the data needed for proper oversight must be identified and the software modifications made to facilitate or enable the collection of the needed data. This element of monitoring may have the longest lead time and may be expensive.

In the foreign militaries we reviewed for our report, oversight and monitoring of the integration of women into combat positions combines monitoring conducted internally (e.g., by military leaders and military organizations themselves) and externally (e.g., by civilian organizations and courts). While internal monitoring helps to ensure consistent attention and leadership commitment, external monitoring provides objectivity, transparency, and accountability. Transparency can help build trust with both personnel within an organization and the public. It can also feed into broader efforts to improve the integration process.

Our findings from the oversight mechanisms in civilian organizations also highlight the need for a high level of authority and autonomy. Many civilian organizations require that their oversight mechanisms have unmistakable support from leadership and unfettered access to any information or individuals that the oversight organizations need to carry out their evaluative tasks. Within the Marine Corps, such an oversight organization will likely require high-level support from Marine Corps leadership (e.g., Commandant of the Marine Corps and Sergeant Major of the Marine Corps), access to all data (including records held at the unit level), and the ability to speak to any individuals with whom the oversight committee or board needs to speak.

Our review also suggests that external monitoring of integration can be extremely valuable and can serve as a powerful catalyst for progress on integration. External reviews conducted by experts, former military personnel, and civilians provide objectivity and accountability that internal reviews sometimes lack. Such an entity can provide an objective assessment of integration progress (or lack thereof) and could play an important independent role in making recommendations. As a result, external reviewers can often be quite powerful in diagnosing problems with the integration process and promoting change where obstacles exist.

As the Marine Corps begins implementation planning, it would be prudent to think about the structure of oversight mechanisms that it could establish to oversee and monitor the integration process. Our findings offer insights that may help the Marine Corps on this front. For instance, our review of internal monitoring in foreign militaries suggests that internal oversight primarily involves audits and reviews of the integration progress mandated by senior leaders and carried out by sources within the military itself. This ensures that various oversight initiatives are integrated and coherent and that leadership commitment to integration is apparent. At the same time, monitoring efforts should "trickle down," meaning that they should incorporate mid-level commanders and leaders as well, to ensure that the oversight of integration becomes consistent.

Monitor Standards and Training

Although our study did not focus on the development or validation of physical fitness standards, the importance of up-to-date, validated gender-neutral physical fitness standards became apparent during several of our project tasks. While many women may not be able to meet gender-neutral standards for entering ground combat occupations, our analyses suggest that gender-neutral standards will likely facilitate task cohesion in integrated units. Gender-neutral standards may actually reduce barriers to integration because they help to establish an equal foundation among all new recruits and help to dispel the notion that women in combat arms occupations are physically unprepared and incapable of completing their jobs effectively.

Our review of the cohesion literature indicates that task cohesion is largely influenced by the ability of team members to effectively carry out their jobs. During integration, the perceived ability of women to effectively carry out their jobs will likely hinge on their ability to meet initial screening criteria, as well as their ability to conduct day-to-day tasks. If women can pull their weight, they will likely be accepted as members of the team. Conversely, if women cannot keep up or if women are given preferential treatment, they will have a harder time establishing themselves as effective members of the unit, and therefore task cohesion will likely be negatively affected. Consequently, it is critical to continue to develop validated gender-neutral standards, regularly update those standards, and enforce them equally. While the Marine Corps may face pressure to allow larger numbers of women into the infantry in order to demonstrate integration "success," our findings suggest that resistance to that pressure would in fact facilitate the integration of those women who do pass the standards.

In several cases, countries have sped up the integration progress by providing additional training for female recruits, either prior to or after enlistment. This helps increase the women's chances of short-term and long-term success in combat arms occupations by ensuring physical readiness. To give women the best chance of success-fully achieving those standards, the Marine Corps could reexamine its training pro-grams to see if any additional changes could better facilitate the physical conditioning women need in order to pass gender-neutral standards. Our review of the experiences of foreign militaries highlights some options that the Marine Corps could try. These include preenlistment training, physical conditioning over longer periods to reduce injuries, segregated training, and integrated training. In particular, integrated train-ing appears to promote progress by improving cohesion and improving the physical readiness of women more than gender-specific training on its own. On a related note, our cost analysis found that training completion rates will have a large impact on the number of women who will enter the infantry. This also reinforces the importance of updated, validated gender-neutral standards to ensure that those training completion rates are an accurate reflection of the physical abilities of women. This is also an area where the Marine Corps could reexamine its training programs to identify potential changes that could give female Marines the necessary physical conditioning to com-plete initial training. Focusing on the training needed to increase those completion rates is one way that the Marine Corps can increase the number of women entering the infantry.

Consider Long-Term Career Progression Issues

While the tendency during the implementation planning process may be to empha-size short-term priorities, we suggest that the Marine Corps keep long-term female career progressions at the forefront of its decisionmaking throughout the entire inte-gration process, from planning to long-term monitoring. One of the primary lessons from the integration experiences of both foreign militaries and civilian organizations is that gender integration is a long process. The evidence from our analysis of civilian organizations indicates that integration challenges evolve over time as women progress through their careers. During the period immediately following integration, challenges tend to focus on issues such as recruiting and hiring, whereas later integration chal-lenges focus on promotion and retention issues as women progress in their careers.

Our analysis of the integration experiences of foreign militaries also found that long-term retention of women in the combat arms is a challenge. In several countries, the number of women in combat arms occupations steadily rose after integration, then leveled off and eventually decreased. This suggests that the Marine Corps should consider these longer-term career progression challenges from the onset of its implementation planning so that it can put the mechanisms in place to mitigate later integration challenges related to promotion and retention. Our study findings indicate that some of those mechanisms could include establishing mentorship programs, as well as ensuring equal access to educational opportunities and leadership assignments throughout a female Marine's career.

Our cost analysis also indicates that the number of women in the infantry is contingent not only on their completion rates for initial training, but also on their continuation rates and retention rates. Career progression issues can influence both continuation rates and retention rates. Tracking retention rates among women and men in combat arms occupations will provide valuable information on integration progress. Also, increasing retention rates has the potential to decrease costs associated with integration by obtaining additional service from fully trained Marines.

Develop Customized Integration Strategies Through Experimentation

One of the key observations from both foreign militaries and civilian organizations is that their integration experiences varied widely. While these experiences can provide insights and signposts for the Marine Corps as it embarks on the path of gender integration in the infantry, none of these organizations is a direct analog to the Marine Corps infantry. Therefore, the Marine Corps will ultimately need to develop integration strategies and approaches that best suit it as an organization and its missions.

While moving forward in the implementation planning process, we suggest that the Marine Corps consider experimenting with different integration strategies and options:

- **Gender-training programs, including content, timing, and delivery:** Different foreign militaries have different gender-training strategies. Some countries have separate gender training, some integrate this training into the basic and refresher courses that all personnel take, and some have special leadership training. In some cases, gender training is really "diversity training," while in others it focuses specifically on gender issues. There are also choices to make in who delivers the training. The same trainers who teach other military courses could do it, or it could be taught by external organizations brought in just to do the gender training. By trying several different approaches and then surveying those who took each training variant about attitudes, both immediately after the training and then periodically, the Marine Corps could determine which approach is most effective.

- **Mentoring programs:** Foreign militaries differ on whether they use formal or informal mentoring networks to support women. Both could be tried and compared based on how women receiving each type of support perform over time.
- **Recruiting strategies:** Different types of recruiting might be more or less effective at attracting women who are well suited to combat occupations. Trying several different strategies at once and then comparing the results (for example, trying different strategies in similar markets) offers a way to identify the best methods.
- **Critical mass:** Since the literature on critical mass does not give the Marine Corps empirical evidence of what the "optimal" number of women might be in a given-size unit, the Marine Corps could assign different numbers and ranks of women to different units. Data from this effort could help to identify whether the number of women in a unit has any impact on both women and the unit as a whole; carrying out similar experiments on matched units of different sizes and missions will help to identify whether effects differ across unit types.
- **Physical training:** Different approaches or types of physical training might better prepare female recruits and promote higher fitness levels that would allow more women to meet the requirements for combat jobs. This might include a pre–boot camp training program or simply different strategies during existing training programs. The effectiveness of each type of training could be compared based on both the completion rates and the physical performance of new recruits following completion of training.

Lastly, if the Marine Corps chooses to use experimentation during the integration process, it should link that experimentation to data collection, analysis, and evaluation. This is significant not only because it is valuable for experiential learning, but also because these data, analyses, and evaluations are the building blocks for near- and middle-term monitoring of the integration process, which we discuss below. These data, analyses, and evaluations can also help to refine the implementation plan and associated policies.

Monitor Integration Progress over Time

In looking across the findings from our studies, we can readily see that monitoring is a key element to integration success over the long term. A strong monitoring plan relies on robust data systems that facilitate the necessary data collection to measure integration progress. As the Marine Corps plans for implementation, it should consider which data systems are already in place to collect the appropriate data to monitor progress over time, and whether any new data systems are necessary.

The monitoring framework presented in Appendix D offers the Marine Corps suggestions on which issues might be included in a monitoring plan, as well as how to measure progress on those issues and what type of data collection methods could be employed. However, in order for a monitoring plan to be effective, it cannot be static. As data are collected and analyzed, new issues and measures may need to be added to or deleted from the monitoring plan.

Another insight from our study is that monitoring needs to be sustained over time. While periodic reviews are valuable, monitoring of integration that occurs every day and on a constant basis is important because it keeps integration as a priority, demonstrates leadership commitment, and helps keep the integration process constantly moving forward. It will be helpful to identify key metrics that leaders should track over time.

Manage Expectations

Lastly, as the Marine Corps begins the implementation planning process, it will need to manage both internal and external expectations. Both proponents and opponents of integration will have particular expectations about how the Marine Corps should handle the decision to integrate the infantry, as well as how to implement any changes. In order to maximize the chances of integration success, the Marine Corps will need to base its decision and implementation strategy on empirical data. This strategy will enable the Marine Corps to set realistic goals and to counter pressure from both proponents and opponents of integration. As evidenced by the number of Marine Corps analytic efforts focused on integration issues, the Marine Corps is already making great headway in developing a broad base of empirical evidence from which it can draw in making its integration decisions and policies. The findings from our study can also assist the Marine Corps in managing both internal and external expectations regarding gender integration.

Of primary importance, the findings from our cost analysis as well as our analysis of foreign militaries suggest that the number of women who are likely to enter combat arms occupations such as the Marine Corps infantry is low. The experiences of foreign militaries indicate that women make up only about 1 percent to 3 percent of combat arms occupations in those countries where these positions are open to women. Our cost analysis also indicates that the growth of women in the infantry is likely to be fairly slow, taking at least seven to ten years to level off. Given these findings, the Marine Corps should manage expectations about the number of women who will likely enter the Marine Corps infantry.

As the Marine Corps embarks on setting its integration goals and defining integration "success," it should keep in mind these findings. If the Marine Corps defines its goals or defines integration success on the basis of having large numbers of women in combat arms occupations, our findings suggest that it may be difficult to achieve those goals or to achieve integration success. Thus, it will be prudent for the Marine Corps to set realistic goals based on input from the various analytic efforts under way, including our study, as well as efforts related to propensity. As the Marine Corps sets expectations regarding what integration "success" means for it as an organization, the experiences of foreign militaries offer cautionary signposts indicating that integration will be a long, slow process and that the number of women entering combat arms positions will likely be relatively low. Our findings from foreign militaries suggest that success was based on institutional factors such as leadership support, plans that were put into place, and the degree to which gender integration became a part of military culture. As it considers how to define integration success, the Marine Corps should again turn to the evidence base that it is building through its various analytic efforts.

Closing Thoughts

As the Marine Corps begins to think about implementation planning, a critical window of opportunity exists to set in place the strategies, plans, and policies that will guide the implementation process. The Marine Corps should take full advantage of this opportunity. During this planning process, both near- and long-term issues should be considered, and the mechanisms put into place during the planning process should be flexible enough to accommodate learning and adjustments. Integration will likely be a process of continual, iterative improvements. Putting the systems in place to collect the appropriate data throughout the integration process will help to build the evidence base for those improvements along the way and will facilitate integration success.

Rubric for Evaluating USMC Infantry Characteristics

Table A.1
Environmental Aspects for Comparison

Aspect for Comparison	Most Similar	Some Similarities	Not Similar
Operating environment	Operates in all environments, to include physically challenging jungle, mountain, and desert terrain	Operates in one or more physically challenging environments	Does not operate in physically challenging environments
Duration of operations	24-hour, remaining in the field for 1–3 weeks	24-hour, remaining in the field for 3–7 days	Short duration (1 day or less)
Austerity	May be completely self-contained, required to carry all sustainment on foot or in vehicles	Requires regular outside sustainment	Wholly dependent on outside sustainment
Adversary	Another armed force *Example: military*	Uncooperative individuals or groups; sometimes outright hostile individuals or groups *Example: patrol officer*	Rarely confronts uncooperative or hostile individuals or groups *Example: fire department*

NOTE: The examples listed may not have all of the characteristics as described in the columns.

Table A.2
Organizational Aspects for Comparison

Aspect for Comparison	Most Similar	Some Similarities	Not Similar
Group dynamics	Nested hierarchies ranging from 13, 43, 120, to 600 individuals that regularly interact with one another	Nested hierarchies, but individuals do not communicate with other levels	Flat organization
Promotion and retention	Required to start at bottom, with little to no lateral entry	Lateral entry is not unusual.	Lateral entry is allowed.

Table A.3
Technical Aspects for Comparison

Aspect for Comparison	Most Similar	Some Similarities	Not Similar
Training	Cyclical training system that moves from individual to collective training repeatedly	Initial training period followed by periodic sustainment, but not cyclical (e.g., police depts.)	Initial training without any sustainment
Personal equipment	Equipment (weapons, protective gear, etc.) plays a large role in how effective the organization is (e.g., fire department).	Personal equipment is a factor but only partially affects the organization as a whole.	Personal equipment not a factor in organization's success
Specialized or crew-served equipment	Significant interaction with equipment that can only be operated by a team, as well as specialized equipment that requires specific training and sustainment	Less significant interaction, or organization does not feature significant specialized equipment or crew-served equipment	Does not require interaction with specialized or crew-served equipment

Summary of FDNY Postintegration Lawsuits

Table B.1
Summary of FDNY Postintegration Lawsuits

Year	Plaintiff	Category	Issue	Resolution
1979	Union	Hiring	Court-mandated retest lowered standards and may endanger public safety.	Union lost suit
1982	Female applicant	Hiring	Physical entrance exam discriminated against women.	FDNY ordered to retest women who failed exam
1983	Female probationary firefighter	Professional development	Training program discrimination. FDNY says firefighter jumped the chain of command in her complaint and subsequently dismissed firefighter.	FDNY ordered to reinstate firefighter
1986	Union	Promotion	Appeals court ruled that promotion system is fair. Since system weighted physical fitness heavily, females were consistently ranked lower for promotion.	FDNY continued its existing promotion practices
1986	Female firefighter	Misconduct	Female firefighter subjected to unequal, unfair, discriminatory work conditions.	FDNY fined and suspended male firefighters
1991	Female firefighter	Misconduct	1986 plaintiff's second complaint—harassment still present.	FDNY fined and suspended other male firefighters
2004	Female firefighter	Misconduct	Harassment at elite fire rescue unit	FDNY awarded damages to female firefighter
2013	Female EMS	Promotion	Promotion ceiling at EMS due to discretionary promotion system above Lieutenant	Pending

SOURCE: *New York Times.*

Regression Results

In this appendix, we include additional information that may be of interest to readers who wish to learn more about the technical details of our calculations of our regression model that determines the number of women likely to enter the Marine Corps in future years. Our regression models·use data on the total number of accessions over time. Specifically, we gathered data on the total number of men and women entering the Marine Corps each fiscal year. Our data source was the Population Representation Reports; these reports utilize data from the Defense Manpower Data Center (DMDC).[1]

The dependent variable in our model is the number of women entering the enlisted Marine Corps each year. Our preferred specification includes time trends (linear, squared, and cubic) as well as the total number of nonprior service (NPS) accessions into the Marine Corps in each fiscal year.

We experimented with data going back to 1978, including variables to indicate key periods (the rescinding of the "risk rule" in the mid-1990s, the drawdown, and the difficult recruiting years of the late 1990s). We also experimented with including the number of women who enlisted in the Army each year (to capture societal trends that might not be included in the time trends). The variations that we tested consistently suggest that the number of female accessions is likely to increase by 75–100 per year in the next few years.

We found that we achieved the best fit by using data from all years, with indications of the "risk rule" period (post-1994), the drawdown (1991–1995), and the difficult recruiting years of the mid-to-late 1990s (1997–1999). Information on Army accessions did not add explanatory power to our model.

The results of this model are quite similar to those suggested by models using data over a shorter time period (2000–forward), as well as those modeling the percentage of accessions who are female (rather than the number). The preferred model suggests that the number of women is likely to increase in the near future by about 100 per

---

[1] See Office of the Secretary of Defense, Personnel and Readiness, *Population Representation in the Military Services 2012*, 2012, Appendix C. Accession data for the most recent years were provided by the Operations Analysis Division, USMC.

year. This estimate also is quite insensitive to small changes in the accession mission; the model's predictions for the near future are very similar when we allow the accession mission to vary between 26,000 and 30,000. Table C.1 includes our regression results.

Table C.1
Regression Results: Dependent Variable: Number of Women Enlisting in the Marine Corps

Independent Variable	Coefficient	Standard Error
Years since 1977	5.15	20.48
Years since 1977 squared/10	−20.03	13.38
Years since 1977 cubed/100	6.10*	2.38
Post-1994 indicator	293.43*	96.33
Drawdown indicator	−255.73*	55.92
1997–1999 indicator	241.94*	67.48
USMC accessions, 1,000's	18.05*	8.80
Constant	1,478.27*	373.66

SOURCE: RAND analysis based on Defense Manpower Data Center personnel files.
Regression includes information from 36 years (N = 36); adjusted R-squared = 0.902.

*Coefficient significant at the 5-percent level or better.

Monitoring Framework

This appendix describes with tables the components of a proposed monitoring framework for the planning and implementation of gender integration of Marine infantry units.

Table D.1
Monitoring Framework: Planning Phase—Individual-Level Monitoring

	Category	Sub-Category	Issue	Metric	Method
Individual	Organization	Readiness	Do data systems to monitor readiness of 03xx Marines exist?	Data systems are in place to track readiness	Review of USMC policy
	Organization	Readiness	Does a methodology exist for determining a baseline readiness rate?	A methodology is established for determining appropriate baseline readiness rate	Review of USMC policy
	Organization	Readiness	What are the baseline deployability rates for 03xx Marines?	The baseline deployability rates for 03xx Marines is identified	Administrative data
	Training	Initial Entry Training	Do data systems exist to collect data on and monitor performance of male and female Marines in infantry and bootcamp, as well as in other training?	Data systems are in place to monitor training performance and completion	Review of USMC policy
	Training	Initial Entry Training	What is the baseline expectation for female Marines passing infantry MOS training?	Establishment of a discrete attrition goal	Administrative data
	Training	Initial Entry training	Does a clear training plan and timeline exist to guide the initial training of female 03xx Marines and to ensure accurate expectations?	Training plan and timeline have been developed	Review of USMC policy
	Training	Initial Entry Training	Have task-based MOS eligibility criteria been developed and tested?	Task-based MOS eligibility criteria have been developed and tested	Administrative data
	Leadership and Education	PME	What data systems need to be put into place to track rates at which female 03xx Marines will achieve MOS roadmap PME goals?	Data systems are in place to track rates at which female 03xx Marines will achieve MOS roadmap PME goals	Review of USMC policy
	Leadership and Education	Career Development	What data systems need to be put into place to track female assignments to desirable/key developmental billets?	Data systems are in place to track female assignments to desirable/key developmental billets	Review of USMC policy
	Leadership and Education	Career Development	Does a methodology exist to define appropriate rates for career development?	Methodology has been defined for determining appropriate career development rates	Review of USMC policy
	Leadership and Education	Career Development	What are the normal rates of career development for 03xx Marines?	Historical 03xx and EPME attendance rates, leadership billets, and their correlation to performance attributes (PFT, pro/con, FITREP, etc.)	Administrative data
	Personnel	Recruitment	Do data systems exist to track recruitment numbers of 03xx's? Of females?	Data system established to monitor recruitment numbers	Review of USMC policy
	Personnel	Recruitment	Do target numbers exist for recruitment of female 03xx's?	Initial target recruitment numbers defined	Administrative data
	Personnel	Assignment	Do data systems exist to monitor and evaluate the assignment of women?	Data systems in place to monitor assignment of women	Review of USMC policy
	Personnel	Promotion	Do data systems exist to track promotion rates of 03xx Marines?	Data systems in place to monitor promotion	Review of USMC policy
	Personnel	Promotion	What is the baseline promotion rate for 03xx MOS's?	Historical 03xx promotion rates by grade and MOS, correlated to performance attributes	Administrative data
	Personnel	Promotion	Do clear criteria exist for what must be accomplished to achieve promotion?	Establishment of clear promotion requirements	Review of USMC policy
	Personnel	Retention	Do data systems exist to track retention rates among 03xx Marines?	Data systems in place to track retention	Review of USMC policy
	Personnel	Attrition	Do data systems exist for monitoring attrition rates?	Data systems in place to monitor attrition rates	Review of USMC policy
	Personnel	Retention	What is the baseline retention target for enlisted and officers?	Historical FTAP and STAP targets, 0302 augmentation rates, female retention rates, male retention rates	Administrative data
	Personnel	Attrition	What is a reasonable first-term baseline attrition rate?	First-term baseline attrition rate is established	Administrative data
	Personnel	Attrition	Does an understanding exist of what causes attrition among male 03xx's? Does an understanding exist of what causes attrition among women in other MOS's?	An understanding is established of the causes of attrition among male 03xx's and among women in other MOS's	Administrative data/Surveys
	Facilities	Infrastructure	What kinds of concerns might female 03xx Marines have regarding any necessary changes to infrastructure?	Identification of concerns that female Marines in other MOS have regarding any necessary changes to infrastructure	Focus Groups/Interviews/Surveys
	Attitudinal	Welfare	Do data systems exist to monitor attitudes towards integration and experiences of female Marines?	Data systems in place to monitor attitudes towards integration and attitudes of female Marines	Review of USMC policy
	Attitudinal	Welfare	What is the baseline perception of current and likely future infantry Marines (both male and female) on integration?	The baseline perception is established of current and likely infantry Marines (both male and female) on integration	Surveys

Table D.2
Monitoring Framework: Planning Phase—Unit-Level Monitoring

	Category	Sub-Category	Issue	Metric	Method
Unit	Organization	Readiness	Do data systems exist to monitor readiness of infantry battalions?	Data systems in place to monitor readiness	Review of USMC policy
	Organization	Readiness	What are the baseline readiness and deployability rates of infantry battalions?	Assessment completed of baseline readiness and deployability rates of infantry battalions	Administrative data
	Organization	Readiness	Do data systems exist to monitor baseline performance rates of infantry battalions?	Data systems in place to monitor performance rates of infantry battalions	Review of USMC policy
	Organization	Readiness	What are the baseline performance rates of infantry battalions?	TTECG assessments, CG assessments, RCT assessments	Administrative data
	Training	Unit Training	Do data systems exist to monitor performance on unit training?	Data systems in place to monitor unit training performance	Review of USMC policy
	Training	Unit Training	Do clear plans, standards and performance expectations exist for unit training?	Clear unit training plans, standards and performance expectations are in place	Review of USMC policy
	Materiel	Equipment and Clothing/ Weapons and Optics	Do data systems exist to track necessary changes at the unit-level to weapons and equipment, past modifications, and their cost?	Data systems in place to collect data on equipment modifications, past modifications, and their cost	Review of USMC policy
	Materiel	Equipment and Clothing/ Weapons and Optics	Have necessary changes to equipment, weapons, or individual optics at the unit-level been identified?	Studies/analyses, recommendations, and implementation plans for necessary changes to individual and unit equipment	Review of USMC policy
	Leadership and Education	Mentorship and Support	Are there advisors to whom unit leaders can turn if they have questions or concerns about gender integration?	Gender advisors in place and unit leaders have access to their expertise	Review of USMC policy
	Leadership and Education	Mentorship and Support	Has the USMC identified and prepared infantry battalions for arrival of female Marines?	An implementation plan is in place down to the battalion level	Administrative data
	Leadership and Education	Mentorship and Support	Has training focused on gender issues been incorporated into unit training?	Training focused on gender issues is a mandatory part of unit training	Review of USMC policy
	Leadership and Education	Mentorship and Support	Have procedures at the unit level been developed to deal with gender-related incidents or complaints?	Procedures in place to address complaints related to gender issues	Review of USMC policy
	Leadership and Education	Mentorship and Support	Has the USMC prepared infantry unit leaders to mentor and counsel female 03xx's?	Program in place to prepare unit leaders (emphasis on enlisted leaders at the Platoon-Battalion level) to perform mentorship and counseling for female Marines	Administrative data
	Leadership and Education	Mentorship and Support	Do clear expectations exist about requirements for mentorship and support at the unit-level?	Clear outline of expectations in place for mentorship and support	Review of USMC policy
	Facilities	Infrastructure	What data systems will be needed to monitor necessary facilities changes at the unit level?	Necessary data systems in place to monitor changes to facilities	Review of USMC policy
	Facilities	Infrastructure	Have changes to billeting or other procedures necessary to support integration been identified?	Existence of studies/analyses, recommendations, and implementation plans of needed changes to billeting and command post areas	Review of USMC policy
	Attitudinal	Misconduct	What are the baseline rates of misconduct in infantry battalions?	Historical rates of Pg11, NJP, CMs, CONGRINTs, IG, etc.	Administrative data
	Attitudinal	Misconduct	What is the baseline rate of gender-related complaints and investigations in gender-integrated units, and in all-male units?	Historical rates of Pg11, NJP, CMs, CONGRINTs, IG, etc.	Administrative data
	Attitudinal	Cohesion and Morale	Do data systems exist to monitor trends in perceived unit cohesion?	Data systems in place to monitor cohesion and morale	Review of USMC policy
	Attitudinal	Cohesion and Morale	Do a methodology and plan exist to study unit cohesion among Marines?	Procedures in place for surveying and interviewing Marines periodically to assess trends in cohesion and morale	Review of USMC policy
	Attitudinal	Cohesion and Morale	What are current issues with unit cohesion?	Identification of current issues with unit cohesion	Surveys/Interviews

Table D.3
Monitoring Framework: Planning Phase—MOS-Level Monitoring

	Category	Sub-Category	Issue	Metric	Method
MOS	Organization	Readiness	What factors limit or compromise readiness of 03xx Marines?	Identification of factors that limit or compromise readiness of 03xx Marines	Surveys of males in combat units and possible female recruits or candidates
	Leadership and Education	PME	What is the baseline for females achieving MOS roadmap PME goals in comparison to their male counterparts?	Establishment of baseline for females achieving MOS roadmap PME	Administrative data
	Leadership and Education	Career Development	Does a clear career development plan exist with specific steps and benchmarks for female 03xx Marines?	A career development plan in place for 03xx Marines	Review of USMC policy
	Leadership and Education	Career Development	What data systems are needed to track career development and progress for female 03xx's in the Marine Corps?	Data systems in place to track career development	Review of USMC policy
	Leadership and Education	Mentorship and Support	Does a plan for mentoring and supporting female 03xx's exist and has it been disseminated among commanders throughout the force?	A mentorship plan is in place	Review of USMC policy
	Leadership and Education	Mentorship and Support	Does a plan exist to ensure the availability of mentors of both genders for female 03xx's?	A mentorship and support plan is in place that promotes presence of both male and female mentors	Review of USMC policy
	Personnel	Assignment	Is USMC prepared to assign female 03xx Marines in a way that supports organizational goals?	A coordinated school break unit fill plan is in place	Review of USMC policy
	Personnel	Assignment	Will enough female entrants select the infantry occupational field to support critical mass?	Survey of female recruiting poolees and MCT graduates	Survey
	Personnel	Recruitment	Does a methodology exist to define and refine target recruitment numbers for male and female 03xx's?	Methodology in place for determining the appropriate recruitment rate	Review of USMC policy
	Personnel	Promotion	Does a methodology exist to define target promotion rates for 03xx's? For females?	Methodology in place for defining appropriate promotion rates	Review of USMC policy
	Personnel	Retention	Does a methodology exist to set and modify target retention targets for 03xx Marines exist?	Methodology in place for setting and modifying retention	Review of USMC policy
	Personnel	Attrition	Does a methodology exist for defining appropriate target attrition rates?	Methodology in place for defining appropriate target attrition rates	Review of USMC policy
	Attitudinal	Cohesion and Morale	What data systems and procedures are needed to monitor morale among 03xx's?	Data systems and procedures (e.g. periodic surveys) in place to monitor morale among 03xx's	Review of USMC policy

Table D.4
Monitoring Framework: Planning Phase—Institutional-Level Monitoring

	Category	Sub-Category	Issue	Metric	Method
Institutional	Organization	Readiness	Has the Marine Corps developed an implementation plan related to readiness issues for female Marines?	An implementation plan is in place that addresses readiness issues for female Marines	Review of USMC policy
	Training	Unit and Initial Entry Training	Is the USMC prepared to assess and potentially revise individual and unit training procedures as needed to support integration?	Plan in place to periodically review and potentially revise training as needed, along with a group of people with the responsibility to conduct this review	Review of USMC policy
	Materiel	Equipment and Clothing/ Weapons and Optics	Do data systems exist to track necessary changes to weapons and equipment, past modifications, and their cost?	Data systems put in place to track changes to weapons and equipment, past modifications, and their cost	Review of USMC policy
	Materiel	Equipment and Clothing/ Weapons and Optics	Does a materiel plan for gender integration exist?	Studies/analyses, recommendations, and implementation plans of needed changes to individual and organizational equipment	Review of USMC policy
	Leadership and Education	PME	Does a PME "roadmap" exist that identifies target rates and types of female PME participation?	PME roadmap developed and implemented	Review of USMC policy
	Leadership and Education	Career Development	Do career "pathways" exist to guide the development and progression of female 03xx's?	Existence of career development pathways for individual Marines	Review of USMC policy
	Leadership and Education	Career Development	Has the Marine Corps developed an implementation plan related to career development issues for female Marines?	An implementation plan is in place that addresses career development issues for female Marines	Review of USMC Policy
	Leadership and Education	Career Development	Do data systems exist to track the participation rate of women in leadership positions?	Data systems in place to track rates of women in leadership roles in place	Review of USMC policy
	Leadership and Education	Career Development	Does a methodology exist to determine the appropriate rate of participation in leadership by women?	Methodology in place to determine appropriate rate of women in leadership	Review of USMC policy
	Leadership and Education	Career Development	What is the baseline participation rate of females in leadership roles in non-infantry MOSs?	Time-series analysis of reported billets of male and female members in gender-integrated units	Administrative data
	Leadership and Education	Career Development	Are the requirements for advancing to a leadership role clearly defined and gender neutral?	Clear and gender neutral standards in place for advancement to leadership positions	Review of USMC policy
	Leadership and Education	Mentorship and Support	Does a system of gender advisors exist to provide guidance to leaders throughout the force on the gender integration process?	System of gender advisors in place	Review of USMC policy
	Leadership and Education	Mentorship and Support	Does the Marine Corps possess the mechanisms for females to seek redress of gender-related issues outside of the chain of command?	Study on the effectiveness of current redress mechanisms outside of the chain of command	Survey
	Leadership and Education	Mentorship and Support	Has a coordinated series of training classes focused on gender issues been developed and integrated into all levels of leadership training and professional development?	Training focused on gender issues is in place as mandatory part of leadership training	Review of USMC policy
	Leadership and Education	Mentorship and Support	Does a plan exist to ensure the availability of mentors of both genders for female 03xx's?	A mentorship and support plan is in place that promotes presence of both male and female mentors	Review of USMC policy
	Leadership and Education	Mentorship and Support	Do mechanisms exist to assess the status of mentorship and support?	Mechanisms (surveys, interviews) in place to assess status of mentorship and support	Review of USMC policy
	Facilities	Infrastructure	Do data systems exist to track necessary changes to existing facilities and plans for modifications?	Data systems in place for tracking necessary changes in facilities	Review of USMC policy
	Facilities	Infrastructure	Has the Marine Corps considered the changes to existing facilities?	Existence of studies/analyses, recommendations, and implementation plans of needed changes to existing facilities	Review of USMC policy
	Policy	Oversight	Has HQMC developed a plan for oversight and assigned responsibility for oversight?	A plan is in place for oversight and responsibility for oversight is assigned	Review of USMC policy
	Policy	Oversight	Do all necessary data systems exist to collect data relevant to monitoring progress on integration?	All necessary data systems in place to collect data on integration progress	Review of USMC policy
	Policy	Integration Execution	Does an implementation plan exist for gender integration?	An implementation plan is in place for gender integration	Administrative data
	Policy	Integration Cost	Do initial budget and resource allocations exist for gender integration?	USMC POM requests and submitted budgets	Budget
	Policy	Communication	Has HQMC developed plans for internal and external communication about gender integration efforts?	Plans in place for internal and external communication	Review of UMSC policy
	Attitudinal	Misconduct	Do data systems exist to track and assess instances of misconduct along with gender-related complaints and investigations?	Data systems in place to monitor instances of misconduct	Review of USMC policy
	Attitudinal	Misconduct	Does a plan exist to minimize and reduce gender-related complaints and instances of misconduct?	A plan is in place to reduce and minimize gender-related complaints and instances of misconduct	Review of USMC policy
	Attitudinal	Misconduct	Do procedures exist to address and investigate instances of misconduct and/or complaints of misconduct?	Procedures in place to investigate and address instances of misconduct	Review of USMC policy
	Attitudinal	Misconduct	How are gender-related complaints currently being addressed?	Study on how gender-related complaints are currently being addressed	Review of USMC policy/ Interviews/Focus Groups

Table D.5
Monitoring Framework: Phase One—Individual-Level Monitoring

	Category	Sub-Category	Issue	Metric	Method
Individual	Organization	Readiness	How do trends in deployability track with baselines identified in planning phase?	Comparison of planning phase baseline of time-series data on individual duty status in Occfield 03xx	Administrative Data
	Training	Initial Entry Training	At what rates are females and males entering and completing bootcamp?	Total numbers of accessions; bootcamp completion or attrition rates	Administrative Data
	Training	Initial Entry Training	What are the primary reasons that male and female trainees fail to meet eligibility requirements?	Reasons men and women do not meet eligibility requirements; Interviews with trainers	Administrative Data, Interviews
	Training	Initial Entry Training	Are female and male trainees completing SOI/IOC at expected rates?	Identification of the rates of completion of female and male trainees completing SOI and IOC	Administrative Data
	Training	Initial Entry Training	What is the career progression of women and men who do not successfully complete SOI/IOC?	Status (serving in the USMC or not); MOS	Administrative Data
	Leadership and Education	PME	Is rate at which females are achieving MOS roadmap PME goals comparable to their male counterparts?	Comparison of planning phase metrics to correlated female rates	Administrative Data
	Leadership and Education	Career Development	How do rates of career progression compare to baselines and targets set in planning phase?	Comparison of planning phase metrics to correlated female rates	Administrative Data
	Leadership and Education	Career Development	At what rates are females being assigned to desirable/key developmental infantry billets? How do these rates compare with baselines set in planning phase?	Comparison to baseline rates established in planning phase	Administrative Data
	Leadership and Education	Career Development	What are rates at which females are progressing through infantry billets compared to their male counterparts?	Comparison of planning phase metrics to correlated female and male rates	Administrative Data
	Leadership and Education	Mentorship and support	Are female 03xx's receiving the mentorship and support they need?	Female 03xx's levels of satisfaction with available monitoring and support	Surveys/Interviews
	Personnel	Recruitment	Are rates at which females are contracting/being selected for 03xx meeting target rate set in planning phase?	Number of 03xx guaranteed contracts, TBS MOS selections compared to planning phase goals	Administrative Data
	Personnel	Promotion	How do 03xx female promotion rates compare to baselines in planning phase?	Comparison of planning phase metrics to correlated female rates for grades E-3 to E-5 and O-1 to O-3	Administrative Data
	Personnel	Promotion	How do 03xx female promotion rates compare to promotion rates of male colleagues? Of females in other occupations?	Comparison of female rates for grades E-3 to E-5 and O-1 to O-3 across MOS and of female rates to male rates in 03xx	Administrative Data
	Personnel	Retention	How do 03xx female retention rates compare to baselines in planning phase?	Comparison of separations before intended End of Active Service between female 03xxs and baseline set in planning phase	Administrative Data
	Personnel	Retention	How do 03xx female retention rates compare to their male counterparts? To women in other MOS?	Comparison of separations before intended End of Active Service between female 03xx, male 03xx, and female non 03xx, comparison of Tier I-IV FTAP 03xxs	Administrative Data
	Personnel	Attrition	How do attrition rates for female infantry Marines compare with baselines set in planning phase?	Comparison of attrition rates with planning phase baselines	Administrative Data
	Personnel	Attrition	How do attrition rates for female infantry Marines compare with those of male 03xx's and females in other occupations?	Comparison of attrition rates with planning phase baselines (male 03xx's, females in other MOS's)	Administrative Data
	Attitudinal	Welfare	What are the perceived effects of integration on morale and welfare in combat units? How do these perceived effects of integration compare with baseline attitudes expressed in planning phase?	Identification of the perceived effects of integration on morale and welfare in combat units; Comparison of planning phase and short-term phase surveys	Survey
	Attitudinal	Welfare	Do females feel they have adequate support in integration?	Identification of whether females feel they have adequate support in integration	Surveys/Focus Groups
	Attitudinal	Welfare	What is the overall level of female 03xx well-being?	Identification of the overall level of female 03xx well-being	Interviews/Focus Groups/Surveys

Table D.6
Monitoring Framework: Phase One—Unit-Level Monitoring

	Category	Sub-Category	Issue	Metric	Method
Unit	Organization	Readiness	How does unit readiness compare with baselines set in planning phase?	Comparison with planning phase metrics	Administrative Data
	Organization	Readiness	What are the perceived impacts of integration on unit readiness?	Perception of females and males in combat units	Surveys/Interviews
	Organization	Readiness	How does unit performance compare with baselines set in planning phase?	Comparison with planning phase metrics	Administrative Data
	Organization	Readiness	What are the perceived impacts of integration on unit performance?	Perception of females and males in combat units	Surveys/Interviews
	Training	Unit Training	Is the unit training plan being implemented?	Extent to which unit training plan is being implemented	Surveys/Interviews
	Training	Unit Training	What are the rates of performance in unit training by military units?	Comparison of rates of performance with standards set in planning phase	Administrative Data
	Materiel	Equipment and Clothing/Weapons and Optics	Are unit-level materiel changes recommended in the planning phase being implemented and are they effectively supporting integration?	Surveys of male and female users	Surveys
	Materiel	Equipment and Clothing/Weapons and Optics	Have new unit-level materiel issues arisen since the start of integration which need to be addressed?	Surveys of male and female users	Surveys
	Leadership and Education	Mentorship and Support	Are Infantry units following the implementation plan for mentorship and support laid out in planning phase for the arrival of female Marines?	Extent to which infantry units are following the implementation plan laid out in planning phase for the arrival of female Marines	Surveys/Focus Groups/Interviews
	Leadership and Education	Mentorship and Support	Has unit-level training on gender issues been implemented and completed by 03xx Marines and their leaders?	Insights from 03xx's and their commanders; Implementation of training procedures	Surveys/Interviews
	Leadership and Education	Mentorship and Support	How have gender-related complaints and incidents been addressed at the unit level?	Insights from male and female 03xx's, their commanders; Documentation about recent complaints	Surveys/Interviews/Review of documentation
	Leadership and Education	Mentorship and Support	Is unit leadership sufficiently and actively supporting gender integration?	Command climate surveys and focus groups with male and female infantry Marines at Platoon-Battalion level	Surveys/Focus Groups
	Leadership and Education	Mentorship and Support	Are standards for mentorship and support being met?	Insights from female 03xx's about mentorship and support received	Surveys/Interviews
	Facilities	Infrastructure	Are unit-level facilities changes recommended in the planning phase being implemented and are they effectively supporting integration?	Surveys of facilities users, maintainers, unit leadership	Surveys
	Facilities	Infrastructure	Have new unit-level infrastructure or facilities issues arisen since the start of integration which need to be addressed?	Surveys of facilities users, maintainers, unit leadership	Surveys
	Attitudinal	Misconduct	What are rates of misconduct at the battalion level? How do these rates compare to targets and baselines set in planning phase?	Rates of misconduct, compared to planning phase	Administrative Data
	Attitudinal	Cohesion and Morale	How does unit cohesion after integration compare with cohesion before integration?	Surveys/focus groups of female 03xx's, their unit leaders, and male peers and subordinates	Surveys/Focus groups
	Attitudinal	Cohesion and Morale	What have been the effects of integration on unit cohesion?	Surveys/focus groups of female 03xx's, their unit leaders, and male peers and subordinates	Surveys/Focus groups

Table D.7
Monitoring Framework: Phase One—MOS-Level Monitoring

	Category	Sub-Category	Issue	Metric	Method
MOS	Organization	Readiness	What factors affect the deployability and/or readiness of female 03xx Marines?	Insights from Female 03xx's, their commanders, colleagues; Administrative data on deployability rates	Administrative data/Survey/Interviews
	Training	Initial Entry Training	At what rates are females and males passing MOS training?	Completion rates of ITB and IOC and comparison to planning phase baselines	Administrative Data
	Leadership and Education	PME	What are the rates at which female 03xx Marines achieve MOS roadmap PME goals?	Analysis of career progression rates of 03xx female Marines	Administrative Data
	Leadership and Education	Career Development	What are the rates of career development for female 03xx Marines? How do these rates compare to targets and baselines set in planning phase?	Female 03xx and PME attendance rates, leadership billets, correlation to performance and comparison to male rates	Administrative Data
	Leadership and Education	Mentorship and Support	Is the mentoring and counseling program defined in planning phase being followed?	Degree to which the mentoring and counseling program developed in the planning phase is being followed	Interviews
	Leadership and Education	Mentorship and Support	Are female 03xx's receiving the mentorship and support they need? What are the primary sources of this support?	Surveys of female 03xx's; Data on usage of existing mentorship and support resources	Surveys/Interviews
	Leadership and Education	Mentorship and Support	Are there mentors and advisors of both genders available to 03xx Marines?	Number of women in mentorship roles; Perception of female 03xx's	Administrative data/Interviews
	Personnel	Assignment	Are enough women entering the infantry MOS to facilitate a "critical mass" in assignments?	Comparison of "critical mass" threshold and entrance rates of women in 03xx positions	Administrative Data
	Personnel	Assignment	Are females are being assigned to infantry battalions according to assignment plan in planning phase?	Comparison to planning phase assignment plan	Administrative Data
	Personnel	Recruitment	Are screening standards fair and fairly applied?	Insights from female recruiting poolees and MCT graduates	Interview/Focus Groups
	Personnel	Recruitment	What are the reasons women are or are not choosing to enter the infantry MOS?	Insights from female Marines	Interview/Focus Groups
	Personnel	Promotion	Are there barriers to promotion of female 03xx Marines?	Insights from female 03xx's, their unit leaders, and male peers and subordinates	Interview/Focus Groups
	Personnel	Retention	What are the reasons female 03xx's are choosing to leave?	Insights from female 03xx's who choose to leave	Surveys/Interviews
	Personnel	Attrition	What are trends of attrition causes in combat units among females? Among male colleagues?	Comparison of causes of attrition in planning phase for both males and females	Surveys
	Attitudinal	Misconduct	How do trends in gender-related complaints and investigations compare with baselines?	Comparison with planning phase metrics; insights from females in combat units about the degree to which gender-related complaints are being sufficiently addressed and they feel comfortable reporting gender-related complaints	Administrative Data/Interviews/Focus Groups/Surveys
	Attitudinal	Welfare	What challenges or obstacles have women experienced since the start of integration?	Insights from female 03xx's about challenges experienced	Interview/Focus Groups
	Attitudinal	Cohesion and Morale	What have been the effects of integration on morale overall?	Insights from 03xx Marines, their commanders	Surveys/Interviews

Table D.8
Monitoring Framework: Phase One—Institutional-Level Monitoring

	Category	Sub-Category	Issue	Metric	Method
Institutional	Organization	Readiness	Has the Marine Corps developed an implementation plan related to readiness issues for female Marines?	Extent to which the implementation plan related to readiness is being implemented	Surveys/Interviews
	Materiel	Equipment and Clothing/ Weapons and Optics	Are materiel changes recommended in planning phase being implemented and are they effectively supporting integration?	Surveys of female users; Data on materiel changes being implemented	Surveys/Administrative Data
	Materiel	Equipment and clothing/ Weapons and optics	Have new materiel issues arisen since the start of integration that need to be addressed?	Surveys of male and female users	Surveys
	Leadership and Education	PME	How does the participation of women in PME compare to original targets and to the "roadmap" established in planning phase?	Comparison of female participation to PME targets and roadmap	Administrative Data
	Leadership and Education	Career Development	How are female 03xx's progressing through the career development pathway established in planning phase?	Comparison of female career progression to pathway and to expectations established in planning phase	Administrative Data
	Leadership and Education	Career Development	Is the implementation plan for dealing with career development issues related to women being followed?	Extent to which the implementation plan related to career develop is being implemented	Surveys/Focus Groups/ Interviews
	Leadership and Education	Career Development	At what rate are women participating in leadership positions? At what rate are females being assigned to desirable/key developmental billets?	Comparison to planning phase baseline rates	Administrative Data
	Leadership and Education	Career Development	What obstacles exist for women seeking to advance to leadership positions?	Insights from female 03xx's seeking leadership roles	Surveys/Interviews
	Leadership and Education	Mentorship and Support	Are there support services available for women making complaints related to gender issues?	Support services made available for women making complaints related to gender issues	Surveys/Interviews
	Leadership and Education	Mentorship and Support	Do women feel that they receive sufficient support? Which avenues of support provide the greatest assistance to female 03xx's?	Women feel they receive sufficient support	Surveys/Interviews
	Leadership and Education	Mentorship and Support	How are gender-related issues and complaints being addressed?	Data on number and types of complaints; Insights from female 03xx's and their commanders	Administrative Data/Interviews
	Leadership and Education	Mentorship and Support	Have force-wide gender-related training courses been implemented and attended?	Insights from 03xx's and their commanders; Administrative data on training attendance	Surveys/Interviews/ Administrative Data
	Leadership and Education	Mentorship and Support	How closely does the mentorship and support infrastructure match what was originally laid out in planning phase, in terms of size, composition (by gender), and availability?	Comparison of mentorship and support in practice and plan laid out in planning phase, including numbers, gender, and specific roles played by individuals in mentorship and support positions	Administrative Data/ Surveys/Interviews
	Facilities	Infrastructure	Are facilities changes recommended in planning phase being implemented and are they effectively supporting integration?	Surveys of male and female facilities users, maintainers, unit leadership; Data on facilities changes being implemented	Surveys/Administrative Data
	Facilities	Infrastructure	Have new infrastructure or facilities issues arisen since the start of integration which need to be addressed?	Surveys of male and female facilities users, maintainers, unit leadership	Surveys
	Policy	Oversight	Is the oversight committee being given adequate support to complete its evaluations?	Oversight committee self-assessment	Surveys/Interviews/ Focus Groups
	Policy	Oversight	Is the oversight plan being executed according to the timeline?	Comparison with oversight plan	Administrative Data
	Policy	Integration Execution	Is the implementation plan being implemented according to the timeline?	Comparison with implementation plan milestones	Administrative Data
	Policy	Integration Cost	Are budget and resourcing plans being followed?	Comparison with planning phase metrics	Administrative Data
	Policy	Integration Cost	Are current budget allocations sufficient for the tasks associated with integration?	Comparison with planning phase metrics	Administrative Data
	Policy	Communication	Are the internal and external communication plans being executed according to timeline?	Comparison with communication plans	Administrative Data
	Attitudinal	Misconduct	What are trends in instances of misconduct and gender-related complaints forcewide?	Analysis of the types and numbers of complaints	Administrative Data
	Attitudinal	Misconduct	Are stated procedures for dealing with gender complaints being followed?	Extent to which implementation plan is being followed	Surveys/Focus Groups/ Interviews
	Attitudinal	Misconduct	How have complaints and instances of misconduct been handled?	Documentation on handling of complaints; Insights from females and males in combat units, and their commanders	Review of documentation/Surveys/ Interviews

Approach to Developing a Monitoring Framework

We began by reviewing the experiences of foreign militaries, domestic organizations, and other U.S. military services in developing and executing monitoring plans for gender integration. We integrated elements from these plans with a wider literature review and search for monitoring plans, and from this, we developed a suggested monitoring framework (Appendix D), along with discussion of strategic monitoring considerations.

Preliminary Inputs

First, we received a preliminary monitoring framework from the Marine Corps with the categories listed in Table E.1.

We reviewed the preliminary Marine Corps monitoring framework to understand the preliminary areas of integration that we needed to consider. We ultimately added and refined additional categories and considerations, but it was important for us to review the Marine Corps' framework in order to understand how Marine Corps leadership was thinking about the monitoring plan.

Second, we drew upon common practices identified by nongovernmental organizations that study military and police practices. Specifically, we adapted some of subcategories from the "Gender Self-Assessment Guide for the Police, Armed Forces, and Justice Sector" in Table E.2.[1]

We used or adapted several elements of this structure for our monitoring framework—particularly the ones dealing with the broader, strategic considerations. However, since this guide is also intended to apply to the police and justice sector, certain elements were not applicable.

With these preliminary frameworks in mind, we moved on to reviewing monitoring plans or gender audits used by foreign militaries, domestic civilian organizations, and other U.S. military services. We then adapted pieces of each to create our own

---

[1] Bastick, 2011. This is a tool developed by the Geneva Centre for the Democratic Control of Armed Forces for assessing the gender responsiveness of a security sector institution.

Table E.1
Preliminary Monitoring Categories

Rates and causes of attrition	Are women attriting from previously closed units or previously closed MOSs at higher rates than other female Marines?
Female career development	Are female Marines pursuing PME and occupying key billets?
Female well-being	Are females in previously closed units or MOSs suffering psychologically?
Readiness trends	What effect does integration have on readiness measures?
Command climate trends	What effect does integration have on command climate?
Misconduct	What effect does integration have on rates of disciplinary actions?
Female MOS populations	What are the rates of entry of females into previously closed MOSs?
Female promotion	What are the rates of promotion for females? Does serving in a previously closed unit or MOS affect promotion rates?
Deployability	What are the deployability rates for men and women? Does integration affect deployability of individuals?
Materiel adaptations	What are the planned materiel adaptations resulting from integrating women? What is the progress of these program changes?
Facilities	What are the required facility changes resulting from integration? What facilities, where, why? Progress?
School screening success	What tools are used to screen for physical or cognitive readiness for an MOS school?
Cost	What is the marginal cost to the Marine Corps of integrating previously closed MOSs?

monitoring framework for gender integration in the USMC. Our review of the monitoring mechanisms used by foreign militaries, domestic organizations, and other U.S. military services is below.

Foreign Militaries

Foreign militaries have conducted reviews of gender integration through gender audits and other reviews that have ranged in scope, length, and depth. Out of the 21 countries selected for in-depth analysis and seven countries selected for a deep-dive discussion in this report, we identified that three of those countries (Canada, Australia, and New Zealand) have carried out particularly rigorous gender-integration assessments that might provide useful insights for our monitoring framework.

The Canadian Forces (CF) did a comprehensive review in 1999 based on the 1989 order of the Canadian Human Rights Tribunal to open all military positions to women (with the exception of submarine service) within ten years. The 1999 CF comprehensive review focused on the following factors: recruitment, training, occupational

Table E.2
Gender Self-Assessment Guide for the Police, Armed Forces, and Justice Sector

Theme	Category
Theme A: Performance effectiveness	1. Capacity and training 2. Access to services 3. Data on gender-related crime
Theme B: Laws, policing, and planning	4. National, regional, and international laws and standards 5. Institutional policy, procedures, and coordination
Theme C: Community relations	6. Public perceptions 7. Cooperation and consultation with the public
Theme D: Accountability and oversight	8. Complaints against security sector personnel 9. Internal and external oversight
Theme E: Personnel	10. Recruitment and selection 11. Retention 12. Assignments, deployment, promotion, and remuneration 13. Mentoring and support 14. Infrastructure and equipment
Theme F: Institutional culture	15. Understanding of gender issues 16. Leadership and public presentation

distributions, career progression, attrition, attitudes toward gender integration, and harassment. Although a large-scale and official review was completed in 1999,[2] there were no interim official reviews to monitor progress through the ten-year mandated integration requirement, and there have been no similar audits completed since. However, there have been several independent and smaller-scale studies that have revealed interesting findings about the CF integration.[3] These studies reveal significant and interesting aspects relevant to monitoring gender integration, even though they were conducted separately from a comprehensive review of the CF integration overall.

The 2014 Australian Defence Force (ADF) audit[4] developed the "Performance Framework for Gender Inclusion in the ADF," which outlines six key areas of focus:

---

[2] Karen D. Davis, "Organizational Environment and Turnover: Understanding Women's Exit from the Canadian Forces," McGill University, July 1994.

[3] For example, Davis (1994) conducted interviews and surveys of women who had left the CF. This study found that Canadian female soldiers with 10–20 years of experience were attriting at a higher rate than their male colleagues, and that married women had the highest rates of attrition in the force. Jane O'Hara, in "Rape in the Military," *Maclean's*, May 25, 1998, documented that, despite the Armed Forces' official position of zero tolerance on sexual harassment, sexual assault accusations plagued the CF. Finally, Lisa Tanner, in *Gender Integration in the Canadian Forces—A Qualitative Analysis*, Ottawa: Department of National Defense, Operational Research Division, 1999, found that while there were more senior-ranking women in the CF in 1998 than in 1989, their average promotion rates remained lower than those of men.

[4] Australian Human Rights Commission, 2013; Australian Human Rights Commission, *Audit Report: Review into the Treatment of Women at the Australian Defense Force*, March 26, 2014

(1) leadership support for gender inclusion, (2) targets to support increased participation by women, (3) career progression, (4) career and personal support, (5) workplace flexibility, and (6) appropriate behavior. There was also a review conducted in 2013 on the treatment of women at the ADF Academy.[5] The findings from interviews, surveys, observations, and data analysis led to 31 recommendations intended to facilitate gender integration, including structure and staffing, health, and well-being.

The 1998 New Zealand Defence Force (NZDF) audit[6] was completed as a result of sexual harassment complaints within the New Zealand Navy. Its recommendations were organized into the following categories:

- attitudinal and perceptual barriers to gender integration
- physical standards
- clothing and equipment
- family-friendly policies and practices
- gender and sexual harassment
- human resource management policies and practices
- leadership on and management of gender integration
- equal employment opportunity.

There was a follow-up independent review in 2005 that found significant advances in gender integration.[7] Finally, an additional NZDF review in 2014[8] focused on recruitment and selection; physical fitness tests; attrition and retention rates; promotion rates; and harassment and discrimination.

We observed that these audits focused on two different types of gender integration impacts that we ultimately designed into our implementation plan: (1) impact on the institution and (2) impact on the individual female service member. In terms of impact on the institution, these audits focused on integration issues that would distract the institution from its operational mission, such as misconduct and acceptance of females into the ranks. In terms of impact on the individual, these audits focused on determining whether the individual was being given an equal opportunity to perform well in the newly integrated institution.

It is important to note that these audits were conducted under different circumstances than the anticipated integration of the Marine Corps infantry. First, some of

---

[5]   Australian Human Rights Commission, 2013.

[6]   Burton, Clare, *Report of the Gender Integration Audit of the New Zealand Defence Force*, Wellington: New Zealand Defence Force and New Zealand Human Rights Commission, 1998.

[7]   J. Burns and M. Hanson, *Review of Progress in Gender Integration in the New Zealand Defence Force*, Wellington: NZDF, 2005.

[8]   New Zealand Ministry of Defence, Evaluation Division, "Maximizing Opportunities for Military Women in the New Zealand Defence Force," February 2014.

these audits were in response to integration problems serious enough to warrant out-side intervention. Second, these audits focused on integration of an entire institution (a military branch, service academy, etc.) rather than a subset of an institution. These caveats are important to take into consideration.

Domestic Civilian Organizations

In terms of domestic civilian organizations, our focus was primarily on fire depart-ments and police departments, since these are the most similar in nature to USMC duties, responsibilities, and challenges to gender integration.[9] We identified several rel-evant reviews from the firefighting community. For instance, in 1993, the *Handbook on Women in Firefighting* reviewed promising practices in gender integration on topics such as recruitment, physical testing, training, policy development, sexual harassment, and cultural diversity training.[10] In 2008, the *National Report Card on Women in Fire-fighting* compiled data from questionnaires and interviews with firefighters represent-ing Kansas City, Los Angeles, Seattle, Minneapolis, and Prince William County. This review discussed treatment as a result of gender, equipment challenges and consider-ations, career advancement, recruiting policies, sexual harassment or complaints, and other gender-related problems.[11]

We also found several relevant reviews from police departments. For instance, the 1998 *Future of Women in Policing* report was conducted based on an ad hoc committee formed to examine the role of women in policing and issues of concern. This report based its findings on a survey of 800 International Association of Chiefs of Police members, and it focused on the following topics:

- status and roles of women in policing
- recruitment and selection of women officers
- supporting and mentoring women officers
- training and supervision as correlates of tenure, success, and promotion of women officers
- attrition and resignation of women officers
- gender discrimination and sexual harassment
- whether a "glass ceiling" exists as a barrier to promotions
- future directions for women in policing.

---

[9]   See Chapter Six for a discussion on why we chose fire and police departments as domestic, civilian analogs to study.

[10]   Dee S. Armstrong, Brenda Berkman, Terese M. Floren, and Linda F. Willing, *A Handbook on Women in Firefighting: The Changing Face of the Fire Service*, Federal Emergency Management Agency, United States Fire Administration, Women in the Fire Service, Madison, Wis., 1993.

[11]   Hulett et al., 2008a.

Of the top five reasons women resigned, family/children/birth ranked first (indicated by 12 percent of respondents). Survey respondents also reported that women leave for reasons of better opportunities, better pay, and career advancement.[12]

The most consistent and organized police review that we found was the series titled *Equality Denied: The Status of Women in Policing*. This series was five annual studies conducted on women's representation in law enforcement, which involved surveying 360 law enforcement agencies (identified in the 1997 Law Enforcement Management and Administrative Statistics as having 100 or more sworn officers). The study focused on hiring, selection, and recruitment policies; physical standards for entrance exams; discrimination and harassment; trends of female representation (overall and in leadership positions); and promotions.[13]

Ultimately, we found that domestic civilian organizations' monitoring plans and audits focused on concerns very similar to the ones that the Marine Corps initially identified. Although there are obvious differences in organizational size, policies, and missions, these monitoring plans further validate the choice of measures that we chose for our proposed monitoring framework.

Other U.S. Military Services

The U.S. military has a long history of integrating new populations, and the USMC could leverage the monitoring efforts from those previous integration efforts. For instance, the Department of Defense produces annual reports on representation in the military and has done or commissioned numerous studies over the years.[14] These could serve as good starting points for designing both ongoing monitoring and periodic deeper assessments. The other U.S services are also currently in the process of considering the implications associated with potentially integrating women into ground combat occupations. While we did not find any concrete monitoring plans in place in any of the other U.S. services, this search was helpful in confirming that we did not miss any open-source information regarding other services' monitoring plans. We did review the other services' required initial implementation plans but did not find any concrete monitoring plans in place.

We also reviewed recommendations made by the Defense Advisory Committee on Women in the Services (DACOWITS) to identify additional potential areas

---

[12] International Association of Chiefs of Police, 1998.

[13] National Center for Women and Policing, 2002.

[14] Examples of such reports include U.S. Department of Defense, Office of Diversity Management and Equal Opportunity (ODMEO*), DoD Diversity and Inclusion: 2013 Summary Report*, 2013; National Guard, *National Guard Diversity and Inclusion Strategic Plan*, 2014; Air National Guard, *Annual Report on Diversity: 2011–2012*, undated; Military Leadership Diversity Commission, *From Representation to Inclusion: Diversity Leadership for the 21st Century Military*, 2011.

to monitor. For instance, DACOWITS has focused on two main issues: wellness and assignments. Wellness issues have focused on the health of women during deployments and prevention of sexual assault and sexual harassment in the military. Assignment issues have focused on the retention gap between men and women in a drawdown environment, and the effective and full integration of women into ground combat units.[15]

---

[15] DACOWITS, *2013 Report*, Washington, D.C.: U.S. Department of Defense, 2013.

References

Air National Guard, *Annual Report on Diversity: 2011–2012*, undated.

Alvarez, Lizette, "Women at Arms: G.I. Jane Breaks the Combat Barrier," *New York Times*, August 15, 2009.

Archer, Emerald M., "The Power of Gendered Stereotypes in the U.S. Marine Corps," *Armed Forces and Society*, Vol. 39, No. 2, April 2013, pp. 359–391.

———, "You Shoot Like a Girl: Stereotype Threat and Marksmanship Performance," *International Journal of Interdisciplinary Civic and Political Studies*, Vol. 8, No. 1, 2014, pp. 9–21.

Armstrong, Dee S., Brenda Berkman, Terese M. Floren, and Linda F. Willing, *A Handbook on Women in Firefighting: The Changing Face of the Fire Service*, Federal Emergency Management Agency, United States Fire Administration, Women in the Fire Service, Madison, Wis., 1993.

Asch, Beth J., Paul Heaton, James R. Hosek, Francisco Martorell, Curtis Simon, and John T. Warner, *Cash Incentives and Military Enlistment, Attrition, and Reenlistment*, Santa Monica, Calif.: RAND Corporation, MG-950-OSD, 2010. As of September 18, 2015:
http://www.rand.org/pubs/monographs/MG950.html

Aspin, Les, "Policy on the Assignment of Women in the Armed Forces," Memorandum to Secretaries of the Military Department, Chairman of the Joint Chiefs of Staff, Assistant Secretary of Defense (FM&P) and Assistant Secretary of Defense (RA), Washington, D.C., April 28, 1993.

Australian Government, Department of Defence, *Removal of Gender Restrictions from ADF Combat Roles: Implementation Plan*, August 2013a. As of April 30, 2015:
http://www.defence.gov.au/Women/ImplementationPlan.asp

———, *Removal of Gender Restrictions on Australian Defence Force Combat Role Employment Categories: Risk Management Plan*, 2013b. As of April 30, 2015:
http://www.defence.gov.au/Women/docs/5%20Risk%20Management%20Plan.pdf

Australian Human Rights Commission, *Audit Report: Review into the Treatment of Women at the Australian Defence Force Academy*, Sydney: Australian Human Rights Commission, 2013. As of May 1, 2015:
http://www.humanrights.gov.au/publications-home/all

———, *Audit Report: Review into the Treatment of Women at the Australian Defense Force*, March 26, 2014. As of April 30, 2015:
https://defencereview.humanrights.gov.au/reports

Author interview with Norwegian military analyst, August 6, 2014.

Author interview with representative of UK Ministry of Defense, April 29, 2014.

Author interview with staff from large U.S. metropolitan police department, October 10, 2014.

Bartone, P. T., B. H. Johnsen, J. Eid, W. Brun, and J. C. Laberg, "Factors Influencing Small-Unit Cohesion in Norwegian Navy Officer Cadets," *Military Psychology,* Vol. 14, No. 1, 2002, pp. 1–22.

Bass, Bernard M., "Does the Transactional-Transformational Leadership Paradigm Transcend Organizational and National Boundaries?" *American Psychologist,* Vol. 52, No. 2, 1997, pp. 130–139.

Bass, Bernard M., Bruce J. Avolio, Dong I. Jung, and Yair Berson, "Predicting Unit Performance by Assessing Transformational and Transactional Leadership," *Journal of Applied Psychology,* Vol. 88, No. 2, 2003, pp. 207–218.

Bastick, Megan, "Gender Self-Assessment Guide for the Police, Armed Forces, and Justice Sector," Geneva: Centre for the Democratic Control of Armed Forces, 2011.

Bastick, Megan, and D. de Torres, "Implementing the Women, Peace and Security Resolutions in Security Sector Reform (Tool 13)," Geneva: Centre for the Democratic Control of Armed Forces, 2010.

Baumeister, Roy F., and Mark R. Leary, "The Need to Belong: Desire for Interpersonal Attachments as a Fundamental Human Motivation," *Psychological Bulletin,* Vol. 117, No. 3, 1995, pp. 497–529.

Beal, Daniel J., Robin R. Cohen, Michael J. Burke, and Christy L. McLendon, "Cohesion and Performance in Groups: A Meta-Analytic Clarification of Construct Relations," *Journal of Applied Psychology,* Vol. 88, No. 6, 2003, pp. 989–1004.

Beckwith, Karen, and Kimberly Cowell-Meyers, "Sheer Numbers: Critical Representation Thresholds and Women's Political Representation," *Perspectives on Politics,* Vol. 5, No. 3, September 2007, pp. 553–565.

Bergeron, Diane M., Caryn J. Block, and Alan Echtenkamp, "Disabling the Able: Stereotype Threat and Women's Work Performance," *Human Performance,* Vol. 19, No. 2, 2006, pp. 133–158.

Berthiaume, Lee, "Canadian Forces to Reduce 'Unattainable' Targets for Recruitment of Women, Visible Minorities," *National Post* (Canada), August 18, 2013.

Boorady, Lynn M., Jessica Barker, Shu-Hwa Lin, Young-A Lee, Eunjoo Cho, and Susan P. Ashdown, "Exploration of Firefighter Bunker Gear," *Journal of Textile and Apparel, Technology and Management,* Vol. 8, No. 2, Summer 2013, pp. 1–12.

Brewer, M. B., and M. D. Silver, "Group Distinctiveness, Social Identification, and Collective Mobilization," in S. Stryker, T. J. Owens, and R. W. White, eds., *Self, Identity and Social Movements,* Minneapolis, Minn.: University of Minnesota Press, 2000, pp. 153–171.

Broome, Lissa, John Conley, and Kimberly Krawiec, "Does Critical Mass Matter? Views from the Board Room," *Seattle University Law Review,* Vol. 34, 2011, pp. 1049–1080.

Browne, Kingsley, *Co-Ed Combat: The New Evidence That Women Shouldn't Fight the Nation's Wars,* New York: Penguin, 2007.

Buddin, Richard J., *Success of First-Term Soldiers: The Effects of Recruiting Practices and Recruit Characteristics,* Santa Monica, Calif.: RAND Corporation, MG-262-A, 2005. As of September 16, 2015:
http://www.rand.org/pubs/monographs/MG262.html

Burns, J., and M. Hanson, *Review of Progress in Gender Integration in the New Zealand Defence Force,* Wellington: NZDF, 2005.

Burrelli, David F., *Women in Combat: Issues for Congress*, Washington D.C.: Congressional Research Service, R42075, May 9, 2013. As of May 1, 2015:
http://fas.org/sgp/crs/natsec/R42075.pdf

Burton, Clare, *Women in the Australian Defence Force: Two Studies*, Canberra: Director Publishing and Visual Communications, Defence Centre, December 1996.

———, *Report of the Gender Integration Audit of the New Zealand Defence Force*, Wellington: New Zealand Defence Force and New Zealand Human Rights Commission, 1998.

Butler, Jack Sibley, *Provide (U) Project Volunteer in Defense of the Nation*, Vol. II, Washington, D.C.: Directorate of Personnel Studies and Research, Department of the Army, 1969.

Caiazza, Amy, "Does Women's Representation in Elected Office Lead to Women-Friendly Policy? Analysis of State-Level Data," *Women and Politics*, Vol. 26, No. 1, 2004, pp. 35–70.

Calderon, Eduardo L., and Maria Hernandez-Figueroa, "Citizen Oversight Committees in Law Enforcement," California State University Fullerton, Center for Public Policy, 2013.

Canadian Air Force, *Gender Integration Strategy*, 1998.

Canadian Army, "Leadership in a Diverse Army—the Challenge, the Promise, the Plan," Army backgrounder, Ottawa, 1998.

Canadian Ministry of Defence, *Annual Report on Regular Force Personnel*, 2010–2011.

———, *Canadian Armed Forces Employment Equity Report*, 2012–2013.

Canadian Navy, Navy VISION 2010, April 1998.

Carless, Sally A., and Caroline De Paola, "The Measurement of Cohesion in Work Teams," *Small Group Research*, Vol. 31, No. 1, February 2000, pp.71–88.

Casey-Campbell, Milly, and Martin L. Martens, "Sticking It All Together: A Critical Assessment of the Group Cohesion–Performance Literature," *International Journal of Management Reviews*, Vol. 11, No. 2, 2009, pp. 223–246.

Cawkill, Paul, Alison Rogers, Sarah Knight, and Laura Spear, *Women in Ground Close Combat Roles: The Experiences of Other Nations and a Review of the Academic Literature*, Defence Science and Technology Laboratory, British Ministry of Defence, DSTL/CR37770 V3-0, September 2009.

Central All-Volunteer Task Force, *Utilization of Military Women: A Report of Increased Utilization of Military Women, FYs 1973–1977*, Washington, D.C.: Office of the Assistant Secretary of Defense (M&RA), AD764510, 1972.

Chaney, Paul, "Critical Mass, Deliberation and the Substantive Representation of Women: Evidence from the UK's Devolution Programme," *Political Studies*, Vol. 54, No. 4, December 2006, pp. 691–714.

Chief Review Services, *Evaluation—Gender Integration in the CF*, June 1998 (revised November 1998) 5000-1 (CRS).

Childs, Sarah, and Mona Lena Krook, "Critical Mass Theory and Women's Political Representation," *Political Studies*, Vol. 56, No. 3, 2008, pp. 725–736.

Childs, Sarah, Paul Webb, and Sally Marthaler, "Constituting and Substantively Representing Women: Applying New Approaches to a U.K. Case Study," *Politics and Gender*, Vol. 6, No. 2, June 2010, pp. 199–223.

Chrobot-Mason, Donna, and Nicholas P. Aramovich, "The Psychological Benefits of Creating an Affirming Climate for Workplace Diversity," *Group and Organization Management*, Vol. 38, No. 6, 2013, pp. 659–689.

Clark, James, "Women Soldiers Judged Too Weak to Join Front Line," *Electronic Daily Telegraph*, March 26, 2001.

Clark, William D., "Women in the Army," memorandum to Acting Assistant Secretary of Defense (MRA&L), Washington, D.C., February 1981.

Crawford, Jamie, "Reports of Military Sex Assault up Sharply," CNN.com, May 1, 2014. As of May 1, 2015:
http://www.cnn.com/2014/05/01/politics/military-sex-assault/

DACOWITS, *2013 Report*, Washington, D.C.: U.S. Department of Defense, 2013.

D'Amico, Francine, and Laurie Weinstein, eds., *Gender Camouflage: Women and the U.S. Military*, New York: New York University Press, 1999.

Dahlerup, Drude, "From a Small to a Large Minority: Women in Scandinavian Politics," *Scandinavian Political Studies*, Vol. 11, No. 4, December 1988, pp. 275–298.

Davis, Karen D., "Organizational Environment and Turnover: Understanding Women's Exit from the Canadian Forces," McGill University, July 1994.

Davis, Kristen, *Chief Land Staff Gender Integration Study: The Regular Force Training and Employment Environment*, Sponsor Research Report 97-2, Personnel Research Team, National Defense Headquarters, Ottawa Canada, K1A OK2, September 1997.

———, "The Integration of Women into the Combat Arms in Canada," remarks made for ADF visit, 2014.

"Defence Force Launches Women's Development Steering Group," New Zealand Defence Force, press release, March 8, 2013.

Defense Manpower Data Center, "Active Duty Marital Status," spreadsheet, April 2010. As of April 29, 2015:
https://www.dmdc.osd.mil/ActiveDuty_MaritalStatus.xls

Devilbiss, M. C., *Women and Military Service: A History, Analysis, and Overview of Key Issues*, Maxwell Air Force Base, Ala.: Air University Press, 1990.

Duffin, Allan T., *History in Blue: 160 Years of Women Police, Sheriffs, Detectives, and State Troopers*, New York: Kaplan, 2010.

Dunigan, Molly, *Victory for Hire: Private Security Companies' Impact on Military Effectiveness*, Stanford University Press, 2011.

Egnell, R., P. Hojem, and H. Berts, *Implementing a Gender Perspective in Military Organisations and Operations: The Swedish Armed Forces Model*, Department of Peace and Conflict Research, Uppsala University, 2012.

Ellemers, N., R. Spears, and B. Doosje, "Sticking Together or Falling Apart: In-Group Identification as a Psychological Determinant of Group Commitment Versus Individual Mobility," *Journal of Personality and Social Psychology*, Vol. 72, No. 3, 1997 pp. 617–626.

Evans, Hannah, "Steyrs and Sheilas: The Modern Role of Women in the Australian Army," *Australian Army Journal*, Culture edition, Volume X, No. 3, 2013, pp. 41–57.

Festinger, Leon, "Informal Social Communication," *Psychological Review,* Vol. 57, No. 5, 1950, pp. 271–282.

Festinger, Leon, Kurt W. Back, and Stanley Schachter, *Social Pressures in Informal Groups: A Study of Human Factors in Housing*, Stanford University Press, 1950.

Gearan, Anne, "Navy Will Soon Let Women Serve on Subs," *Associated Press*, February 23, 2010.

German Federal Minister of Defense, "Joint Service Regulation ZDv 10/1: Leadership Development and Civic Education (Innere Führung)," DSK FF140100255, January 2008.

Greed, Clara, "Women in the Construction Professions: Achieving Critical Mass," *Gender, Work, and Organization*, Vol. 7, No. 3, July 2000, pp. 181–196.

Grey, Sandra, "Women and Parliamentary Politics: Does Size Matter? Critical Mass and Women MPs in the New Zealand House of Representatives," paper written for the 51st Political Studies Association Conference in Manchester, United Kingdom, April 10–12, 2001.

Gustafsson, D. M. S., *Gender Integration and the Swedish Armed Forces: The Case of Sexual Harassment and Prostitution*, Aalborg: FREIA—Center for Kønsforskning, Institut for Historie, Internationale Studier og Samfundsforhold, Aalborg Universitet, 2006.

Gustavsen, Elin, "Equal Treatment or Equal Opportunity? Male Attitudes Towards Women in the Norwegian and US Armed Forces," *Acta Sociologica*, Vol. 56, No. 4, November 2013, pp. 361–374.

Hagedorn, Linda, Winny Chi, Rita Cepeda, and Melissa McLain, "An Investigation of Critical Mass: The Role of Latino Representation in the Success of Urban Community College Students," *Research in Higher Education*, Vol. 48, No. 1, February 2007, pp. 73–91.

Harel, Amos, "Is the IDF Ready for Women in Combat?" *Haaretz*, April 29, 2007.

Haring, Ellen, "Insights from the Women in Combat Symposium," *Joint Forces Quarterly*, Vol. 70, 2013, pp. 55–58.

Harrell, Margaret C., and Laura L. Miller, *New Opportunities for Military Women: Effects Upon Readiness, Cohesion, and Morale*, Santa Monica, Calif.: RAND Corporation, MR-896-OSD, 1997.

Harrington, Penny E., *Recruiting and Retaining Women: A Self-Assessment Guide for Law Enforcement*, National Center for Women and Policing, 2001.

Harrison, David A., Kenneth H. Price, and Myrtle P. Bell, "Beyond Relational Demography: Time and the Effects of Surface- and Deep-Level Diversity on Work Group Cohesion," *Academy of Management Journal*, Vol. 41, No. 1, February 1998, pp. 96–107.

Harries-Jenkins, Gwyn, "Women in Extended Roles in the Military: Legal Issues," *Current Sociology*, Vol. 50, No. 5, September 2002, pp. 745–769.

Hauser, Orlee, "'We Rule the Base Because We're Few': 'Lone Girls' in Israel's Military," *Journal of Contemporary Ethnography*, Vol. 40, No. 6, 2011, pp. 619–647.

Hay, Mary Sue, and Charles G. Middlestead, *Women in Combat: An Overview of the Implications for Recruiting*, U.S. Army Research Institute for the Behavioral and Social Sciences, Research Report 1568, July 1990.

Hays, Robert B., "The Development and Maintenance of Friendship," *Journal of Social and Personal Relationships*, Vol. 1, No. 1, March 1984, pp. 75–98.

Hendricks, Cheryl, and Kristin Valasek, "Gender and Security Sector Transformation—From Theory to South African Practice," in Alan Bryden, and 'Funmi Olonisakin, eds., *Security Sector Transformation in Africa*, Geneva: Geneva Centre for the Democratic Control of Armed Forces (DCAF), 2010, pp. 69–88.

Hirschfeld, Robert R., Mark H. Jordan, Hubert S. Feild, William F. Giles, and Achilles A. Armenakis, "Teams' Female Representation and Perceived Potency as Inputs to Team Outcomes in a Predominantly Male Field Setting," *Personnel Psychology*, Vol. 58, No. 4, December 2005, pp. 893–924.

Holden, Nikki, "Retention of Air Force Officers in the Canadian Forces," briefing, International Military Testing Association, Defense Research and Development, 2010.

Hollander, Edwin P., "Leadership, Followership, Self, and Others," *Leadership Quarterly*, Vol. 3, No. 1, 1992, pp. 43–54.

Holm, Jeanne, *Women in the Military: An Unfinished Revolution*, revised ed., Novato, Calif.: Presidio Press, 1992.

Hulett, Denise M., Marc Bendick Jr., Sheila Y. Thomas, and Francine Moccio, *A National Report Card on Women in Firefighting*, International Association of Women in Fire and Emergency Services, April 2008a. As of May 1, 2015: https://i-women.org/wp-content/uploads/2014/07/35827WSP.pdf

———, "Enhancing Women's Inclusion in Firefighting in the USA," *International Journal of Diversity in Organisations, Communities and Nations*, Vol. 8, No. 2, 2008b: pp. 189–207.

"Increasing Women in Army," Army News and Media, Australian Army website, January 2013. As of May 3, 2015: http://www.army.gov.au/Our-work/News-and-media/News-and-media-2013/News-and-media-January-2013/Increasing-women-in-Army

International Association of Chiefs of Police, *The Future of Women in Policing: Mandates for Action*, Fairfax, Va.: International Association of Chiefs of Police, November 1998.

Ivarsson, Sophia, Armando Estrada, and Anders Berggren, "Understanding Men's Attitudes Toward Women in the Swedish Armed Forces," *Military Psychology*, Vol. 17, No. 4, 2005, pp. 269–282.

Jacoby, Tami Amanda, "Fighting in the Feminine: The Dilemmas of Combat Women in Israel," in Laura Sjoberg and Sandra Via, eds., *Gender, War and Militarism: Feminist Perspectives*, Santa Barbara, Calif.: Praeger Security International, 2010.

Jehn, Christopher, *Women in the Military*, hearing before the House Armed Service Committee, Subcommittee on Military Personnel and Compensation, 101st Congress, 2nd Session, Washington, D.C., March 20, 1990.

Joecks, Jasmin, Kerstin Pull, and Karin Vetter, "Gender Diversity in the Boardroom and Firm Performance: What Exactly Constitutes a 'Critical Mass?'" *Journal of Business Ethics*, Vol. 118, 2013, pp. 61–72.

Johnston, Lucy, and Miles Hewstone, "Cognitive Models of Stereotype Change: Subtyping and the Perceived Typicality of Disconfirming Group Members," *Journal of Experimental Social Psychology*, Vol. 28, No. 4, 1992, pp. 360–386.

Kanter, Rosabeth, "Some Effects of Proportions on Group Life: Skewed Sex Ratios and Responses to Token Women," *American Journal of Sociology*, Vol. 82, No. 5, March 1977, pp. 965–990.

Kearney, Eric, and Diether Gebert, "Managing Diversity and Enhancing Team Outcomes: The Promise of Transformational Leadership," *Journal of Applied Psychology*, Vol. 94, No. 1, January 2009, pp. 77–89.

Konrad, Alison, Vicki Kramer, and Sumru Erkut, "Critical Mass: The Impact of Three or More Women on Corporate Boards," *Organizational Dynamics*, Vol. 37, No. 2, April 2008, pp. 145–164.

Korb, Lawrence J., "Women in the Military," information memorandum to Secretary of Defense, Washington, D.C., August 16, 1982.

Kunda, Ziva, and Kathryn C. Oleson, "Maintaining Stereotypes in the Face of Disconfirmation: Constructing Grounds for Subtyping Deviants," *Journal of Personality and Social Psychology*, Vol. 68, No. 4, April 1995, pp. 565–579.

Laurenceau, Jean-Philippe, Lisa Feldman Barrett, and Paula R. Pietromonaco, "Intimacy as an Interpersonal Process: The Importance of Self-Disclosure, Partner Disclosure, and Perceived Partner Responsiveness in Interpersonal Exchanges," *Journal of Personality and Social Psychology,* Vol. 74, No. 5, June 1998, pp. 1238–1251.

Lewis, Adrian R., *The American Culture of War,* New York: Routledge, 2007.

Lien, Diana S., Aline O. Quester, and Robert W. Shuford, "Marine Corps Deployment Tempo and Retention from FY04 Through FY07," Center for Naval Analyses, Research Memorandum D0018757.A2, 2008.

Lonsway, Kimberly A., Rebecca Paynich, and Jennifer N. Hall, "Sexual Harassment in Law Enforcement: Incidence, Impact, and Perception," *Police Quarterly,* Vol. 16, No. 2, June 2013, pp. 177–210.

Lord, Charles G., and Delia S. Saenz, "Memory Deficits and Memory Surfeits: Differential Cognitive Consequences of Tokenism for Tokens and Observers," *Journal of Personality and Social Psychology,* Vol. 49, No. 4, October 1985, pp. 918–926.

MacCoun, Robert J., and William M. Hix, *Unit Cohesion and Military Performance,* Santa Monica, Calif.: RAND Corporation, MG-1056-OSD, 2010.

MacCoun, Robert J., Elizabeth Kier, and Aaron Belkin, "Does Social Cohesion Determine Motivation in Combat? An Old Question with an Old Answer," *Armed Forces and Society,* Vol. 32, No. 4, July 2006, pp. 646–654.

Martin, Patricia, Dianne Harrison, and Diana Dinitto, "Advancement for Women in Hierarchical Organizations: A Multilevel Analysis of Problems and Prospects," *Journal of Applied Behavior Science,* Vol. 19, No. 1, March 1983, pp. 19–33.

Marx, David M., and Jasmin S. Roman, "Female Role Models: Protecting Women's Math Test Performance," *Personality and Social Psychology Bulletin,* Vol. 28, No. 9, September 2002, pp. 1183–1193.

McGregor, Jena, "Military Women in Combat: Why Making It Official Matters," *Washington Post,* May 25, 2012.

"Military Leaders Lift Ban on Women in Combat Roles," Fox News, January 24, 2013.

Military Leadership Diversity Commission, *From Representation to Inclusion: Diversity Leadership for the 21st Century Military,* 2011.

Miller, Laura L., Jennifer Kavanagh, Maria C. Lytell, Keith Jennings, and Craig Martin, *The Extent of Restrictions on the Service of Active-Component Military Women,* Santa Monica, Calif.: RAND Corporation, MG-1175-OSD, 2012.

Moelker, René, and Jolanda Bosch, *Hidden Women: Women in the Netherlands Armed Forces,* Netherlands Defence Academy, Publications of the Faculty of Military Sciences, No. 2008/01, 2008.

Moran, D. S., Eran Israeli, Rachel K. Evans, Ran Yanovich, Naama W. Constantini, and Nogah Shabshin, "Prediction Model for Stress Fracture in Young Female Recruits During Basic Training," *Medicine and Science in Sports and Exercise,* Vol. 40, No. 11 Suppl., November 2008, pp. S636–644.

Morden, Bettie, *The Women's Army Corps, 1945–1978,* Washington, D.C.: Government Printing Office, 1990.

Morris, Madeline, "By Force of Arms: Rape, War, and Military Culture," Duke Law Journal, Vol. 45, 1996, pp. 651–781.

Mudrack, Peter E., "Defining Group Cohesiveness: A Legacy of Confusion?" *Small Group Research,* Vol. 20, No. 1, February 1989, pp. 37–49.

Mullen, Brian, and Carolyn Copper, "The Relation Between Group Cohesiveness and Performance: An Integration," *Psychological Bulletin,* Vol. 115, No. 2, 1994, pp. 210–227.

National Center for Women and Policing, *Equality Denied: The Status of Women in Policing: 2001,* April 2002.

National Defense Research Institute, *Sexual Assault and Sexual Harassment in the U.S. Military: Top-Line Estimates for Active-Duty Service Members from the 2014 RAND Military Workplace Study,* Santa Monica, Calif.: RAND Corporation, RR-870-OSD, 2014. As of April 27, 2015: http://www.rand.org/pubs/research_reports/RR870.html

National Guard, *National Guard Diversity and Inclusion Strategic Plan,* 2014.

New Zealand Ministry of Defence, Evaluation Division, "Maximizing Opportunities for Military Women in the New Zealand Defence Force," February 2014.

Norwegian Report to Committee on Women in NATO Forces, *Year in Review: 2001,* Brussels, Belgium, updated March 26, 2002.

Norwegian Report to the NATO Committee on Gender Perspectives, *National Report 2012 from Norway's Armed Forces to NATO Committee on Gender Perspectives (NCGP),* Brussels, Belgium, 2013.

Office of the Assistant Secretary of Defense (Health Affairs), "Per-capita DoD Costs for TRICARE Programs in FY2012," unpublished spreadsheet provided to authors.

Office of the Secretary of Defense (Personnel and Readiness), *Population Representation in the Military Services 2012,* 2012.

Office of the Under Secretary of Defense (Personnel and Readiness), *Report to Congress on the Review of Laws, Policies and Regulations Restricting the Service of Female Members in the U.S. Armed Forces,* February 2012.

Office on Women in the NATO Forces, *Women in the NATO Armed Forces, Year-In-Review, 1999–2000,* Brussels, Belgium: NATO Headquarters, 2000.

O'Hara, Jane, "Rape in the Military," *Maclean's,* May 25, 1998.

O'Leary-Kelly, Anne M., Lynn Bowes-Sperry, Collette Arens Bates, and Emily R. Lean, "Sexual Harassment at Work: A Decade (Plus) of Progress," *Journal of Management,* Vol. 35, No. 3, June 2009, pp. 503–536.

Oliver, Laurel W., Joan Harman, Elizabeth Hoover, Stephanie M. Hayes, and Nancy A. Pandhi, "A Quantitative Integration of the Military Cohesion Literature," *Military Psychology,* Vol. 11, No. 1, 1999, pp. 57–83.

Parfyonova, Natasha, and Andrea Butler, "The 2012 CF Retention Survey: Descriptive Results," Human Resource Systems Group, Ltd 6 Antares Drive, Phase II Suite 100 Ottawa, Ontario, K2E 8A9, Canada.

Pazy, Asya, and Israela Oron, "Sex Proportion and Performance Evaluation Among High-Ranking Military Officers," *Journal of Organizational Behavior,* Vol. 22, No. 6, September 2001, pp. 689–702.

Pfalzer, Janina, "Swedish Army Turned Professional Tempts More Female Recruits," *Bloomberg,* August 21, 2013.

Police Assessment Resource Center, "Review of National Police Oversight Models for the Eugene Police Commission," Police Assessment Resource Center, February 2005.

Poggione, Sarah, "Exploring Gender Differences in State Legislators' Policy Preferences," *Political Research Quarterly*, Vol. 57, No. 2, June 2004, pp. 305–314.

Presidential Commission on the Assignment of Women in the Armed Forces, *The Presidential Commission on the Assignment of Women in the Armed Forces: Report to the President, November 15, 1992*, Washington, D.C.: Government Printing Office, 1992a.

———, "Section II—Alternative Views: The Case Against Women in Combat," *The Presidential Commission on the Assignment of Women in the Armed Forces:Report to the President, November 15, 1992*, Washington, D.C.: Government Printing Office, 1992b.

"Promoting Women's Roles in Peace and Security," Government Offices of Sweden, 2014. As of May 4, 2015:
http://www.government.se/sb/d/2174/a/138957

Public Law 77-554, An Act to Establish a Women's Army Auxiliary Corps for Service with the Army of the United States, May 14, 1942.

Public Law 95-485, Department of Defense Appropriation Authorization Act, 1979, October 20, 1978.

Public Law 625, Women's Armed Services Integration Act, June 12, 1948.

Public Law 689, H.R. 6807 [Chapter 538], Establishment of Women's Reserve, July 30, 1942.

Public Law 103-160, National Defense Authorization Act for Fiscal Year 1994, Sec. 543, Gender-Neutral Occupational Performance Standards, November 17, 1993.

Public Law 113-66, National Defense Authorization Act for Fiscal Year 2014, Sec. 523, Establishment and Use of Consistent Definition of Gender-Neutral Occupational Standard for Military Career Designators, December 26, 2013.

Qualitative Report for the Study of Women in Combat, Berkshire Consultancy, United Kingdom, November 2009.

Quester, Aline O., "Marine Corps Recruits: A Historical Look at Accessions and Bootcamp Performance," Center for Naval Analyses, annotated briefing, D0023537.A1, 2010.

Quester, Aline O., Anita Hattiangadi, Gary Lee, Cathy Hiatt, and Robert Shuford, "Black and Hispanic Marines: Their Accession, Representation, Success, and Retention in the Corps," Center for Naval Analyses, D0016910.A1, September 2007.

Radebe, Hopewell, "Defence Force 'Struggling' to Meet Gender Equity Targets," *BusinessDay Live*, August 13, 2013.

Randazzo-Matsel, Annemarie, Jennifer Schulte, and Jennifer Yopp, *Assessing the Implications of Possible Changes to Women in Service Restrictions: Practices of Foreign Militaries and Other Organizations*, Alexandria, Va.: Center for Naval Analyses, DIM-2012-U-000689-Final, July 2012.

Raver, Jana L., and Michele J. Gelfand, "Beyond the Individual Victim: Linking Sexual Harassment, Team Processes, and Team Performance," *Academy of Management Journal*, Vol. 48, No. 3, 2005, pp. 387–400.

Remmington, Patricia Weiser, "Women in the Police: Integration or Separation?" *Qualitative Sociology*, Vol. 6, No. 2, summer 1983, pp. 118–135.

Report on the Review of the Exclusion of Women from Ground Close-Combat Roles, British Ministry of Defence, November 2010.

Richman, Laura Smart, Michelle vanDellen, and Wendy Wood, "How Women Cope: Being a Numerical Minority in a Male-Dominated Profession," *Journal of Social Issues*, Vol. 67, No. 3, September 2011, pp. 492–509.

Ricks, Thomas E., *Making the Corps*, New York: Scribner, 1997.

Rix, Sarah E., ed., *The American Woman 1990–1991: A Status Report*, for the Women's Research and Education Institute, New York: W.W. Norton and Company, 1990.

Rogers, John G. S., Maj, Royal New Zealand Infantry Regiment, *Gender Integration in the New Zealand Infantry*, thesis presented as part of completion of Master of Military Art and Science degree, Fort Leavenworth, Kan., 2001.

Rosen, Leora N., and Lee Martin, "Sexual Harassment, Cohesion, and Combat Readiness in U.S. Army Support Units," *Armed Forces and Society*, Vol. 24, No. 2, winter 1998, pp. 221–244.

Rosen, Leora, Doris Durand, Paul Bliese, Ronald Halverson, Joseph Rothberg, and Nancy Harrison, "Cohesion and Readiness in Gender-Integrated Combat Service Support Units: The Impact of Acceptance of Women and Gender Ratio," *Armed Forces and Society*, Vol. 22, No. 4, summer 1996, pp. 537–553.

Rosen, Leora N., Kathryn H. Knudson, and Peggy Fancher, "Cohesion and the Culture of Hypermasculinity in U.S. Army Units," *Armed Forces and Society,* Vol. 29, No. 3, Spring 2003, pp. 325–351.

Rostker, Bernard, *I Want You! The Evolution of the All-Volunteer Force*, Santa Monica, Calif.: RAND Corporation, MG-265-RC, 2006. As of April 24, 2015:
http://www.rand.org/pubs/monographs/MG265

Rostker v. Goldberg, 453 U.S. 57, 1981.

Rudman, Laurie A., and Kimberly Fairchild, "Reactions to Counterstereotypic Behavior: The Role of Backlash in Cultural Stereotype Maintenance," *Journal of Personality and Social Psychology,* Vol. 87, No. 2, 2004, pp. 157–176.

Rudman, Laurie A., and Julie E. Phelan, "Backlash Effects for Disconfirming Gender Stereotypes in Organizations," *Research in Organizational Behavior,* Vol. 28, 2008, pp. 61–79.

Sandhoff, Michelle, Mady Wechsler Segal, and David R. Segal, "Gender Issues in the Transformation to an All-Volunteer Force: A Transnational Perspective," University of Maryland, working paper, 2010.

Sasson-Levy, Orna, "Feminism and Military Gender Practices: Israeli Women Soldiers in 'Masculine' Roles," *Sociological Inquiry*, Vol. 73, No. 3, August 2003, pp. 440–465.

Sasson-Levy, Orna, and Sarit Amram-Katz, "Gender Integration in Israeli Officer Training: Degendering and Regendering the Military," *Signs*, Vol. 33, No. 1, 2007, pp. 105–133.

Schjølset, Anita, "NATO and the Women: Exploring the Gender Gap in the Armed Forces," PRIO Paper, Peace Research Institute Oslo, July 2010.

Schmader, Toni, "Gender Identification Moderates Stereotype Threat Effects on Women's Math Performance," *Journal of Experimental Social Psychology*, Vol. 38, 2002, pp. 194–201.

Schmitz, Edward J., Michael J. Moskowitz, David Gregory, and David Reese, "Recruiting Budgets, Recruit Quality, and Enlisted Performance," Center for Naval Analyses Research Memorandum D0017035.A2, 2008.

Scoppio, Grazia, "Diversity Best Practices in Military Organizations in Canada, Australia, the United Kingdom, and the United States," *Canadian Military Journal*, Vol. 9, No. 3, 2009. As of May 4, 2015:
http://www.journal.forces.gc.ca/vo9/no3/05-scoppio-eng.asp

Segrave, Kerry, *Policewomen: A History*, Jefferson, N.C.: McFarland and Co., 1995.

Sekaquaptewa, Denise, and Mischa Thompson, "Solo Status, Stereotype Threat, and Performance Expectancies: Their Effects on Women's Performance," *Journal of Experimental Social Psychology*, Vol. 39, 2003, pp. 68–74.

Selenich, Sarah, *Women in Combat: A Plan to Implement the Repeal of Combat Exclusion Policies*, master's project, Sanford School of Public Policy, Duke University, 2012.

Shils, Edward A., and Morris Janowitz, "Cohesion and Disintegration in the Wehrmacht in World War II," *Public Opinion Quarterly*, Vol. 12, No. 2, summer 1948, pp. 280–315.

Siebold, Guy L., "The Essence of Military Group Cohesion," *Armed Forces and Society*, Vol. 33, No. 2, January 2007, pp. 286–295.

———, "Key Questions and Challenges to the Standard Model of Military Group Cohesion," *Armed Forces and Society*, Vol. 37, No. 3, July 2011, pp. 448–468.

Siebold, Guy L., and Twila J. Lindsay, "The Relation Between Demographic Descriptors and Soldier-Perceived Cohesion and Motivation," *Military Psychology*, Vol. 11, No. 1, 1999, pp. 109–128.

Simić, Olivera, *Moving Beyond the Numbers: Integrating Women into Peacekeeping Operations*, Executive Summary, Norwegian Peacebuilding Resource Centre, March 2013.

Sims, Carra S., Fritz Drasgow, and Louise F. Fitzgerald, "The Effects of Sexual Harassment on Turnover in the Military: Time-Dependent Modeling," *Journal of Applied Psychology*, Vol. 90, No. 6, November 2005, pp. 1141–1152.

Smith, Heather J., Tom R. Tyler, and Yuen J. Huo, "Interpersonal Treatment, Social Identity, and Organizational Behavior," in S. Alexander Haslam, Daan van Knippenberg, Michael J. Platow, and Naomi Ellemers, eds., *Social Identity at Work: Developing Theory for Organizational Practice*, New York: Psychology Press, 2003, pp. 155–171.

Smith, Hugh, "The Dynamics of Social Change and the Australian Defence Force," *Armed Forces and Society*, Vol. 21, No. 4, summer 1995, pp. 531–551.

Smith, Hugh, and Ian McAllister, "The Changing Military Profession: Integrating Women in the Australian Defence Force," *Journal of Sociology*, Vol. 27, No. 3, December 1991, pp. 369–391.

Stewart, Greg L., "A Meta-Analytic Review of Relationships Between Team Design Features and Team Performance," *Journal of Management*, Vol. 32, No. 1, February 2006, pp. 29–54.

Stremlow, Mary V., *A History of the Women Marines, 1946–1977*, Washington D.C.: United States Marine Corps, 1986.

Study of Women in Combat—Investigation of Quantitative Data, Berkshire Consultancy, United Kingdom, June 2010.

Summers, Anne, "The Lady Killers: Women in the Military," *The Monthly*, December 2011.

"Swedish Women Troops Want 'Combat' Bra," *Australian Associated Press*, September 23, 2009.

Symons, Ellen, "Under Fire: Canadian Women in Combat," *Canadian Journal of Women and Law*, Vol. 4, 1990–1991, pp. 477–511.

Tanner, L., *Gender Integration in the Canadian Forces—A Qualitative Analysis*, Ottawa: Department of National Defense, Operational Research Division, 1999.

Torchia, Mariateresa, Andrea Calabro, and Morten Huse, "Women Directors on Corporate Boards: From Tokenism to Critical Mass," *Journal of Business Ethics*, Vol. 102, 2011, pp. 299–317.

Treadwell, Mattie E., *The Women's Army Corps*, Washington, D.C.: U.S. Army Center of Military History, 1954.

Turner, J. C., M. A. Hogg, P. J. Oakes, S. D. Reicher, and M. S. Wetherall, *Rediscovering the Social Group: A Self-Categorization,* Oxford: Blackwell, 1987.

Tyson, Ann Scott, "Panel Votes to Ban Women from Combat," *Washington Post*, May 12, 2005.

U.S. Air Force, "Air Force High Level Implementation Plan on Gender Integration," April 2, 2013.

U.S. Commission on Civil Rights (USCCR), *Sexual Assault in the Military*, Washington, D.C.: USCCR, September 2013.

U.S. Department of Defense, "Memorandum for Secretaries of the Military Departments; Acting Under Secretary of Defense for Personnel and Readiness; Chiefs of the Military Services. Subject: Elimination of the 1994 Direct Ground Combat Definition and Assignment Rule," January 24, 2013.

U.S. Department of Defense, Office of Diversity Management and Equal Opportunity, *DoD Diversity and Inclusion: 2013 Summary Report*, 2013.

U.S. Department of Justice, Office of Justice Programs, "Recruiting and Retaining Women: A Self-Assessment Guide for Law Enforcement," *Bureau of Justice Assistance Bulletin*, 2001.

———, "Women in Law Enforcement," *Community Policing Dispatch*, COPS Office, July 2013.

U.S. Department of the Navy, "Department of the Navy Releases Fiscal Year 2015 Budget Proposal," Navy News Service, March 4, 2014. As of September 16, 2015:
http://www.navy.mil/submit/display.asp?story_id=79466

———, Headquarters U.S. Marine Corps, "Organization of Marine Corps Forces," MCRP 5-12D, October 1998. As of April 23, 2015:
http://www.marines.mil/Portals/59/Publications/
MCRP%205-12D%20Organization%20of%20Marine%20Corps%20Forces.pdf

———, Assistant Secretary of the Navy, Financial Management and Comptroller website, undated. As of April 29, 2015:
http://www.finance.hq.navy.mil/fmb/pb/books.htm

———, Office of the Chief of Naval Operations, OPNAV Instruction 1300.17B: Assignment of Women in the Navy, Washington, D.C., May 27, 2011.

U.S. General Accounting Office, *Information on DoD's Assignment Policy and Direct Ground Combat Definition*, Washington, D.C.,: U.S. General Accounting Office, 1988.

———, *Women in the Military: Deployment in the Persian Gulf War*, Washington, D.C., GAO/NSIAD-93-93, July 1993.

U.S. Marine Corps, MARADMIN 493/14: *Announcement of Change to Assignment Policy for Primary MOS 0803, 0842, 0847, 2110, 2131, 2141, 2146, 2147, 2149, 7204, and 7212*, September 30, 2014.

———, *MCIP 3-11.01: Combat Hunter*, February 4, 2011.

———, *MCIP 3-11.01A: Infantry Company Operations*, December 5, 2013a.

———, *MCWP 3-15.5: MAGTF Antiarmor Operations*, November 27, 2002a.

———, *MCO 1200.17E: Military Occupational Specialities Manual (Short Title: MOS Manual)*, Aug 8, 2013b.

———, *MCWP 3-11.2: Marine Rifle Squad*, Nov 27, 2002b.

———, *NAVMC 3500.44A: Infantry Training and Readiness (T&R) Manual*, July 26, 2012.

Van den Heuvel, Ella, and Marten Meijer, *Gender Force in the Netherlands Armed Forces*, paper presented at the RTO Human Factors and Medicine Panel Symposium, Antalya, Turkey, October 13–15, 2008.

Vecchio, Robert P., and Donna M. Brazil, "Leadership and Sex-Similarity: A Comparison in a Military Setting," *Personnel Psychology*, Vol. 60, No. 2, summer 2007, pp. 303–335.

Vivian, Kevin R., *From the Past and into the Future: Gender Integration in the Canadian Armed Forces 1970–1999*, Ottawa: Department of National Defense, Directorate of Military Gender Integration and Employment Equity, 1998.

Warner, John, Curtis Simon, and Debra Payne, "Enlistment Supply in the 1990s: A Study of the Navy College Fund and Other Enlistment Incentive Programs," DMDC Report No. 2000-015, Arlington, Va.: Defense Manpower Data Center, 2001.

Watson, Warren E., Kamalesh Kumar, and Larry K. Michaelsen, "Cultural Diversity's Impact On Interaction Process and Performance: Comparing Homogeneous and Diverse Task Groups," *Academy of Management Journal*, Vol. 36, No. 3, June 1993, pp. 590–602.

Weaver, Matthew. "Women Could Get Combat Roles in British Army by 2016," *Guardian*, December 19, 2014.

Weinberger, Caspar W., "Women in the Military," memorandum to Secretaries of the Military Departments, Washington, D.C., January 1982.

Weinberger, Caspar W., "Women in the Military," memorandum to Thomas K. Turnage, Washington, D.C., 1983.

Winslow, Donna, and Jason Dunn, "Women in the Canadian Forces," in Gerhard Kummel, ed., *The Challenging Continuity of Change and the Military: Female Soldiers—Conflict Resolution—South America*, Proceedings of the Interim Conference 2000 of ISA RC 01, 2001.

"Women in the IDF," Israel Defense Forces website, March 7, 2011. As of September 17, 2015: https://www.idfblog.com/blog/2011/03/07/women-in-the-idf/

Wong, Leonard, Thomas A. Kolditz, Raymond A. Millen, and Terrence M. Potter, *Why They Fight: Combat Motivation in the Iraq War*, Carlisle Barracks, Pa.: Strategic Studies Institute, U.S. Army War College, July 2003.

Yoder, Janice, "Rethinking Tokenism: Looking Beyond Numbers," *Gender and Society*, Vol. 5, No. 2, June 1991, pp. 178–192.

Zaccaro, Stephen J., and Charles A. Lowe, "Cohesiveness and Performance on an Additive Task: Evidence for Multidimensionality," *Journal of Social Psychology*, Vol. 128, No. 4, 1988, pp. 547–558.

Zaccaro, Stephen J., and M. Catherine McCoy, "The Effects of Task and Interpersonal Cohesiveness on Performance of a Disjunctive Group Task," *Journal of Applied Social Psychology*, Vol. 18, No. 10, August 1988, pp. 837–851.

Zaccaro, Stephen J., James Gualtieri, and David Minionis, "Task Cohesion as a Facilitator of Team Decision Making Under Temporal Urgency," *Military Psychology*, Vol. 7, No. 2, 1995, pp. 77–93.

Zhao, Jihong "Solomon," Ni He, and Nicholas P. Lovrich, "Pursuing Gender Diversity in Police Organizations in the 1990s: A Longitudinal Analysis of Factors Associated with the Hiring of Female Officers," *Police Quarterly*, Vol. 9, No. 4, December 2006, pp. 463–485.

Zimmer, Lynn, "Tokenism and Women in the Workplace: The Limits of Gender-Neutral Theory," *Social Problems*, Vol. 35, No. 1, February 1988, pp. 64–77.